Algrove Publishing Limited
36 Mill Street, P.O. Box 1238
Almonte, Ontario, Canada K0A 1A0

Telephone (613) 256-0350
Fax: (613) 256-0360
Email: sales@algrove.com

Library and Archives Canada Cataloguing in Publication

Laughton, L. G. Carr (Leonard George Carr), 1871-1955
   Old ship figure-heads & sterns : with which are associated galleries, hancing-pieces, catheads and divers other matters that concern the "grace and countenance" of old sailing-ships / by L.G. Carr Laughton.

(Classic reprint series)
Reprint. Originally published: London : Halton & T. Smith, 1925.
Includes indexes.
ISBN-10   1-894572-74-2
ISBN-13   978-1-894572-74-3

   1. Figureheads of ships. 2. Ship decoration. I. Title. II. Title: Old ship figure-heads and sterns. III. Series: Classic reprint series (Almonte, Ont.)

VM308.L38 2003   736'.4   C2003-901447-9

Printed in Canada
#1-9-06

PUBLISHER'S NOTE

The 1925 edition of "Old Ship Figure-heads & Sterns" was handsomely bound, but badly designed typographically, making it difficult to read. Another publisher since undertook a photographic reprint, but this perpetuated the bad typography.

This edition has been completely reset in a double-column format with an easy-to-read type face complemented by suitable kerning and leading. A few small errors have also been corrected and we have considerably expanded the index subject matter and ship names. Of equal interest for anyone doing research, we have included a key (page 3) to the more obscure footnote references in the 1925 edition. The original superb contents remain unchanged except as noted.

Leonard G. Lee, Publisher
September 2006
Almonte, Ontario

OLD SHIP FIGURE-HEADS & STERNS

WITH WHICH ARE ASSOCIATED GALLERIES, HANCING-PIECES,
CATHEADS AND DIVERS OTHER MATTERS THAT CONCERN THE
GRACE AND COUNTENANCE OF OLD SAILING-SHIPS

By

L. G. CARR LAUGHTON
1871-1955

ORIGINALLY PUBLISHED IN 1925

CONTENTS

LIST OF ILLUSTRATIONS
(At end of the book)

PLATES IN COLOUR

PLATES IN MONOCHROME

PREFACE

This book has grown so much in the making that its ultimate bulk greatly exceeds what was originally intended. The object proposed was to illustrate systematically the development of ship ornamentation by bringing all available forms of the principal features into their proper sequence. Success in this attempt would show both where ideas and forms originated, and how far the several nations influenced one another. It would also afford a useful guide whenever, as often happens, an unknown ship, whether in a picture or in a model, was to be identified.

The evidence available for the purpose is so vast, and so widespread, that anything like a complete search was clearly impossible. It seemed best therefore to rely chiefly on the English collections and records, using foreign collections as far as possible in order to illustrate the genesis of ideas and the interrelation of forms. Thus the book is primarily a history of English development; from which point of view it will, it is hoped, be found to be moderately complete. What is added of foreign practice should be regarded rather as notes introductory to a serious study of those branches of the subject, than as a complete statement of the methods even of the more important nations. To attempt more was impossible on account of both lack of opportunity and of space. The same limitations of time and space ruled out any attempt at original research into pre-Tudor conditions. The summary of the practice of antiquity and the Middle Ages, though of the shortest, yet is perhaps representative of the known evidence.

In acknowledging my indebtedness to many friends and correspondents, my first duty is to Mr. Cecil King, whose share in the book goes far beyond the drawings which he has contributed to it. The drawings speak for themselves: but they leave it to me to testify to the extent of the research work which he has performed, especially during visits to the collections of Holland and France, and to the frequent advantage I have drawn from consultation with him on almost every feature included in the work.

Our joint thanks are due to Mr. W. G. Perrin, both as Admiralty Librarian and as Editor of "The Mariner's Mirror," for manifold assistance throughout the progress of the work: to the Director of Naval Construction at the Admiralty, for permission to use and photograph the records of his department, and especially for his loan of the newly-discovered draught of the *Victory* of 1765 (Plate 16), the only draught which shows the original carved works: and to Mr. C. Knight, Curator of original drawings in the Naval Construction Department, for facilities and assistance freely given. We are indebted to Admiral Sir Sydney Fremantle, Commander-in-Chief at Portsmouth, for permission to take photographs and sketch on board the *Victory*; and to the Curator of the R.N. Museum at Greenwich for the help which he gave us in our use of that valuable collection of models.

Our thanks are due for facilities given and help rendered to: Col. Sir Arthur Leetham, Curator of the Museum of the Royal United Service Institution, Whitehall; to Mr. G. L. Overton and Mr. G. Laird Clowes, of the Science Museum, and Mr. G. Palmer of the Art Library, at South Kensington; to the Librarian of the Pepysian Library at Cambridge; and to

Commander C. B. Fry, Superintendent of the "Mercury" training ship.

We have received much kindness and invaluable assistance from Mr. R. C. Anderson, who both put his collections at our disposal and allowed us to draw freely on his extensive knowledge; from Mr. A. G. H. Macpherson, who generously gave us access to his unrivalled collection of naval prints; and from Lt.-Col. Harold Wyllie, who lent valuable drawings and useful photographs, and gave welcome information on more than one difficult point. We received similar help from Mr. Gregory Robinson; and from Mr. G. Wheatly Cobb, to whose kindness the photograph of the *Foudroyant's* figure-head and the sketch of her cathead-end are due. Mr. Philip Castle made us free of the extensive and interesting collection of original figure-heads and carvings belonging to his firm, and allowed us to profit by his unique knowledge. Mr. R. Lionel Foster has given us the use of his collection of Nelsoniana, from which four remarkable water-colour drawings by R. Livesay are reproduced. Mr. Augustus Walker has given us access to, and photographs of, several ship models. Mr. H. H. Brindley has lent a copy of the rare book of engravings of naval ornaments issued by Laurie & Whittle in 1799; and Mr. Edward Fraser has generously placed at our disposal his considerable collection of notes on figure-heads. To all of these gentlemen we offer our sincere thanks.

We are greatly indebted to Col. Rogers for the loan of an admirable series of photographs of the ship models in his collection, and for permission to reproduce from them. To Mr. Junius S. Morgan, Junr., we owe especial thanks for permission to reproduce the magnificent drawing by Van de Velde of the *Sovereign of the Seas.*

We are particularly indebted to the Directors of the Rijks and Scheepvaart Museums at Amsterdam, and of the Prenten-Kabinet in the Rijks Museum; of the Franz Hals Museum in Haarlem; of the Boymans Museum, and of the Naval section of the Prins Hendriks Museum at Rotterdam, for the generosity with which they granted facilities for using those collections and for making drawings. To the Directors of the Scheepvaart Museum and of the Naval section of the Prins Hendriks Museum our especial thanks are due for much valuable information, and for photographs of models and pictures in their collections. We owe a similar debt of gratitude to Messrs. C. G. 't Hooft and Mr. G. C. E. Crone for access to their collections, and for information and advice.

Through the kind offices of the French Naval Attaché in London, Capitaine-de-vaisseau Comte de Ruffi de Pontevès-Gevaudan, D.S.O., similar assistance was given to us by the Director of the Service Historique of the French Admiralty, by the Director of the library, and by other officials of that department; notably by Monsieur J. Destrem, Conservateur of the Musée de Marine at the Louvre, through whose kindness it was permitted to make notes and drawings on days when the Museum was closed to the public; and by Capitaine-de-vaisseau Vivielle, of the library of the Section Hydrographique of the Ministère de la Marine. We had equal facilities in Brussels through the courtesy of the Inspecteur Général de Marine, and of the Director of the Musée de l'Armée.

EXPLANATION OF CERTAIN SHORT FORMS

The footnotes and text contain many references to sources that are not obvious:

Reference	Source
Ad. Sec.	Admiralty Secretary
Admy.	Admiralty
Anthony Roll	*The Anthony Roll of Henry VIII's Navy*; A pictorial survey of Henry VIII's navy compiled in 1546 by Anthony Anthony, a clerk in the ordnance office.
Auquier	Auquier, Philippe; several books on Pierre Puget, French sculptor, architect, carver of ships' figureheads and decorator of ships.
Cal. S. P. Dom.	*Calendar of State Papers, Domestic* (the accumulated papers of the Secretaries of State of England, relating to home affairs)
Chatterton	Chatterton, E Keble. *Sailing Models, Ancient And Modern*.
Declared Accounts	Declared Accounts of the Office of Works
Exch. T. R.	This may be the 'Treasury of the Receipt' in Westminster, which was the repository for various Exchequer records, including miscellaneous books.
M.M.	*The Mariner's Mirror*, a quarterly publication by the Society for Nautical Research (founded 1910)
Nance	Nance, R. Morton, *Sailing Ship Models*
Nav. Chron.	*Naval Chronicles*: British naval news and views including action reports, intelligence of foreign naval matters, and biographies of officers, published every year from 1793 to 1815.
Nicolas	Nicolas, Sir Nicholas Harris, *A History of the Royal Navy*
Oppenheim	Oppenheim, M., *A History Of The Administration of the Royal Navy and of Merchant Shipping in Relation to the Navy; from MDIX To MDCLX, with an Introduction Treating of the Preceding Period.*
P.R.O.	Public Record Office (currently the national archive of England, Wales and the United Kingdom)
Rev. Marit.	Revue Maritime et Coloniale
Ronciere	de la Ronciere, Charles, *Histoire de la Marine Francaise*.
S. P. Henry VIII	State Papers of Henry VIII (Public Records Office at Kew)

CHAPTER I

——— INTRODUCTORY ———

A MAN who undertakes to write about Jane Austen, or Westminster Abbey, or Shakespeare and the musical glasses, or any of the subjects that have attracted many pens, is probably justified in writing with Roget on his desk; but when he comes to break new ground he will undoubtedly do well to remember the old rule that the more unusual the subject in hand, the more matter of fact should be his statement of it. The subject of this book, which is a history of naval architecture in its decorative aspect, is certainly unusual; and the statement of it is intentionally plain and matter of fact.

Further, as the subject is necessarily highly technical, no attempt has been made to avoid the use of the appropriate terms of art. The reader who starts in entire ignorance of the difference between a hair-bracket and a lower finishing need feel no alarm when those, and many other strange terms of shipwrightry, stare at him from these pages; for he will find them explained in the simplest and most pleasant of ways. As the terms involved are all names of concrete things, it seems best to avoid attempting to introduce them in the usual manner by a table of definitions – the more so as it is quite difficult to make "definitions" define – and to prefer the pen of the artist to that of the author. It is confidently believed that the three pages of key drawings,[1] which show respectively the two ends and the middle of the ship, will make the technicalities of the subject clearer to the reader, and with less effort, than a dozen pages of text could have done.

It would not be possible to go very far in an enquiry of this nature without taking it into account that of all things the ship is the most cosmopolitan. From some date which may be said to have been so early as to be beyond the reach even of conjecture, she was already fit to go from one country to another; and in the intermingling of cultures begun by that intercourse the ship herself was of necessity influenced. During the whole of the period of which we have authentic record it is found that the ships of nations in constant inter-communication tended to approach each other in type, such differences as remained being due chiefly to the local conditions of their own coast and harbours.

Examples might easily be multiplied, but a few will suffice. Thus in Henry VIII's reign we find Antoine de Conflans recording that there was no appreciable difference between French and English ships; and we see such important types as the carrack, in the 15th century, and the gallion, in the 16th, adopted by all the maritime powers. For the most part such adoptions proceeded from the ordinary interchange of ideas, and were made so gradually as hardly to attract notice; but there have been, probably at all stages of the world's history, many examples of the deliberate adoption of foreign methods. The Romans did this when they built their first war fleet from the model of a stranded Carthaginian trireme; Gustavus Vasa did a similar thing when he imported Venetian shipwrights into Sweden early in the 16th century; the French did the same thing in another way a hundred years later

1. Pages 32, 88, 158.

by buying their men-of-war ready made from Holland, just as the minor naval powers bought cruisers from Elswick at the end of the 19th century. Peter the Great's visits to the shipyards of Holland and England, and the subsequent foundation of a Russian navy which in most essentials was either Dutch or English, will at once occur to the memory; so too will the perennial dependence of Spain on the other maritime powers, from which, from at least the 16th to the 20th century, she impartially acquired ships or borrowed shipwrights.

When allowance has been made for the intrusion of national taste in such minor matters as applied ornament, it will still be easy to see why in the early 17th century the men-of-war, and probably the more important merchantmen, of all the powers of Northern Europe should have had much in common; why a Spanish fleet of the 18th century should have looked like a collection of English and French ships: or why the Japanese navy in the war with Russia should in all its more obvious features have represented English practice.

It will perhaps be noticed that very few printed books are cited as authorities. It would no doubt have been possible to quote all or most of the authors enumerated by Mr. R. C. Anderson in a recent article on "Early Books on Shipbuilding",[1] but it has not been found necessary. Such authors, addressing themselves to the professional shipwright, had relatively little to say concerning the decorative aspects of naval architecture: their chief problem was to make the ship big

enough and strong enough to bear the weights put into her, though always with an eye to her comeliness. Such written detail as was needed for the present purpose has had to be collected laboriously from MS. sources, of which by far the most important is the records of the Navy Board, which during the old wars discharged the duties now performed by the technical branches of the Admiralty. There are many thousands of volumes of these papers, of which only a small proportion has been laid under contribution. Since it began publication in 1911 the Society for Nautical Research has completed ten volumes of its journal "The Mariner's Mirror", in which is to be found a wealth of detail concerning naval architecture which is not to be had elsewhere. For this reason "The Mariner's Mirror"[2] has proved the most indispensable of printed sources, and it will be seen that very frequent reference has been made to it both for documentary and for pictorial evidence. Frequent reference has also been made to the illustrations in Mr. R. M. Nance's recent book on "Sailing Ship Models"; and occasionally to models in several collections of which no representation is offered. For the most part this course has been followed only in regard to confirmatory evidence.

The plan of the book is that, as far as possible, the pictures should illustrate the text. This they certainly do; but always with this reservation, that had it been possible to multiply their number threefold, still many would have been omitted which one would have wished to include. The mass of available evidence, both documentary and pictorial, is so great

1. M.M. X, 53.   2. Cited throughout as M.M.

that it will be long before it is exhausted: meanwhile, in what is necessarily a preliminary, and in many respects an incomplete, survey of the subject, it has seemed best to devote as much of the available space as possible to material which has hitherto remained unpublished. It will thus be found, by all but the very few who are close students of naval archæology, that the great majority of the illustrations are unfamiliar, and that most of the new light thrown on the process of evolution is drawn from material dug out from the records, at the Public Record Office and elsewhere.

To an extent which will hardly be appreciated by those who have not tried to solve some problem in nautical archæology, it has been necessary to create much of the necessary raw material before using it. This is because models and unnamed and undated drawings of ships form a great part of the evidence; evidence which is extremely valuable when it can be understood, and is proportionately misleading when it cannot. Now it is no exaggeration to say that hardly 10 per cent. of the models in English collections have been identified, while a considerable number have not even been assigned correctly to the classes and periods to which they belong. In Holland, thanks to the work of a keen group of students, and perhaps to some degree because there is a less complicated history to unravel, the position is better; but in countries where devotees are few, the models which survive bear for the most part merely traditional names, in many cases of ships neither of their class nor of their

period, while others are vaguely referred to a century. For Spain we have Señor Artiñano's recent important work, which, amongst other good things, gives a list of line-of-battle ships built for the Spanish Navy since 1700. Such lists are invaluable. It is a matter for regret that none such either for the Dutch or French navies are available in any printed source.

Pains have been taken to decide as nearly as possible what each model or picture represents before using it; but the best that can be hoped is that no ship has been placed out of her proper sequence. One cannot always be hedging; and quite frequently, in order to avoid a tiresome repetition of various phrases expressing doubt or reservation, statements have been made more categorically than the evidence strictly justifies. It may appear that this is the case even in some instances where the evidence is in fact adequate, for on account of space it has often been impossible to quote the numerous examples on which an opinion is based. In the circumstances I confidently anticipate that some of my friends of the Society for Nautical Research will wish to challenge some of the conclusions: as to which I have the permission of the Editor to say that the pages of "The Mariner's Mirror" will be open to them for the purpose.

The method of dividing the subject which has been adopted has perhaps given rise to some small degree of overlapping. That, however, is no great matter: it seems more important to point out that it has necessarily tended to obscure the fact that development in the Royal Navy usually was not by an even flow of orders, but by leaps and bounds. Thus in the 18th century there were three short periods, each of them less than five years in length, when a considerable number of changes affecting the appearance of the king's ships were made; and conversely there were also periods, some of them extending to more than 20 years, in which no very noticeable changes took place. Unless the actual order governing procedure has been discovered, it is not always possible to date a change exactly; but usually if enough models and drawings are available, as is generally the case for English ships in the 18th century, a very close approximation to the actual date can be made. The list which forms an appendix to this chapter will, it is hoped, prove useful; it is an amplification of that which was printed in "The Mariner's Mirror" in January, 1925 (XI, 8, 9). From this it will readily appear that the three short periods of maximum change were 1705-10, 1756-60, and 1796-1800.

APPENDIX TO CHAPTER I
A list of the principal changes in the appearance of H.M. ships

1703.   Order greatly reducing carved works.

1706.   Order to raise the channels above the middle deck guns in all three-decked ships.

1705-10   (the exact dates not having been found): –
Introduction of the steering wheel; of round houses on the beakhead bulkhead; of standard pattern stern lanterns; of the central gangway from the quarter-deck to the main mast; of the screen bulkhead; of the carrying of the rudder-head up through the counter; of the flat or dummy gallery upper finishing to the quarter gallery; of a fife rail on the forecastle; of volute terms to the drift rails; and of double halliards to the port lids of the heavier guns.

1710.   Order to fill the rooms between the floor timbers.

1716.   Order to make a model of every ship built or rebuilt.

1727.   Order permitting the use of a figure instead of the lion head, especially in small ships.

1737.   Order further reducing the prices allowed for carvings.

1737.   Introduction of terms as supports for the stern galleries.

1742.   Order to raise the heads, to fit a third pair of cheeks, and to make the carvings of the tafferel, quarter pieces, and figure-head as small and as light as may be.

1744.   Order to fit gangways from the quarter-deck to the forecastle in all two and three-decked ships.

1745. Raising of the channels of all two and three-decked ships above the upper-deck guns.

1756-60. Introduction of 74-gun ships and of the new type of frigate as established classes; and of a lighter type of head. Standardisation of the form of stern galleries, with close quarters. The central gangway to the mainmast dropped owing to the lengthening of the quarterdeck. The third pair of cheeks dropped. The channels lowered again to below the upper-deck in three-decked, but not in two-decked ships. There must also have been an order about 1756 regulating the cost and extent of carved works. Introduction of the round bow in frigates.

1773. Order regulating the price of carvings.

1779. Order establishing carronades; and the consequent introduction of a high poop rail in line-of-battle ships.

1780. General introduction of coppering, which had been experimental since 1762.

1782. Order that the gangways be raised flush with the quarter-deck and forecastle, and that the gunwales in the waist be raised to correspond.

1787. The channels of three-decked ships again raised above the upper-deck guns.

1796. Order "to explode carve works altogether" and fit scrolls instead of figure-heads. As far as concerned the figure-heads this order was so unpopular that it was not enforced, but from this time busts were substituted for whole figures in frigates and smaller ships.

1797. Introduction of close sterns.

1800. Order introducing high bulwarks in place of the old drift and fife rails in line-of-battle ships.

1811. Order introducing round bows.

1813. Order reintroducing open stern galleries, but without the screen bulkhead.

1817. Order introducing round sterns.

The dates of the several ship-building establishments are 1706, 1719, 1733, 1741 and 1745; and of the gunning establishments are 1677, 1703, 1716, 1734, which was not fully carried out till 1743, and several partial establishments of later date. Summaries of these have been printed in Derrick and other books readily accessible.

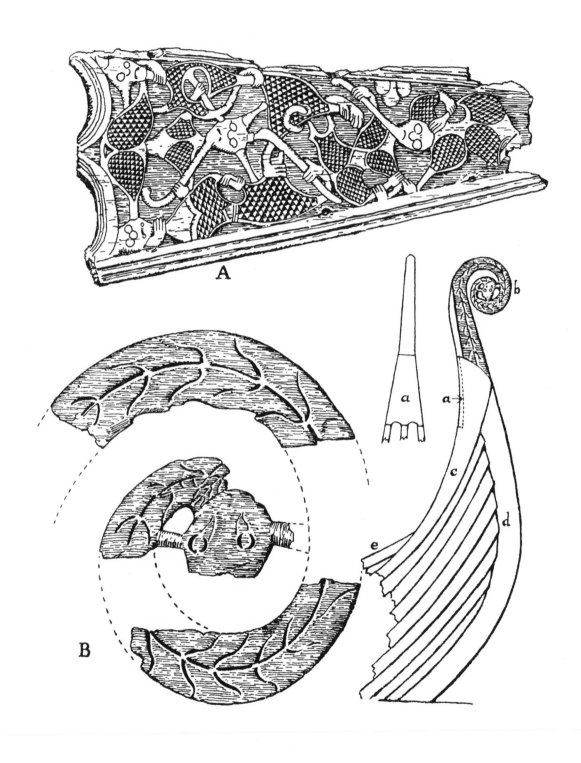

ORNAMENTAL DETAILS OF THE OSEBERG SHIP

CHAPTER II

FASHION IN ORNAMENT

Unless it could be proved, as it cannot, that the decorative tradition of the Græco-Roman era had been preserved unbroken at sea though it failed entirely on land, it would not be worth while here to hark back to the period of classical antiquity. As far as we know applied art afloat simply represented artistic progress, or decline, ashore. This was probably also the case in the dark period of the Middle Ages, but our records are of the scrappiest. We have only one example of carving from a Viking ship, that found at Oseberg, which is believed to date from about 800 A.D. The same *motif* (somewhat suggestive of Wimbledon) runs throughout, except on the stem-head itself, (b) and (B), which represents a snake. Its detail is shown (facing page) from what may perhaps be termed the apron (A), the place of which in the ship was at (a); but the same design was carved also on the stems in wake of the planking (d), on the sheering end of the gunwale (c), and possibly also on the washboard (e). This unique relic is of great value both as illustrating Viking practice, and for the hint that it gives of the method of decoration that is likely to have been employed by our ancestors of Celtic Britain, whose ornaments were of somewhat similar nature.

The principal development of ships in the 13th and 14th centuries consisted in the erection of "stages" at their ends, which gradually developed into "castles". At first fitted merely temporarily to merchant ships, in order to fit them for war, these stages seem to have amounted to little more than a piece of scaffolding. They began to be permanent structures in the 13th century, when, as far as can be decided from such inadequate representations as seals and monkish MSS. afford, they were raised above the hull by open arches based upon the gunwale,[1] – which at that date cannot have been called the "gunwale", but may have been called the "arch-board". Inevitably these arches were of Gothic design, with corresponding ornaments, borrowed directly from architectural designs ashore.

In the 14th century in northern waters, but a good deal earlier in southern, these stages became integral parts of the ship, and developed into "castles", of which the forecastle has kept its name after it has ceased to exist, while the after-castle a century later came to be known as the summer-castle, and a century later still as the half-deck or quarter-deck, according to its length. But the tradition of the arches on which the open structure had been raised survived these changes and centuries, and in Elizabeth's reign,[2] as well as in the later 15th century, we find the sides of the after-castle arcaded. These latter-day arches were small and of uniform size, and they survived partly as an ornamental tradition, but chiefly because they served to give light and air under the half-deck. When guns were introduced on board ship they also became available as ports for them, and were indeed the earliest gun-ports used. Such applied ornament as there was before the 16th century was almost certainly extremely simple: diaper pattern, trefoils and the like were carved on the bulwarks of the after-castle as may be seen from pictorial records, but we only hear of anything more elaborate

1. Pp. 57, fig. (l); and 87, fig. (h).   2. Plates 1, 5, 6.

from written sources. About 1400 very occasional mentions begin of "personages" carved in timber, which personages appear usually to have been saints, and of the royal leopards or badges similarly carved. At the same time we hear too of the decoration of ships by paintwork, but beyond a mention of the colours used, we get little detail.

Such detail as does survive entirely confirms the belief, formed from other sources, that in the 14th and 15th centuries the greatest profusion of decoration, afloat as ashore, was heraldic. It was the era of painted sails,[1] of the royal badges painted on the king's ships, sometimes all over them, of private ships painted in the colours of their owners, and of a gorgeous display of flags of all kinds, banners, standards, streamers, penoncelles, according to the nature of the ship, her ownership, and her employment.[2]

The fashion of painted or coloured sails was a very old one, reaching back into the remotest times. We need only concern ourselves here with the striped sails of the Norsemen, to which devices were occasionally added; with the particoloured sails of the 14th century – which apparently sometimes used one colour for the sail and another for the bonnets; with the heraldic paintings of the later Middle Ages, and with the religious emblems or devices which in the 16th century superseded all but national emblems.[3] Yet it is well to remember that in representations of ships of all these periods white sails are always in the majority. It may be doubted indeed if painted sails were ever very much more common, though

admittedly more elaborate, than they were in the middle of last century, when packet ships put a red cross, a black ball, or other device into their fore top-sail.

Perhaps the relic of pure mediævalism which survived the longest was the shark's tail or albatross head at the jib-boom end of the South-Spainer. It may be that these particular decorations were commonly mere trophies, with perhaps a reference to the horns talisman in the case of the shark's tail; but it is tempting to imagine for them a direct descent from the ornaments which were placed on the bowsprit, presumably from the date of its origin, till well into the 17th century, and with the masthead ornaments which preceded and no doubt suggested those of the bowsprit. Thus we would have in the simple emblems of the last few years the direct descendants of the masthead vanes in the shape of birds with extended wings which graced Sweyn's ships in 1004; of the large gold eagle with a crown in its mouth which stood on the end of the bowsprit of the *Goodpace of the Tower* in 1400; of the masthead religious emblems of Spanish ships of the 16th century; of the armillary sphere at the bowsprit end which betokened the East Indiaman of the 17th; and perhaps of the wooden crosses which the Spanish ships hung from their spanker-booms at Trafalgar.

It is probable that in the later Middle Ages the ornamentation of galleys was considerably in advance of that of contemporary ships. Duro, in speaking of the improved galleys built early in the 16th century for the war against Barbarossa, says that:[4]

1. Nicolas, Hist. of the R.N., II, 446-7.   2. (Original) Frontispiece.   3. M.M. III, 347.   4. Duro, Armada Española, I, 324, 328.

"The Capitañas [flag-ships] were distinguished by their external adornment, especially those which accompanied Charles V. This was the time of the Renaissance, and ships were not exempt from its influence. This was evident from the figures carved on the prows, in the work in relief and the gilding on the sterns, in the elegant form of the lanterns, in the painting of the pavesses, and the beauty of the tilts, standards and streamers. The fact that Barbarossa sent to the Sultan the scutcheon from the stern of the galley of Portuondo, as a precious work of art, shows what labour was spent on them; and yet this was surpassed by the decoration of the galley in which Don Felipe was at Genoa, which was the work of the best Italian artists."

When, however, he comes, to speak of the size and magnificence of the new gallions of the Bazan type, he does not mention carving and gilding, but says that those in which were Charles V and his son Philip had painted sails (which therefore, by implication, the ordinary run of ships had not), tapestries of cloth of gold and silver in their cabins, and immense standards. Presumably the painting of the hulls was decorative, but he does not speak of it. The ships, as he describes them, were still in the mediæval tradition. Fortunately we are now able to remedy Duro's omission by reference to the contemporary coloured drawings of the ships of Queen Elizabeth's navy.[1] These, drawn and coloured by a master shipwright, it is believed by Matthew Baker, who began his apprenticeship under Henry VIII and survived till the reign of James I, are both of the highest authority and are the earliest detailed representations of the hulls of ships which have survived.

As will be seen there is no ornament but such as is gained from the fashions of the ship and from paint work. If there were any applied carvings they must have been of the slightest, and perhaps confined to the stern, where we would expect to find at least some of the royal badges if not the coat-of-arms and its supporters. But the paint work is much more elaborate than any which is known to have been used for Henry VIII's ships. They appear to have been content with a modest frieze of herring-bone or diagonal pattern, with the addition of some badges on the counter and pavesses along the rails; but the queen's ships were painted elaborately in the conventional style of the period, with geometrical patterns, with strap ornaments, and with the arcading picked out in bright colours. It is believed that none of these ships is of later date than 1587, so that unfortunately we are still to seek for the fashion of the later years of this reign, when we know the expenditure on ornamentation, including carvings, to have been greatly increased.

One of the ships represented seems, in the form of her hull, to approach to the galleass type, and perhaps suggests Mediterranean influence; but her decorative scheme is entirely in accordance with English practice. In her indeed the straight line ornaments of herring-boning and diagonals are so pronounced as to remind us of the dazzle painting of the late war; but if any such idea was entertained in the 16th century, its purpose, at the utmost, can only have been to mask the position of the upper guns.

1. Plates 1, 5, 6.

We do know that the shipwrights of this period, as no doubt of all times, thought much of the appearance of their ships, which they set themselves to improve both in their technical design, and by attention to such features as could be made to combine use with ornament. They spoke of the "countenance" of their ships; of their "goodly port"; and in minor matters, such as the finishing of the upper works, were careful "to fit the ship with comeliness". They wished their ships to carry an impression of their "terror and majesty" to their enemies, and indeed to all beholders; and they were careful to examine any suggested innovation lest, in the literal sense, it should prove "disgraceful". A study of these drawings suggests that they achieved a far greater measure of success than is conveyed by any other known representation of their handiwork. Their ships look shapely, and far more snug and seaworthy than such sources as the Armada tapestries or Visscher's engravings would have us believe. We cease to wonder at their remarkable record of immunity from serious harm either from the sea or at the hands of the enemy.

It is at first sight remarkable that Elizabeth's ships show nothing of the compartmenting or panelling which was so prominent a feature in late Tudor domestic architecture. The explanation seems to be that the sea is not the land; that seamen, especially English seamen, are cautious and conservative by training and tradition, and that they have almost always been slow in adopting a new thing. It is ingrained in their nature to play for safety: if the old thing is safe,

and will serve its purpose, it will do: the new thing may serve the purpose better, but it may not be so safe: the sea does not understand experiments, and exacts the full penalty for mistakes. Such a habit of mind, acquired in dealing with essentials, is reflected also in the attitude towards non-essentials such as ornament. It concerns itself with the abandonment of old friends as much as with the adoption of new. It took the prestige of Trafalgar to reconcile seamen to the new method of painting their ships; and in the latter part of the 19th century they showed themselves as unwilling to abandon the figure-head as they were to see the masts and yards go over the side.

Vroom and other Dutch painters show, in much greater detail than is to be had from English sources, the fashions connecting Elizabeth's reign with the great ships of 1610 and 1637. We see the advance of Tudor ornament, the strap design of lozenge and circle, and the gradual introduction of compartmenting till it reaches its zenith in the *Sovereign of the Seas*. The sea, it would appear, was a generation behind the land. Even the elaborate carvings of the period recall for the most part the methods of Tudor Gothic rather than of the Renaissance; and though the effect of the Renaissance on architecture and ornament was slow in making itself felt in England, it had already well begun its vogue ashore. One particular feature common in Tudor architecture was the ogee dome. This found its way eventually into the royal ships as an ornament for the turrets of the galleries, and in modified form as a cap for belfries; but it hardly appears before 1637, and once adopted it held its place almost till the end of the century.

It has been said that the Commonwealth severity of taste was reflected in the reduction of carving and gilding on board ship no less than in civilian dress. That there was a great reduction of cost is certainly true, but this was almost entirely due to the substitution of a form of gold paint for gold leaf. It would be difficult from a consideration of such of the Commonwealth ships as are pictorially available to say in what the alleged reduction consists. Indeed they appear to show more ornament than any pre-Commonwealth ship save the *Sovereign* herself; and in the extent of their decoration they compare very favourably with ships of the Restoration period, with which, in the matter of the cost of ornament, they were very much on a par. That there was a certain degree of stiffness about the decorative schemes of the Commonwealth was natural enough, for the art of the ship carver was passing through the intermediate stage between the formality of the Tudor manner and the freedom of the Restoration artists.

The seamen were very slow in turning pilaster work to account. Even allowing for the inevitable lag of novelties in finding their way afloat, we might have expected to see pillars introduced decoratively in the Restoration navy. We do not, in fact, so find them, though Puget and his contemporaries were making important use of them in the decoration of French ships before 1670. But Puget, though a great artist, was no seaman. He

could not appreciate that his decorations represented so much dead weight which the ship had to carry. He was a very long way from the Gothic tradition of decorating the structure: he constructed the decoration. Thus we find ornaments which interfered with the handling of the ship, disproportionately heavy figures which overloaded her, and massive pillars which had no corresponding weight to support. In France both the sword and the pen protested, and from protest advanced to actual hostilities. We hear of a captain who, as soon as he got to sea, sawed off his great stern figures and let them go overboard. We find Colbert, then at the head of the Ministry of Marine, in 1670 repeatedly warning the superintendents of the dockyards against Puget. The stern ornaments used, he says, have been far too large, and must be reduced to a minimum. The carvers think more of their own reputations than of the good of the service. Puget goes a little too fast and has too fervid an imagination: be very careful therefore that he does not make the ships sumptuous where strength and efficiency are what is needed.

In England, no doubt, men thought with Colbert. They knew what the French ships were like, but they adopted from them only such features as seemed useful. They did not adopt the pillar, for Puget's use of it was not of a nature to commend itself. Thus though Restoration ships were profusely ornamented, extravagantly so to modern ideas, they continued under the Renaissance to respect the old tradition of ornamenting the structure, and they adopted no new feature till they saw a distinct use for it. Thus they continued with relatively small carved figures, and applied most of their decoration to mullions, rails, brackets, and other essential parts of the ship. The only new feature introduced in this period was a simple balustrading for the galleries, imitated, like the galleries themselves, from the French.

When one is identifying either models or drawings with individual ships, a difficulty which constantly arises is that the carvings do not seem to agree with what is known of them from other sources. Thus the *St. Michael* of 1669,[1] as interpreted by Van de Velde, has what looks like a feminine angel on her tafferel; while the tafferel carving of the *Katherine* of 1664[2] looks masculine.

As the identification of the Van de Velde drawing with the *St. Michael* appears to be certain, I consulted a friend, whose knowledge of 17th century ships is exceptional, as to my difficulty about the angel. He answered that he would not worry about the sex: that he thought ship carvers liked to use the best features of both sexes, and that certainly model makers did so to a ludicrous extent. It would be easy to cite many instances in support of this opinion: such as the wild men supporters in the stern of the little Danish ship of *c.* 1680,[3] reproduced from a Van de Velde drawing, which at first sight are easily mistaken for Adam and Eve; or the official draught of H.M.S. *Achilles* of 1795, the figure-head of which exhibits a decidedly feminine leg, perhaps because the draughtsman remembered the hero's school adventure,

perhaps because he took his wife for his model.

Under William III the rivalry of shipwrights and carvers succeeded in introducing an extravagance of ornament which left the Restoration navy quite in the shade. Ornament was certainly overdone, not because the artists, for they were artists, introduced decorations which were individually heavy, but because they tried to put more into the limited space at disposal than the space would stand. A ship is not a picture, to be regarded from a chosen distance and at the best angle. She will be seen from any angle, and more often at a considerable distance than from close at hand. Thus by a profusion of small ornament the artists defeated themselves: also they enhanced the cost of their carvings so enormously that the administration rose in its wrath and tied them down to very strict limits.

"Baroque" has been defined as "art with knobs on", and the knobs at this period were much in evidence. This is true to a considerable extent of all the carvings of the ships built in William's reign, and especially so of the elaborate figure-heads of the largest ships. When the order of 1703 greatly reduced the profusion of carving, it did not harm the appearance of the ship, for as much detail was left as the space could carry. A comparison, for instance, of the tafferel of the *St. George* of 1701 with that of the *Royal George* of 1715 should bring conviction of this to most minds. But unfortunately an exception to the order was commonly made with regard to the figure-heads of first rates which for more

1. Plate 27.   2. Plate 11.   3. Plate 36.

than half a century to come continued the old tradition. It was a tradition that they must be anything rather than simple. They must be symbolic to a high degree; and this symbolism was only attained by the crowding of a profusion of figures, human and divine, mythological and monstrous, into an entirely inadequate space. Such figure-heads were in no way effective: the mass of detail defeated its purpose. It was art with knobs on with a vengeance, and from any probable distance it was impossible to discover more than a mere congeries of knobs.

But in the main the restrictive order brought relief. Now for the first time the carvers were deprived of their elaborate mullions and told to use plain mouldings. They turned to domestic architecture for a hint, and discovered the fluted pillar and the plain arch; and they adopted these features apparently with enthusiasm. The ships of Anne and George I show the advance of these forms and their modifications, such as the keystone arch, the arch broken by the introduction of an ornament, frequently a shell, which was now put to very good use afloat. The history of naval ornament in the 18th century is one of gradual reduction, abroad as well as at home, for it was a century of almost continuous wars, and extravagances could not be borne. England apparently was less affected than any other nation. French carvings after 1700, for instance, were light, following the convention of the period; but sometimes the imperative need for economy resulted in a ship having none at all, but a mere pretence of painted canvas.

A curious and unexplained fashion found its way into naval ornament a little before 1720 and, as far as may be inferred from such models as exhibit it, had a vogue of some twenty years at most. This was the introduction of Chinese painted figures, which are found on the counters, on the bulkheads, and on the inside of the port lids.[1] The same fashion also extended to the lion, who, as may be seen from the contemporary carver's drawing,[2] and from another representation taken from the draught of an actual ship in which a dragon is also introduced,[3] assumed an extremely Chinese and most decorative appearance. In the figure-head the Chinese influence lingered after it had passed away from the painted works; but whence it came is at present a mystery. It had come and gone before the same influence began to show itself in English furniture. It does not seem to have been felt abroad at this time, though in the second half of the century it certainly affected the form of French belfries;[4] but that apparently was a natural extension of development ashore.

Reference seems necessary to the fashion for Oriental ornament which is seen both in East Indiamen and in men-of-war built in the East. From about 1720 it seems to have been the regular practice in Holland to give them Oriental carvings,[5] just as was the case with many ships trading regularly to the East in the middle of last century. This however never represented a national fashion; it was inspired entirely by the occupation of the ships or their origin, and, as far as can be seen, exercised

1. P. 18.   2. Plate 10.   3. Plate 25.   4. P. 208, figs. (D), (F).   5. Plate 15.

CHINOISERIE: FROM 3 MODELS

1. A 70 g. ship of *c.* 1720. (*R.U.S.I.*); 2. A 60 g. ship ascribed to 1738. (*R.U.S.I.*); 3. The later of the models called *R. William*, of 1719, which is perhaps the *R. Sovereign* of 1728. (*Greenwich*).
(a) (b) (c) are the inside of the portlids from 1, 2, 3.   (d) from the beakhead-bulkhead of 3.
(e) (f) from the beakhead-bulkhead of 2.   (g) from the upper works of 3.   (h) from the counter of 1.

no influence beyond the small circle directly concerned. Its purpose probably was in part politic, as was Colbert's in 1670 when he caused rich carvings to be placed on ships built for his new East India Company, because he thought that their magnificence would impress the natives of those parts to which they were bound. This, it will be noticed, was at the time when he was doing his best to reduce ornament in men-of-war.

All through the 18th century pilasters of classical form, and pseudo-classical trophies were very freely used in the decoration of English ships; and thus it happened that the intensification of the classical influence which marks the encyclopædic period was hardly felt in England. In France there was a decided swing in the direction of a severe Roman style, which was exaggerated at the end of the century, and may be said to have

been unintentionally caricatured by Ozanne;[1] but in England the movement expended itself, as far as the navy was concerned, in the choice of classical names, symbolised by the figure-heads, and to some small extent by the other carvings, of the ships which bore them.

The decadent classicism of the Regency period affected our men-of-war the less because by the beginning of the 19th century decoration had been reduced to a minimum. Thereafter there was little ornament beyond the figure-head, which sufficed to show that the period was not one from which great artistic results were to be expected. But the weakness of this period shines by comparison with some of the results of early Victorian utilitarianism and realism. The more pretentious of the figure-heads from about the date of the Great Exhibition are deplorable alike for their stiffness and the

1. Plate 20.

lack of imagination which they betray; while as to the other ornaments of the ships of the period, it need only be said that when a design for "carved work" was to be repeated, sometimes a pattern was made, and the thing cast in iron like so many fireplace ornaments. It was perhaps well that the coming of steam and the armoured ship freed the navy from the need of such "ornaments."

Except for the figure-head, which in merchant ships sometimes reached a high standard of grace or dignity, such efforts as were made after this date to beautify ships concerned themselves with the structure and with the best mode of setting it off by paint work. Some of the last of the sailing men-of-war, especially of the smaller classes, and many of the clipper ships, achieved to a high degree that kind of beauty which is the outward symbol of perfect fitness for the work in hand.

A question that is sometimes asked is as to what wood was used for the carvings of ships, and very different answers have been given. The earliest certain evidence I have met with is of 1640, and then elm was used,[1] twenty loads of it being needed for the carved works of the *Prince Royal*. Such evidence as has come to light for the Restoration period and the early 18th century shows that oak was then the regular use; but at some time unspecified oak was superseded by soft wood. Probably there are documents among the unsearched records which will settle the point, but as they have not yet been found it may be thought legitimate to guess. There was an important

Navy Board order in 1742 directed to the strengthening of ships,[2] and easing them of superfluous weight in their carvings: in particular the carvings of the stern and quarters were to be made "small and very light". It seems possible that some of the lightening process may have consisted in the substitution of pine or other soft light wood for oak.

It is easy to see why elm proved unsatisfactory; for it was always a difficulty that water got under the carvings, and elm when alternately wet and dry soon becomes of the consistency of putty. Oak on the other hand stands even those conditions fairly well, and it would appear that in the days of oak the carvings often outlasted the ship. The Restoration surveys show much replacement of carved works, but nearly always on the ground of damage suffered in action; and the order of 1700 for the curtailment of the cost of carvings contemplated that when ships were "rebuilt" – this was an administrative fiction meaning when they were broken up and new ships built in their place – much of the carved work of the old ships would be available for the new. But when soft wood was used the boot was on the other leg, and it is common to find it reported that such and such a ship being in hand for repair, it has been found on survey that her carved works are rotten and must be replaced. This was, for instance, the case with the *Howe* in 1835, only 20 years after her launch.

Mr. Philip Castle has told me that of the very many figure-heads and carvings of which he has personal knowledge, all

1. Add. MS. 9294. f. 409.   2. Admy.; Navy Bd. 2507, No. 344.

have been of soft wood, the only exception being that in a few of the largest pieces a core of oak was used for the sake of strength. Perhaps the oldest of the carvings which Mr. Castle has today are two stern gallery brackets from the *Téméraire*, launched in 1798, the form of which is that of an Atlas; but it may be taken that the professional memory of his firm extends to departed relics of even earlier ships.

CHAPTER III

THE LIMITATION OF ORNAMENT

Although a considerable degree of ornamentation had been introduced into the King's ships by 1400, as will be seen later,[1] it is not likely that this in itself was felt to be an extravagance. Ship decoration as yet included neither carving nor gilding on any appreciable scale, and even an elaborate coat of paint, with a complete outfit of banners and streamers, cost but a minute fraction of the value of the hull. We cannot expect therefore to find any attempt made to reduce cost along these lines until the expenditure on ornament had risen to be a serious burden. We can imagine Queen Elizabeth ordering the Navy Board to stop the painting of sails, but rather as a thing that was beginning to look un-English than as one which was useless and extravagant; and it almost seems possible that the use of extravagant streamers may have been restrained by order in this reign. But there was nothing more to be done, and the tendency of the reign was rather to increase ornament than to reduce it. Carving and gilding virtually began under Elizabeth, and in the few years before her death were carried to considerable lengths. It is of some importance to remember this, in order to understand that the relatively high cost of the ornaments of the *Prince Royal* of 1610 was not a thing that stood alone. On the contrary, there was something approaching to a regular progression in extravagant expenditure on carvings and gildings. Thus in 1598-9 the *White Bear* cost £377; in 1610 the *Prince Royal* cost £1,309, and in 1641 £3,327; while in 1637 the *Sovereign of the Seas* cost £6,691.

After which, as would inevitably have happened even had not England been in a turmoil over more serious matters, there came the deluge. We have not the exact accounts for the period of the first Dutch war, but clearly the painting of the largest ships was then costing only two or three hundred pounds, instead of thousands as had been the case a few years before. This great reduction[2] was made possible chiefly by the abandonment of the lavish application of gold leaf. A far more economical method was adopted, which appears to have given satisfactory results. It seems to be a well-established fact that even the ships of the Commonwealth, and of the early Restoration period, which were designedly kept plain, had as much or more carved work about them, and in general were more highly ornamented, than any early Stuart ship save the *Sovereign* only.

The Restoration Navy inherited the methods of building and ornamenting ships which had been developed under the Commonwealth, but it inherited also a heavy debt which was destined to hamper it in every way. The new administration went to work at first in a sober mood, determined apparently not to spend money on non-essentials. Thus when on 20 September, 1661, the Duke of York ordered the Navy Board to prepare an estimate for building two second-rates,[3] he added that "His Majesty intends them very plain, without any other carving or gilding than the arms on the stern". These ships were the *Royal Katherine* and *Royal Oak*, both launched in 1664. Whether as completed they were as plain as the King's good resolve had intended

1. P. 89.   2. P. 216.   3. Ad. Sec.; Out Letters, 1745.

is very doubtful, for before 1664 most of his good intentions had gone to form pavements. There are no models of these ships to show what they looked like when first built; but there is a Van de Velde drawing,[1] of uncertain date, which shows the *Katherine* with what from its form must be decided to be her original stern. Some economy of ornament on her sides can be noticed, but the stern apparently has been treated as sacrosanct, and retains all the usual ornaments of the period.

In general, however, it seems to have been the rule that any ship built for the Navy in the 17th century was heavily ornamented. There were exceptions, but these prove on examination to have been either prizes or ships bought into the service. For instance, the *Algier* reported in 1672[2] that "by taking in her colours, jack staff, ancient staff and guns", she had decoyed a privateer within reach and captured her. The *Algier* came into the Navy as a prize made from the Algerines, but, doubtless, like most of their ships, was built as a merchantman. There were again exceptions in the other direction, bought ships which looked like men-of-war. The *Mordaunt*, bought in 1683, was such an exception, for being built for a privateer she was finished like a man-of-war, though as her model in the Mercury Museum proves, not precisely like an English man-of-war.

It resulted from this profuse ornamentation that a man-of-war was easily recognised: it was by no means easy for her to disguise herself as a merchantman, though we do occasionally meet with instances of her attempting it,

by spreading tarpaulins over her carved works. This difficulty of disguise was a serious drawback in dealing with the Barbary corsairs, whose ships habitually sailed so well that the prospect of catching them in a fair chase was small. One expedient adopted was to equip all cruisers sent against them with auxiliary oars, in the hope of giving them an advantage in calms and light airs; another, which certainly had at least one notable success, was to build a Q ship.

This Q ship (which was, so far as is known, the first of her kind) was the *Kingfisher*, built in 1676 on the model of a flyboat,[3] *i.e.*, of a merchantman. She was made snug, with her upper tier of guns firing over the gunwale, and with waistboards to take off and on; so that when they were shipped the upper-deck guns were hidden. She also had "irons placed on her quarters with painted canvas to take off and on, and her head fitted in such manner as that it may likewise be taken off and on". The action of 1681, in which after 12 hours' hard fighting and the loss of her captain, Morgan Kempthorne, she beat off a squadron of seven Algerines, lives in history; but it has been forgotten that, had not her disguise beguiled the pirates into attacking her, there would probably have been no fight; and it is generally neglected also that she had other notable successes against the corsairs.

Both under the Commonwealth and in Charles II's reign carved works were a good deal cheaper than might be supposed. Thus in 1655 the carver's bill for a second rate was £150, and for a fifth

1. Plate 11.   2. Cal. S.P. Dom., 19 Sep. 1672.   3. Ad. Sec.; Out Letters, 1746, 23 Jan. 1673.

rate £25. The second rates of 1664 no doubt cost a little less than the average, but there is no reason to suppose that the sum of £140 spent on each of them was greatly exceeded in other cases. Two volumes of surveys[1] give valuable information for a later date, and show that in 1678 the English *Ruby*, a fourth rate, was charged no more than £10 "for fixing and carving two supporters for the belfry, a new cap, 1 new counter bracket, 2 counter heads, 15 new gallery and stern brackets, one badge for the middle counter, and one head bracket"; while for £20 the *Success*, a fifth rate, received practically a new outfit of carvings: "For carving the King's arms and two quarter pieces, a tafferel, the beast, trail board, supporters, a carved frieze, bulkhead brackets, hancing pieces, other brackets, ports, prince's arms, and several other carved works new in the stern". In no case did these figures include the cost of painting and gilding, which at both these dates cost about the same as the carvings. There was in fact very little gilding properly so called; but apparently the rest of the ship which was not gilded was painted to look as much like gold as possible. The models by showing this paint-work as gold have been seriously misleading.

Mentions of a carved frieze frequently occur in this period, in ships as well as in yachts. It is possible that painted friezes were already common, though it was not till after 1703 that carvings for this purpose were laid aside. In the yachts, as in the ships, the carved friezes were painted, the only exceptions being such yachts as were intended for the royal use. This distinction was still made in the 18th century; and indeed as long as the royal yacht was a sailing vessel she had carvings and gilt work far in excess of anything used for any other class of ship. The *Royal George* of 1817, familiarly known as the "Little George", had elaborate gilt carvings: the royal arms from her tafferel, the figures from between her stern windows, and her figure-head, all heavily gilt, are preserved in the museum of the Royal United Service Institution, and serve as an excellent illustration of what such things might be.

There seems to be little doubt that ornamentation became more extravagant towards the end of Charles II's reign, that is after the conclusion of the series of wars with the Dutch. The increase, it was said, was caused by the rivalry of the shipwrights, which was not restrained. James II seems to have issued the first general order in restraint of this profusion. This was in March, 1686; but the order was for one thing unimportant, dealing only with a minor point, and secondly it was not obeyed. There was virtually no shipbuilding in this reign; but that of William III began with a war against France, and with a good deal of building of the lower rates, followed in 1690 by a Naval Defence Act which provided 27 capital ships, to which 3 more were immediately added.

The Dutch were our allies instead of our enemies in this war, and it is tempting to try to account, at least in part, for the growth of expenditure on ship ornamentation by suggesting that something in the nature of rivalry may have existed between the two

1. Admy.; Navy Bd. Misc. 3118, 3119.

services. Dutch ships of this war[1] were still highly ornamented, though very different in appearance from English ships; and at the very beginning of the next century the Dutch, like the English, began to economise in the matter of decorations. However that may be, it is at least known fact that the cost of ship carvings continued to go up, and in this reign stood higher than it had ever done before. In the years before 1700 the sums paid for the carved works of the several rates were as follows:[2] –

1st rate		£896		
2nd rate		£420		
3rd rate	(80 g.)	£293	to	£164
3rd rate	(70 g.)	£277	to	£160
4th rate	(60 g.)	£157	to	£144
4th rate	(50 g.)	£103	to	£75
5th rate		£93	to	£65
6th rate		£52	to	£42

The models of this reign, of which there are several very fine examples in the Naval Museum at Greenwich, and a few elsewhere, confirm these figures by exhibiting a greater profusion of decoration than at any other period either before or after.

A set of contracts from 1692 to 1695 for the building of ships of different rates from 80 guns to 24 is available.[3] The only hint of a reduction of carvings which occurs in any of these is that while in the case of the *Newark*, of 80 guns, carved round ports are specified for the half-deck, poop and forecastle,

it is added that they shall be supplied "also for the upper tier if thought necessary". We have two models of the *Newark's* sister ships, which show that wreath ports for the upper-deck were still thought necessary, though their day was nearly done. It would seem that the Navy Board must have had in mind the little order of 1686, which forbade carved upper-deck ports in ships of 50 guns and under. It is part of the same specification "to gild the lion of the head and the King's arms in the stern. To trible paint the ship within and without board with good oil colour, and in like manner all the joiners' works … bulkheads and carved works within board".

This contract was made at the beginning of a war, when the experience of the Dutch wars had been forgotten. A few years of war with France served to remind the Navy Board that inboard carvings were undesirable, and on 4 November, 1700, they issued an important order:[4] –

"Whereas notwithstanding the many cautions which have been given by this Board to the officers of H.M. Yards against the increasing of H.M. charge in the ornamental works of H.M. ships, and the many injunctions to them to use all possible good husbandry therein, several of H.M. ships are found to have carved works in their cabin coaches and other improper places, which upon any prospect of action are torn to pieces by the sailors, and consequently a very unnecessary charge; and whereas upon examination of the bills passed for carved works for new ships and ships rebuilt for some time backward, some are thought to be very extravagant and few of a rate observed to agree in charge one with another, which renders it absolutely necessary to have some regulation made therein; we have, upon mature consideration had thereof, thought fit not only to prohibit for the future the putting up of

1. Plate 49.   2. M.M. IV, 27.   3. Admy. Library, MS. No. 44.   4. Admy.; Navy Bd. 2507, No. 150.

any carved work in the cabin coaches and other improper places of H.M. ships, but also to put a limitation to the charges of the said works by establishing such sums for the several rates and ranks of ships as are not to be exceeded when any of the said ships shall be built or rebuilt, viz.: –

For a 1st rate		£500
For a 2nd rate		£300
For a 3rd rate of	80 guns	£150
For a 3rd rate of	70 guns	£130
For a 4th rate of	60 guns	£100
For a 4th rate of	50 guns	£ 80
For a 5th rate		£ 50
For a 6th rate		£ 25

… Likewise in the reparation of H.M. ships for the time to come … you are carefully to survey their carved work … and save what can be saved and will or may be made to serve again … so as H.M. may have the benefit thereof in as full and ample manner as is hereby intended."

This was the thin end of the wedge, which was driven home by Admiralty order within 3 years:[1] –

"16 June, 1703. Whereas it was some time since recommended to you [the Navy Board] by his Royal Highness [the Lord High Admiral] to consider how the great charge of carvers' and joiners' and other ornamental works may be lessened on board her Majesty's ships for the future; to which you have made the following report: –

That the carved works be reduced to only a lion and trail board for the head, with mouldings instead of brackets placed against the timbers: that the stern have only a tafferel and two quarter pieces, and in lieu of brackets between the lights of the stern, galleries and bulkheads, to have mouldings fixed against the timbers; that the joiners' works of the sides of the great cabin, coach, wardroom, and round-house of each ship be fixed only with slit deals without any sort of moulding or cornice, and the painting be only plain colour….

We have considered of these propositions, and very well approving thereof do … hereby desire and direct you to cause the same to be put in execution as soon as conveniently may be, and that no other carvers', joiners' or painters' works be allowed or put in any of H.M. ships for the future, without particular and especial orders for the same…."

Both models and pictures prove that this order was well observed; which is perhaps curious, seeing that the other general orders to the same effect, from 1686 to 1700, had uniformly failed of their purpose.

Students of ship models are familiar with the effect of the restrictive order of 1703, but those who would like to gain a good general impression of the extent of the change may with advantage compare an 80-gun ship built under the Act of 1690[2] with a ship of the same class built to the establishment of 1706.[3] The model of the *Boyne* of the former class is at Greenwich, one of the 1706 establishment is at South Kensington. Though the change is very noticeable in all classes, it is perhaps more obvious in the 80's than in any other class or rate.

It may be taken for granted that a schedule of prices to be allowed for carvings in the several rates was issued in connection with the order of 1703, but no copy of it has yet been discovered. It also seems likely that there may have been some further reduction about 1710, from which date the wreaths round the

1. M.M. III, 20.   2. Nance, Plate 46.   3. *Id.* Plate 71.

quarter-deck ports disappear. In the absence of detailed information on these points it is useful to have a list kept by John Hayward, one of the master shipwrights, showing what ships he built or rebuilt, and what sums were expended on their carving and painting. This list covers a period of eighteen years, from 1712 to 1730, and includes all classes of ships, from first rates to sloops, and as nothing else of the kind has come to light it seems to be of interest enough to be worth quoting: –

Rate	Ship	Guns	Date	Carving			Painting		
1	Royal George	100	23.04.1712 to 20.09.15	£323	7	0	£273	5	10½
3	Cambridge	80	18.11.1713 to 17.09.15	£ 56	0	0	£104	11	10½
4	Panther	50	03.03.1714 to 26.04.16	£ 20	15	0	£ 41	6	7½
4	Dartmouth	50	11.08.1714 to 07.08.16	£ 24	4	6	£ 38	2	8
4	Guernsey	50	10.10.1716 to 24.10.17	£ 24	0	0	£ 35	4	5
3	Revenge	70	27.03.1717 to 13.10.18	£ 59	16	0	£ 87	8	6¼
4	Weymouth	50	30.10.1717 to 26.02.18	£ 24	5	0	£ 60	5	2½
1	Britannia	100	27.02.1716 to 03.10.19	£290	5	0	£179	18	11
6	Shoreham	20	28.10.1719 to 25.08.20	£ 18	2	0	£ 38	12	11½
4	Leopard	50	23.09.1719 to 18.04.21	£ 25	7	0	£ 36	14	5
Sl.	Ferret		20.03.1721 to 06.05.21	£ 4	0	0	£ 5	12	10
3	Northumberland	70	09.09.1719 to 13.07.21	£ 69	17	0	£ 63	10	11¼
4	Argyle	50	18.05.1720 to 05.07.22	£ 24	18	6	£ 44	10	0¼
3	Stirling Castle	70	12.07.1721 to 23.04.23	£ 70	5	0	£ 72	7	3¼
3	Kent	70	02.05.1722 to 10.08.24	£ 78	5	0	£ 64	18	0¼
4	Superb	60	13.05.1720 to 10.11.21	£ 25	0	0	£ 55	13	9
5	Ludlow Castle	40	30.05.1722 to 01.02.23	£ 30	12	6	£ 37	8	7¼
5	Lark	40	09.01.1724 to 02.08.26	£ 30	12	0	£ 39	9	5
6	Rose	20	09.01.1723 to 08.09.24	£ 22	13	6	£ 17	19	0¼
2	Neptune	90	.02.1725 to 15.10.30	£132	0	0	£124	18	8½
5	Princess Louisa	40	12.10.1726 to 08.08.28	£ 26	17	0	£ 40	12	2
4	Falmouth	50	20.07.1726 to 03.04.29	£ 40	2	0	£ 41	4	11¼
Sl.	Salamander	8	02.07.1729 to 07.07.30	£ 17	0	0	£ 15	6	5¾
6	Squirrel	20	05.04.1727 to 19.10.27	£ 22	13	6	£ 26	18	5

The sums spent on carving are in most cases unexpectedly small, and it is a little surprising to find that painting in general cost more than carving. One or two items suggest doubts: for instance, the £25 set down for the carvings of the *Superb* of 60 guns; and the great discrepancy between the sums allotted for the two sloops. In the first-named case it may be that a token sum was entered; as regards the sloops, the explanation is that the *Ferret* of 1721 measured only 67 tons, while by 1730 sloops had grown to be sizable ships.

It will be seen that on the average the price of the carved works tended to rise: in a 70-gun ship from £60 to £78, and in the 50's from £20 to £40. This may partly be accounted for by a rise of prices; but if so, some explanation is needed why the tendency of the cost of painting was rather to fall than to rise. It is not unlikely that this fall may be due to a decline in the amount of labour expended on purely decorative work, such as friezes, which would naturally be the most expensive part of the painters' works.

The recent rise in the cost of carved work was recognised by a Navy Board order of 8 July, 1737,[1] and a new schedule of prices was fixed which, it will be seen, showed an advance upon those in Hayward's list for all ships but first rates: –

Guns	Lion			Trailboard			Tafferel			Quarter pieces			Total		
100	£44	8	0	£7	4	0	£55	8	0	£57	12	0	£166	12	0
90	£39	0	0	£5	6	0	£45	0	0	£47	8	0	£136	14	0
80	£31	14	0	£4	5	0	£38	16	0	£40	0	0	£114	15	0
70	£23	18	0	£2	16	2	£30	18	0	£30	4	0	£ 87	16	2
60	£17	10	0	£2	11	2	£22	16	0	£22	10	0	£ 65	7	2
50	£13	2	0	£2	1	5	£16	4	0	£16	4	0	£ 47	11	5
40	£10	2	0	£1	13	4	£12	7	0	£13	0	0	£ 37	2	4
20	£ 7	4	0	£1	4	8	£ 9	8	0	£10	7	0	£ 28	3	8

1. P.R.O., Ind. 10665. f. 559.

There had been a slight change in the regulations as to carved works in 1727, but as it only affected figure-heads, another opportunity will be taken of referring to it.[1] An order of considerable importance was issued to all the dockyards on 15 April, 1742. It altered the appearance of the ships in more ways than one; and by the great reduction which it made in the carved works of the stern, must have had an appreciable effect on their cost. It may be suspected, however, that when ornament was reduced in one direction, the carvers took an opportunity of adding to it in another. The order was as follows:[2] –

"In order to prevent as much as possible H.M. ships from complaining at sea, these are to direct and require you as ships come into port to refit, or are building, rebuilding, or under repair, … to strengthen the sterns all that is possible, make the quarter pieces and taffrails small and very light, and in order to secure the head of the ships … to place an additional pair of cheeks to all ships of 50 guns and upwards, and to make the lion or figures of the head as light and as small as possible; keep the knees of the heads of all three-decked ships so high as to have one pair of cheeks above the hawse holes."

If, for example, the stern of the *Royal William*[3] of 1719 is compared with that of the *Victory*[4] of 1765, the great reduction of the tafferel and quarter pieces brought about by this order will be readily appreciated. It seems certain that a new schedule of costs must have been got out in consequence of this order, but it has not yet been found. Similarly there must have been a revision of the schedule in or soon after 1756, in order to include the new types of ships,

especially the 74-gun ships of the line, and the 32 and 28-gun frigates, which were then first established as classes; but this too has not yet come to light. There was a further modification in 1773, when the prices for figure-heads were again altered, being made more generous for ships of the line; but the prices already established for quarter pieces, tafferels and trail boards were continued. This order remained in force till 1796, so that it is approximately true to say that – save for a reduction in the case of first rates made in 1737 and the change of 1742 – there was little if any difference in the amount of ornament applied to the King's ships between 1703 and 1796.

When Lord Spencer's Board of Admiralty took office it began to play the part of a new broom, and on 18 August, 1796, issued an order to "explode carve work altogether on board H.M. ships that may be built or repaired in future, except what may be necessary for the mouldings about the scroll or billet head, and the stern and quarters". On the single point of the billet, or fiddle, head this order was of small effect, for this particular change was so unpopular that it became virtually a dead letter; but in general the order stood, and for some time to come ships of war lost the small ornaments which they had retained so long. Ornamental rails, hances, trail boards, and the like vanished entirely; all that remained was a greatly reduced tafferel, an equally reduced figure-head, with almost vestigial quarter pieces and finishings to the galleries. The gradual process by which these several features

1. P. 68.   2. Admy.; Navy Bd. 2507, No. 344.   3. Plate 28.   4. Plate 29.

declined and fell will be described in the separate chapters assigned to them.

But the order of 1796 had in fact tried to do too much, and after a few years of extreme plainness, ships, in the concluding period of the war, regained an appreciable amount of what they had lost.

From actual examples it may be decided that the increase of prices allowed for carvings in 1815, as compared with 1796, represented no sudden change, but only the regulation of what had become customary for some years past. A comparison of the carvings of the *Nelson* 1814 model at Greenwich with that of the project for lengthening the *Victory* in 1802, which is in the Royal United Service Institution, will show this clearly. Prices as fixed on 7 April, 1815, were: –

Class of Ship		Tafferel and Quarter pieces			Upper Finishing			Lower Finishing		
1st rate	120-100 guns	£40	0	0	£ 4	0	0	£6	0	0
2nd rate	90 guns	£37	10	0	£ 3	15	0	£5	10	0
3rd rate	80 guns	£21	0	0	£ 3	5	0	£3	15	0
	74 guns	£16	14	0	£ 3	3	0	£3	10	0
4th rate	50 guns	£13	0	0	£ 3	0	0	£3	0	0
5th rate	38 and 36 guns	£10	10	0	£ 2	10	0	£2	5	0
	32 guns	£ 8	10	0	£ 2	10	0	£2	5	0
6th rate	24 and 20 guns	£ 7	0	0	£ 2	7	0	£2	3	0
Ship sloops with Q.D.		£ 6	10	0	£ 2	5	0	£2	0	0

The prices of figure-heads were not included, but were £50, £35 and £21 in the first three rates, £6 for frigates, and £3 for sloops.

FOREIGN PRACTICE

As this is a branch of the subject concerning which very little is available in printed sources, it has been thought better not to attempt any systematic treatment of it. Without access to the naval records of the several nations, the result of such an attempt would be so incomplete as probably to be seriously misleading. The reader will be able to infer from the examples illustrated that there must have been orders issued in Holland, as we know already was the case in France, comparable to the great English restrictive order of 1703. To discuss the matter in detail is essentially a task for the naval antiquaries of each country concerned, the result of whose researches will be awaited with interest.

Cathead end of the "*Prince*", 1670.

CHAPTER IV

THE HEAD

§ 1. ITS FORM

The head, which is so striking a feature in all contemporary ship-models of earlier date than the 19th century, only came into existence in the reign of Henry VIII. Before then great ships, apparently whether classed as ships or carracks, had that projection of the forecastle beyond the stem head[1] which by general consent is said to be carrack fashion. It is not certainly known how far back that fashion originated; but it is enough for the present purpose to know that it was already well established in the 14th century. Before its day it is believed that sailing ships had no projection whatever before the stem head.

The term gallion begins to be applied to sailing ships early in the 16th century,[2] at first to small ships, but by 1540 to ships of six or seven hundred tons. It is not too clear how these very early gallions differed from ships. The portrait of the *Santa Ana* of 1525, or rather of that ship as she was in 1535,[3] shows her with a very elaborate projection of the carrack forecastle, and – as a distinctive feature – with a galley's ram or beak only a few feet above the water-line. It is supposed that this beak was adopted by sailing ships so that they might be able to meet oared galleys with their own weapon; but what is not clear is whether this feature alone differentiated the gallion from the ship. The beak as a simple spur seems rapidly to have become very general: it is found within the next few years combined with the carrack forecastle in French,[4] English,[5] and Portuguese ships. The carrack

forecastle itself in its last days did what it could to complicate the issue, for it extended itself to an abnormal length outboard, and took to itself an upper story in the form of a square structure which stopped short abaft the stem.[6] This form of forecastle looks very like the later head, but differs from it in the essential point that its lower edge ranged with the gunwale, or at least with the upper-deck of the ship; whereas the beakhead which grew out of the galley spur was originally placed a deck lower. If we may judge by English ships of Elizabeth's reign, there was a considerable period of overlapping fashions, some keeping to a high beakhead derived from the last development of the carrack forecastle, others, especially the later ships, having the very low beakhead which owed its origin to the galley.

The galley spur as first introduced seems to have been a mere open framework,[7] and its development from that point to have proceeded much as did the bird's nests in the fable. At first men thought that the thing was complete as it stood, and even put a figure-head, not at its outboard end, but on top of it, so that – unless as a fore-tack bumkin – the spur could serve no other than its original purpose. But presently there came the idea of decking the framework of the spur, so that it might be used both for handling some of the head-gear and as a platform for small-shot men. It is not clearly known when this was first done; but it seems likely that it may have been one of the improvements introduced by Alvaro de Bazan in 1540 to 1550,[8] and in general that the purpose of those

---

1. P. 57, fig. (n); and p. 59.   2. Duro: Armada Española, I. 352, 416-7.   3. M.M. X, 212.   4. M.M. II, 72 (11).   5. The Anthony Roll.
6. M.M. II, 68, 72, 74; and p. 57, fig. (m) below.   7. P. 177, fig. (a).   8. Duro: *Op. cit.* 1., 440-1.

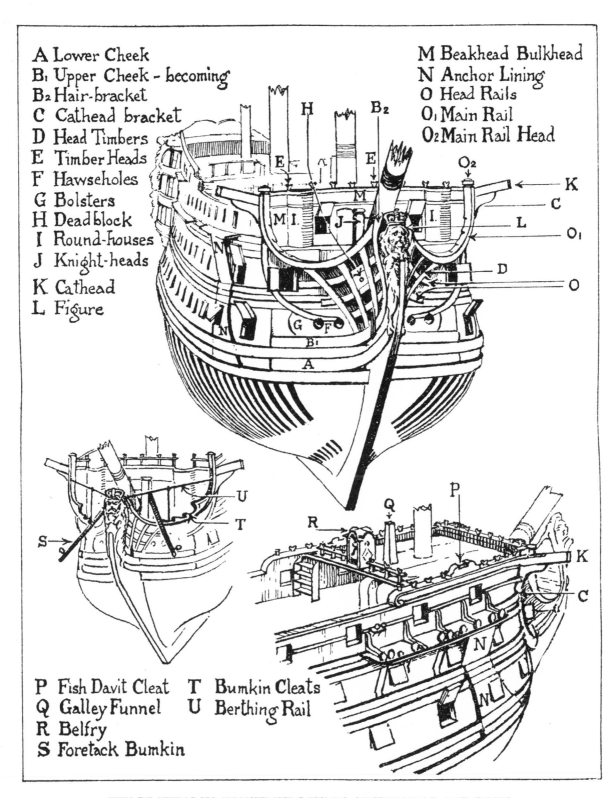

A Lower Cheek
B₁ Upper Cheek – becoming
B₂ Hair-bracket
C Cathead bracket
D Head Timbers
E Timber Heads
F Hawseholes
G Bolsters
H Deadblock
I Round-houses
J Knight-heads
K Cathead
L Figure

M Beakhead Bulkhead
N Anchor Lining
O Head Rails
O₁ Main Rail
O₂ Main Rail Head

P Fish Davit Cleat   T Bumkin Cleats
Q Galley Funnel   U Berthing Rail
R Belfry
S Foretack Bumkin

KEY DRAWING TO ILLUSTRATE DETAILS OF THE HEAD AND BOWS

changes was to develop in the broadside ship the offensive end-on strength of the galley. It was at that time within living memory that the galley had been much improved by the mounting of heavy guns on the forecastle, which gave her a powerful fire directly ahead. No similar fire had yet been developed in sailing ships; and indeed the idea that it was possible to mount bow chasers in the round of the bow did not occur till the 17th century, nor was it carried to its logical conclusion till the beginning of the 19th century.

The Spanish idea seems to have been to cut the bows of the ship away square right down to a low-placed beakhead, thus making it possible to have guns firing directly ahead from as many as three decks. This arrangement is shown in the "treasure frigate" of the latter part of the 16th century,[1] and probably derives from Bazan. Northern ships did not at that time place the beak so low, no doubt owing to the rougher seas in which they usually worked. The beak in them was level with that part of the upper-deck which lay under the forecastle. This does not necessarily mean that it was level with the waist, for commonly the upper-deck had a fall of a foot or two at the forecastle bulkhead, which meant that the head would be correspondingly below the normal level of the upper-deck. This is best shown in the *Ark Royal*[2] of 1587, and in the *Phœnix*[3] of 1612, in which the draughtsman has dotted in the position of the decks; but in the other 16th century ships represented[4] it can be deduced from the position of the ports.

As the bows were not cut away at all, it followed that the "beakhead-bulkhead" – that being the name of the flat bulkhead in which the ship ended above the beakhead – was only the height of the forecastle, which might, according to the size of the ship, have two decks or only one. In order to understand how it was that in the 17th and 18th centuries the beakhead of English and other ships was, relatively to the height of the ship in the waist, lower than it was in the 16th, it is necessary to remember that the whole course of the development of the man-of-war was in an upward direction. Ships added deck to deck more or less unconsciously by building up the waist; and until it came to be admitted that these built-on portions were part of the hull proper, and not mere superstructures like the fore and after castles, external features of the ship, such as the channels, the beakhead, and the entering port, remained in their original positions. They were not lowered, but left behind by the course of development.

Very shortly after the beakhead was formed by adding a floor to the spur it was seen to be necessary that this floor should have rails. A bulwark therefore was carried along each side of the structure, and the resulting head was in section a rectangular trough.[5] This vertical bulwark of the head was divided into compartments by timbers which were a continuation of the brackets supporting the floor; it was ornamented on the panels,[6] the whole arrangement being considered to be a frieze. The form of the head was greatly changed in the 17th century, but its frieze survived

---

1. Hakluyt, X, 160 (Maclehose edition).   2. Plate 6.   3. Plate 1.   4. Plates 1, 5.   5. P. 34, fig. (b).   6. Plate 2.

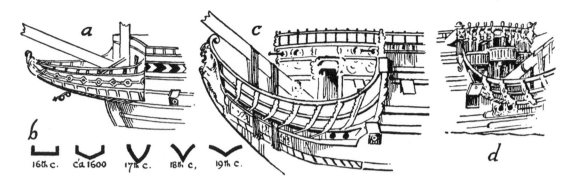

DETAILS OF 17TH CENTURY HEADS

these changes and is still found till about the end of Charles II's reign. It is well shown in the model of the *Prince* of 1670,[1] and is frequently mentioned in the surveys of 1674-8.

The first change made in the form of the head was by steeving up the knee, and consequently the whole structure, so that from being horizontal it came to make an angle of about 30 degrees with the water-line. Doing so made it necessary to curve the rails, and also caused the brackets to form an obtuse instead of a right angle with the knee. The head thus became a shallow V in section (fig. b, above), but its friezed bulwark was still raised vertically on the ends of the brackets. This change, which was accompanied by a considerable shortening of the projection of the head before the stem, seems to have begun about 1640, and was the regular practice under the Commonwealth (fig. c).

After the Restoration the same tendency continued; and as the cheeks of the head still remained low, while with the raising of the knee the rails became higher and more curved, the head became more markedly V-shaped in section (fig. b).

The brackets however were convex, not straight, so that the section was not truly a V, but intermediate between a V and a U. These heads were deep, especially in three-deckers, the beakhead-bulkhead being flat in some cases to the middle deck; but owing to the high curve of the rails they look less low than the later heads of the Anne period.

At the end of the century the brackets straightened out, and then took up a reverse or concave curve, thus making the head narrow below, but spreading out aloft to the main, or upper rails, which in plan ran straight from the figure to the corners of the forecastle. From about 1700 there was little or no essential alteration in the form of the head. The tendency continually was to raise it, and to make it lighter, and its appearance, especially in profile, served to indicate its date; but the same general arrangement lasted till wooden ships came to an end.

Several of these minor changes are illustrated. The heads of Anne's and George I's reigns were notoriously deep and clumsy looking, and this was especially the case in the three-decked ships. The *Ossory* of 1711 illustrates this.[2] It

1. P. 64, fig. (A).   2. P. 35, fig. (b). The *Ossory* began rebuilding in 1706, was renamed *Princess* in that year, and launched 1711.

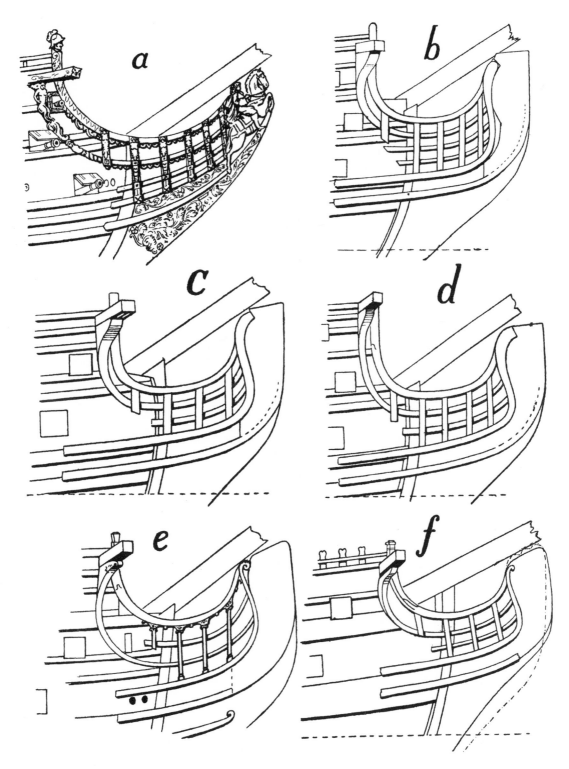

ENGLISH HEADS

(a) Deane's First rate, *c.* 1670.   (b) *Ossory*, 90, 1706-11.   (c) *Resolution*, 70, 1708.
(d) *Cumberland*, 80, 1710.   (e) *Ramillies*, 90, 1748.   (f) *Canada*, 74, 1759.

will be seen that the reason for the heavy look lies in the lowness of the cheeks, which in a three-decker made four rails, instead of the usual three, necessary to raise the upper edge to the desired height. Even so the head was very low, the main rail dipping to about 3ft. below the upper-deck, which soon afterwards came to be considered as its normal level. This meant that there was a break in the floor of the head, the after part, abaft the stem head, being on the exposed end of the upper-deck, and the fore part laid level with the rail.

The 80-gun ship *Cumberland* of 1710[1] shows an interesting thing. She was one of the earliest of the 80-gun ships designed as three-deckers, and she preserved the tradition of her two-and-a-half-decked ancestors. So she had her main rail and the floor of the head very slightly above the level of the middle deck, the stem stopping short just above the middle deck, and the bows of the ship above being cut back to form a beakhead-bulkhead nearly two decks deep. There were many of these 80-gun ships, and it is in great measure from pictures of them that we draw the impression of the extreme lowness of the heads of this period. They were in fact three-decked ships with the three rail heads of two-deckers, and their heads may be regarded as a tacit protest against the mistaken policy which loaded them with an extra deck.

The *Resolution*, 70, of 1708,[2] will stand as a type of the two-decked ship of the period. The main rail is only about a foot below the upper-deck, and

the head in general differs little from that of forty years later. When this head is compared with that of the *Ramillies*, 90, of 1748[3] it will be seen that the chief difference of form consists in the greater rounding of the rails in elevation, and in the increased rake aft of the hair bracket. A similar thing is shown in the draught of the *Canada*, 74,[4] which, designed in 1759, had a distinctly old-fashioned head for her date. She has the same rake aft of the hair bracket, and of the fore side of the knee; and the dotted line on the same draught shows for comparison the profile of the head knee of the *Culloden* of 1744. It is interesting to see from this that the rake aft of the knee, and consequently the lean back of the figure-head itself, was a feature of the middle years of the century rather than, as is perhaps commonly supposed, of the George I period.

It will be noticed that the *Ramillies*, though a three-decker, has only a three-rail head, which however is not low like that of the *Cumberland*, but in about the same position as that of the *Ossory*. This raising of the head was procured by an order of 15 April, 1742,[5] which instructed the yard officers "in order to secure the head of the ships ... to place an additional pair of cheeks to all ships of 50 guns and upwards, and to make the lion or figure of the head as small and as light as possible; keep the knees of the heads of all three-decked ships so high as to have one pair of cheeks above the hawse-holes". The *Ramillies* shows this order in force: there had been an experimental period from 1733. The third pair of cheeks did not last after 1761, presumably because with

---

1. P. 35, fig. (d).   2. *Ibid.* fig. (c).   3. *Ibid.* fig. (e).   4. *Ibid.* fig. (f).   5. Admy.; Navy Bd. 2507, No 344.

the further lightening of the head they ceased to be necessary, but the head was permanently raised, and the placing of the hawse-holes between the cheeks was extended to all classes of ships.

A lighter form of head became common in about 1756, and with very slight modifications continued to the end of the century. In it the rake aft, both of the knee itself and of the hair bracket ceased, and, with the cheeks remaining in their raised position, the head itself grew shallower. Two successive stages of this are illustrated from the *Albion*, 74, of 1778, and from the *Courageux*, 74, of 1796.

After 1800 the head was placed still higher and became lighter. The projection of the head knee was increased, and these features caused the flattening of the rails. Additional cheeks also were reintroduced, the two pairs of the last century becoming three in the opening years of the 19th century, four in the largest ships by 1815,[1] and even five still later. It will be seen that the introduction of round bows by the order of May, 1811,[2] did not affect the form of the head, which though high placed and very shallow was essentially as in 1756.

About 1815 there were slight changes, the most noticeable being that owing to the height to which the head had been raised, and the consequent straightening of the rails, it was no longer possible to curve round one of the lower rails to reconcile with the cathead bracket, which in future had a simple square hanging knee. Similarly the carrying of the main rail head to the corner of the forecastle, where in the 17th century it had formed a carved ornament,[3] and in the 18th a bollard,[4] ceased, because the introduction of round bows left the forecastle without a corner. An attempt was indeed made for a few years to carry it up to the old place, but after 1815 it was abandoned and the rail carried straight to the side to butt against the cathead bracket.[5]

About 1760 a berthing rail was introduced, this being a light iron or wooden rail running horizontally from the corner of the forecastle to the back of the figure-head and serving to spread a canvas screen down to the main rail. It was then a mere detail of equipment and is rarely represented in models or draughts; but in the 19th century it came to be the practice to berth up, that is to board up, the space between it and the

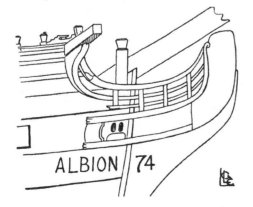

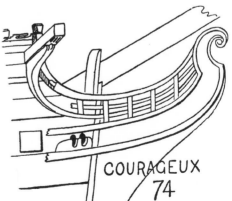

1. As in the *St. George* of 1840.   2. M.M. X, 183.   3. P. 34, figs. (c) and (d); p. 35, fig. (a).   4. P. 35, figs. (b) to (f); p. 37.
5. *Cp.* the *Belleisle* and *Cornwallis*, p. 38.

main rail, which by then instead of being nearly semi-circular had become flat and almost parallel to the berthing rail. This berthing is the most conspicuous feature in the heads of the latest period, the old head-rails being nearly masked by it, especially in one-decked ships, which since the Seven Years' War had had only one rail below the main rail.

The latest form of the rails of the head had thus become not unlike that of the Commonwealth period. The head was placed high instead of low, but it was again a shallow V in section with a vertical bulwark. There the resemblance stopped, for the latest structure was severely utilitarian and quite plain instead of being, as formerly, one of the most ornamental parts of the ship.

The trail board lay between the cheeks, or, if there were more than two pairs of cheeks, between the upper pairs. It belongs to the head, but is only worth consideration for the ornament applied to it, which was a sort of extension of the carved figure-head, in conjunction with which it will be treated.

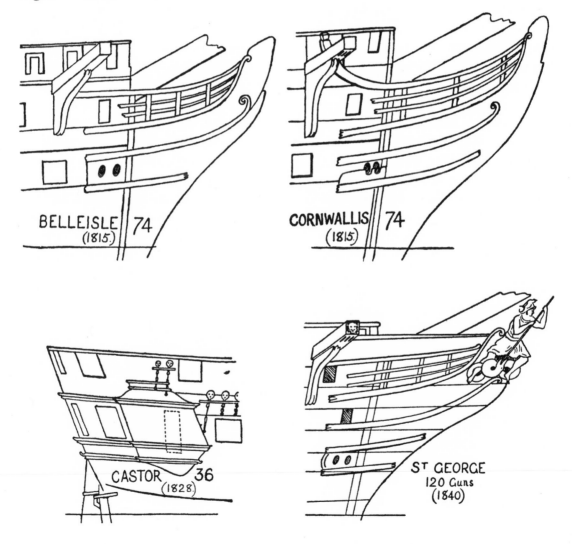

BELLEISLE 74 (1815.)

CORNWALLIS 74 (1815)

CASTOR 36 (1828)

St GEORGE 120 Guns (1840)

Down to the order of 1703 the head was a highly ornamental feature, the rails and the brackets, besides other features which will be discussed presently, being heavily carved. The brackets were particularly decorative, often being given the form of whole figures or of terms.[1] The rails were either moulded or carved in some light design of foliage or the like. The main rail had special features at both its ends, the after end at the corner of the forecastle being always carved, often into a human head; and the fore end being carried up to the figure, where it sometimes was decorated with a rose, a helmet, or other conspicuous knob.[2] Under the Commonwealth this was replaced by a small spiral.[3] Commonly during the decorative period the carvings of the figure came far enough aft to cover the end of the rail, as well as the upper part of the upper cheek which formed the fore side of the frame of the head; but after 1703 this upper part of the cheek, called the hair bracket – perhaps from its contact with the mane of the lion – was usually carved in a volute. But even this small attempt at ornament was abolished by order in 1817.[4]

The stem came up in the middle of the head, and as long as the bowsprit was to one side of it a carved ornament was often placed on top of it. Thus the *Prince* of 1670 had a lion in that position.

But soon after this time – the exact date has not been determined – it became the practice to bed the bowsprit directly down on the stem-head, and to bring a pair of cheeks up on each side of the stem to embrace and thus help to secure the bowsprit. These were the knight-heads, so called, it is said, because they were often carved in the semblance of a man in armour. Evidence of this is lacking; and it is more likely that they drew their name from the pre-existing "knights" on the forecastle and elsewhere inboard, which were undoubtedly so carved.

FOREIGN PRACTICE

As Spanish ships were those with which the gallion head originated, it seems natural that they should have been the first to vary its form. During the war with England they were already steeving up the head till it made an angle of some 30 degrees with the water-line;[5] but the northern nations did not at first follow their example. Even after 1600 Dutch heads, and consequently those of the other nations which took their maritime fashions from the Dutch, were horizontal or nearly so;[6] and by the middle of the century the northern powers had not passed beyond the angle of steeve which the Spaniards had adopted half a century

STEM-HEAD CARVING, 1670

1. P. 35, fig. (a); and p. 64, fig. (A).   2. Plate 2.   3. P. 34, fig. (c).   4. M.M. X, 199.   5. Nance, Plate 10.
6. P. 34, fig. (a), and *cp.* M.M. III, 376.

earlier. Dutch pictures of the campaign of 1639 show the heads of their ships beginning to turn up, and it was very doubtful whether as late as 1637 any other nation would have built a ship with so flat a head as the *Sovereign of the Seas.* Apparently the Dutch ceased very early to frieze the head. When they did so they commonly placed a small open rail or half rail above the frieze;[1] but by about 1630 the frieze seems to have been entirely discontinued, the rails and timbers to have been left quite plain, save for the ends of the main rail, and the head to have become a simple V in section.

Though at the time of the first Dutch war there was little difference in profile between English and Dutch heads, yet on close inspection certain well marked differences are noticed. Dutch ornament was confined to the main rail head, which was heavily carved, usually into a gigantic human head; and to the fore end of the rail, which was turned back in a spiral over the head of the lion. In English ships the spiral is occasionally found after 1660, but then is generally placed lower, so that it is much less conspicuous. Then, as has been mentioned, there was the presence or absence of the frieze; also that the carvings which the English applied to the head brackets were fixed on outside the rails, while the Dutch brackets, being almost always unornamented, appear inside the rails. But what was perhaps the greatest difference was that with the Dutch the forecastle was more cut back than in English ships, so that with them the upward curve of the after part of the main rail was less marked than

with us. This will appear by comparing the head of the *Rainbow*, Van de Velde's drawing of which must have been made in 1652-3,[2] with that of the *Amaranthe*[3] model at Gothenburg. This ship, though Swedish by ownership, is as Dutch as can be desired in her fashions.

French practice at this time was virtually Dutch, and there is nothing to show that the French had evolved a national fashion before they were seriously set to work by Colbert to design and build their own ships. Then they very quickly evolved new forms, which in their turn influenced the practice of their neighbours. Thus the design of a head, reproduced from the Colbert book,[4] is original in its carrying up of the rails and cheeks of the head to a point at their fore ends. It is also noticeable for its carrying up the ends of the main rails to the side of the forecastle abaft the cathead, a practice which much exaggerated the apparent length of the head. It is possible that the deeper curve of the rails in this design represents a French adaptation of the deep English Restoration head, with its almost semi-circular rails;[5] for the design belongs to the period of the alliance with England against the Dutch, when the advice of English experts was eagerly sought. Anthony Deane was chief among those consulted, for which reason it is of interest to compare the typical Deane head with the design of the Colbert book.

Towards the end of the century a new form of head is found both in French and in Dutch ships. It is not clear who originated it; but as it is much nearer

1. P. 34, fig. (a).　　2. *Ibid.* fig. (b).　　3. Plate 15.　　4. Plate 14.　　5. P. 35, fig. (a); P. 64, fig. (A); and Plate 12.

to the intermediate French form, which has just been described, than to the old Commonwealth form, which the Dutch kept till they forsook it for this type, the probability seems to be that its origin was French. It is illustrated here from the *Soleil Royal*[1] and the *Terrible* of 1692;[2] and it will be seen that it is peculiar in having all the rails close together, curving down in a semicircle, with their after ends all carried up to a large carved boss abaft the cathead. The Dutch imitation, if such it was, of this form was half-hearted. The arrangement of the rails was similar, but only the main rail was continued aft to the forecastle, where its head was treated in the old-established manner, and the curve was less deep than in the French design. This is well shown in Mr. R. C. Anderson's model of one of the Dutch three-deckers of about 1685.[3] It occurs also in a model of a small three-decked ship of about the same date, which may perhaps also be Dutch.[4] This model is decidedly French about the stern and quarter, though appearing in other respects to be Dutch, and its identification is likely to throw some light on the interchange of styles at this period. The Dutch only built three-deckers between 1683 and 1695, for the type was not successful with them and was not repeated. In the circumstances it is not remarkable to find that these ships had the head placed very low, in fact where it would have been in a two-decker. As we have seen, it took Englishmen, long familiar with three-decked ships, a considerable time to realise that as decks were added the head ought to go up; and they had not fully accepted this proposition when they built 80-gun three-deckers in Anne's reign.[5]

This fashion of close parallel rails was altogether unlike anything ever found in English ships. It is found in French ships down to about 1755, but with the Dutch it seems to have had but a short vogue. It occurs in Spanish ships, notably in the *Princesa*, built in 1730, and no doubt indicates French influence, for throughout the 18th century the Spaniards evolved no national style of naval architecture, but borrowed all their forms from the great shipbuilding powers. The *Princesa* was French in form throughout; but it is not uncommon to find a Spanish ship combining two styles: the *Fenix*, for example, of 1749, which in 1780 became by capture the English *Gibraltar*, was English as to her head, hances, and other features, but had a decidedly un-English stern.

The Dutch did not abandon this form of head abruptly, for it occurs, with some modification, in the East Indiaman of the 1720's, though by that time there was already a strong tendency towards the English fashion. Thus in the *Ary*[6] we find all three rails brought up parallel at the back of the figure to end in a modification of the old spiral which served when only one rail was so brought up; and the gathering of two rails to a boss at the corner of the forecastle is distinctly like French practice; but the curve of the rails, the treatment of the main knee, and of the trail board, are more suggestive of English usage. English shipbuilding influence was in fact growing strong in Holland, as may be seen from existing ship models and draughts; and it is not surprising to find *'t Wickelo*,[7] a contemporary of the *Ary*, with a

---

1. P. 42, fig. (B).　2. Plate 14.　3. Nance, Pl. 39; and *cp*. P. 54, fig. (b). In E. Indiamen *c*. 1720 two rails were carried up to the boss; *cp*. p. 41 below.
4. From a photograph lent by Mme. Enthoven.　5. P. 36.　6. Plate 15.　7. Plate 14.

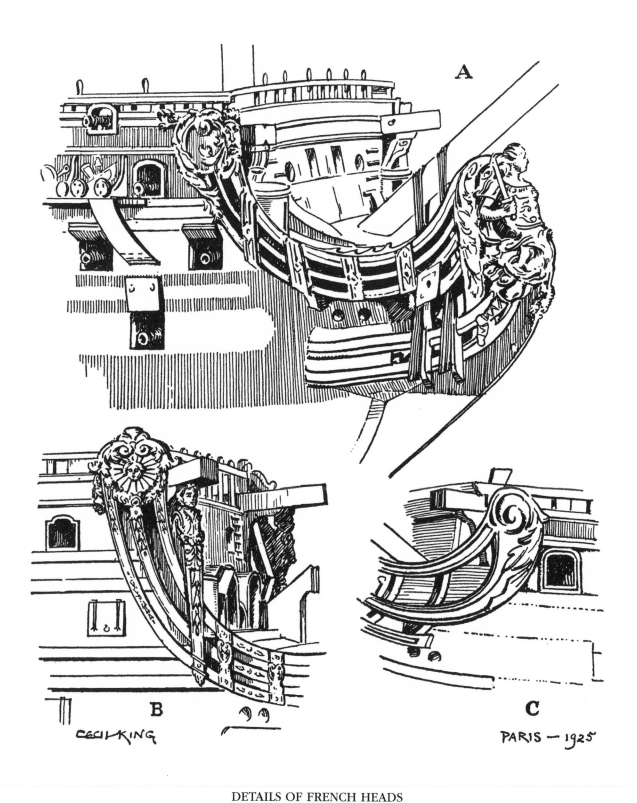

DETAILS OF FRENCH HEADS

(A) *R. Louis*, 1758.   (B) *Soleil Royal*, 1690.   (C) Model presented to the Louvre by M. Marcotte.

head approaching quite nearly to the English pattern, and even with her head timbers carved as half figures. It almost invariably happened, when one nation consciously adopted the fashions of another, that it continued to follow those fashions after they had been laid aside in the country of their origin; and this was the case after the Dutch, towards the mid-eighteenth century, had adopted the English form of head. The form adopted was early Georgian – the model of an English 6o-gun ship of about 1720 is in the Rijks Museum, and was probably one of the actual models from which such details were taken; – and, though definitely superseded in England about 1756, this form continued in use in Holland till quite late in the century. It is shown by draughts in the Scheepvaart Museum of a *'s Lands schip* of 1767,[1] and of a 64-gun ship of 1778;[2] also in a British Admiralty draught of the *Hercules*, 64,[3] which was captured at Camperdown in 1797 and became the *Delft* in the Royal Navy.

During the war of the French Revolution the Dutch would seem to have continued to follow English practice, but with the difference that they abandoned the old early Georgian model and chose a new one which was up-to-date. The head of the *Washington*, for instance, as seen from the model in the "Mercury" Museum, is no longer short and deep, but light, pointed, and rather long, as were the heads of contemporary English ships. It does not seem necessary to follow Dutch practice beyond this point.

A slight change is seen in the head of the *St. Louis* of 1721,[4] which, in addition

to stopping the lower rail short so that only two came to the ornamental boss, carried the main rail in a reverse curve over the head of the figure, forming what may almost be called a small canopy. This seems to be the first inkling of changes to come; for during the 50's of this century a new form of head was introduced, and very shortly entirely superseded the old pattern. The 74-gun ship *Monarque*,[5] captured by England in 1747, is the earliest in which the new form has been noticed. It will be seen that her head, though the fore ends of the rails are obscured by the figure, is not essentially different from that of the *Pompée* of 1788,[6] which may be stated to represent standard French practice for the second half of the century. The earlier ship carries two rails to the ornamental boss on the forecastle, whereas soon after only the main rail head was so treated; but she shows the essential feature which serves as a distinguishing mark of French ships. The main rail at its fore end makes a reverse curve, and the lower rails are gathered up to meet it at the same point. The *Bertin*,[6] captured in 1761, shows what is perhaps a transitional form: her lower rails stop short in the new fashion, and the main rail has the reverse curve; but, save for the fore end of the main rail, the old method of parallel rails is preserved. She was, however, built as an East Indiaman, though taken later into the navy, and departs from navy practice in several respects, those which affect the head being the round bow, the main rail to the cathead, and the uncrowned lion.

There are three other models at the Louvre which illustrate the transitional

1. P. 44, fig. (B).   2. *Ibid*. fig. (A).   3. *Ibid*. fig, (C).   4. Plate 14.   5. Plate 25.   6. P. 47.

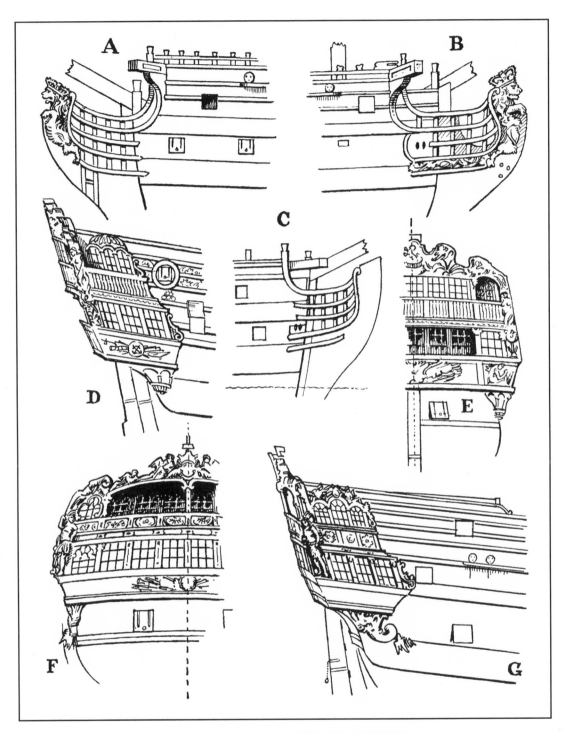

DUTCH HEADS, QUARTERS AND STERNS

(A) A 64-gun ship of 1778. (B) A *'s Lands schip* of 1767. (C) *The Hercules*, 64, taken in 1797.
(D) and (E) *The Boeken Roode*, of 1732. (F) and (G) A 64-gun ship of 1749.
(C is from an Admiralty draught; the others from draughts in the Scheepvaart Museum).

period between these styles. What is perhaps by a little the earliest in design is described as the *Royal Louis*,[1] a three-decker. She shows what is entirely the old form, save that the main rail has the reverse curve at its fore end. The other two models are unidentified. One is known as the "Pic" model, and represents a 74-gun ship of 1755; the other, of a 60-gun ship, is known as the "Marcotte" model,[2] from the name of its donor. This last is dated late 17th or early 18th century, but seems rather to be of about the same date as the "Pic". Each of these two agrees with the *Monarque* in carrying up two rails to the boss, while the third ends short; the "Pic" model also shows a method of twisting the head timbers round the rails[3] which has not been noticed except in French ships, and was probably rare even in them.

The head shown in the *Pompée*[4] lasted till after the peace of 1815 as much the commonest form. It varied a little, the rails sometimes being wider apart, *e.g.*, in the *Centaure* of 1759; and sometimes closer together than those of the *Pompée*, as in the *Spartiate* of 1796. When the rails were close together the reverse curve naturally became much less, as in the *Genoa* of 1814,[5] or was entirely omitted; and sometimes, as in the *Diane*,[6] which shows a late type of frigate head, the rails were not gathered up to a point. The two-rail head of small ships is illustrated from a corvette, the *Vésuve*,[7] of the Empire. The form of head illustrated from the Louvre model which is known as the "vaisseau à rames" of 1785 is unusual in a French ship.[8] It is almost entirely English, with the sole exception that it carries up

the main rail, instead of one of the lower rails, to form the cathead bracket. This practice became very common during the wars of the Revolution and Empire, but did not entirely supersede the old fashion of an independent cathead with an ornamental boss for the main rail head abaft it.

This old fashion had a long vogue and died hard. As we have seen, at first all three rails went to the boss; then from about 1750 two only. As early as 1759 (the *Centaure*) only one went to the boss in some ships; and by 1788, as seen in the *Pompée*, the ornament was very much reduced. The *Genoa*[9] shows the last stage. There is no ornamental boss, as the rail goes to the cathead; but the upper part of the rail which forms the bracket is lightly carved: "in memoriam", as it were.

From 1756, as has been seen, English frigates used only two rails for their heads. The French did not adopt this distinction, but – as the reduced freeboard of a frigate did not give room for a normal three-rail head – they got over the difficulty by putting the rails very close together and making the whole head very light. The "vaisseau à rames", though a frigate, is an exception, for she is in fact a two-decked ship, though with a very incomplete lower deck of guns. Still she is entitled to, and has, the head of a two-decker; but has the round bows of a frigate.

Spanish ships in the second half of the 18th century appear to have taken their fashions almost entirely from English

1. P. 42, fig. (A).   2. *Ibid.* fig (C).   3. P. 46.   4 to 7. P. 47. With the *Vésuve cp.* the head on p. 30.   8. P. 46.
9. P. 47. But *cp.* p. 30, which shows that there was some latitude in respect of ornament.

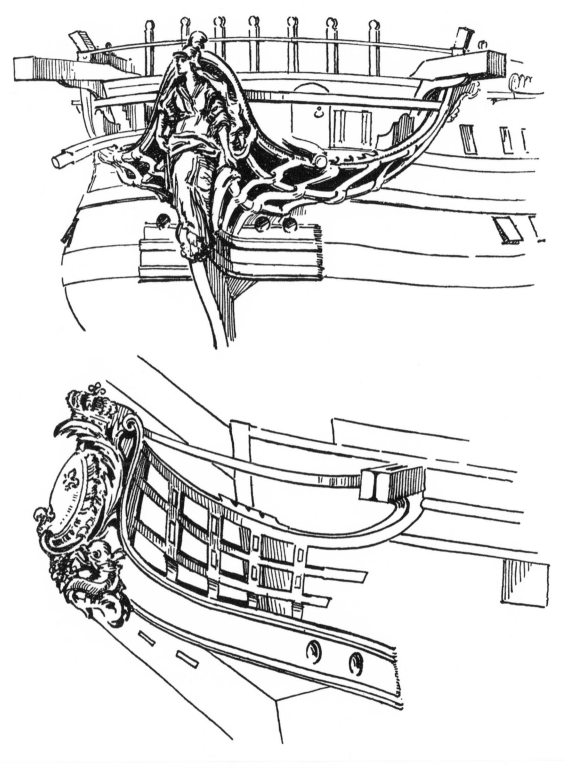

FRENCH HEADS AND FIGURES
From the "Pic" model, 1755; and the "vaisseau à rames", 1785.

ships, and especially so for the heads. One small point, which might serve to differentiate a Spanish from an English ship, is that the Spaniards kept to the early Georgian or Anne form of head generally similar to that of the *Resolution* of 1708;[1] and they kept this form, with flat rails, even in their frigates which, like English frigates after 1756, had only two head rails. But English frigates never had two rails with the Queen Anne form of head.

The Danes, who adopted the round bow for ships of the line a few years before we did, used a two-rail head in two-decked ships both with the beakhead-bulkhead and with round bows. This head was like the English form but lower, as if the main rail had been entirely omitted: in it the upper of the two rails formed the cathead bracket. In the *Norge*, a round-bowed ship taken in 1807, the forecastle deck was carried above the head to end at the back of the scroll which served for a figure-head. The advantage gained by this low form of head was that a pair of upper-deck guns could be fired in chase.

As to Swedish ships there is little to be said; for from the time of Chapman onwards English fashions prevailed so

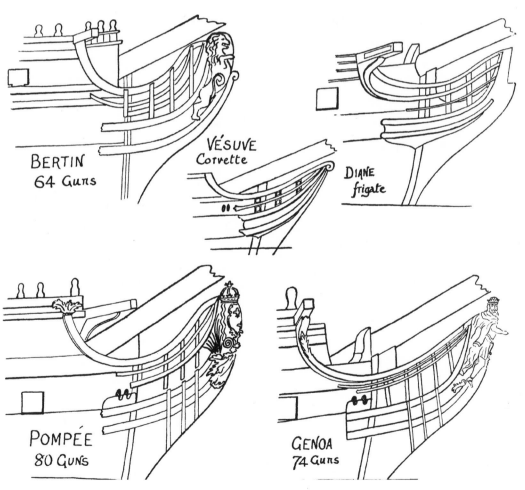

BERTIN
64 Guns

VÉSUVE
Corvette

DIANE
frigate

POMPÉE
80 Guns

GENOA
74 Guns

1. P. 35, fig (c).

entirely with them that the difference between a Swedish and an English ship were minute; and such as there were belonged rather to the after part of the ship.

Most American frigates differed very little in appearance from English, but a few of the earlier ships had French forms. In the War of Independence there was some small variation, as for example in the *Raleigh*, 32, which though in most respects like an English ship, allowed the lower head rail to meet the cathead bracket at an angle of about 120 degrees instead of reconciling with it.[1] The like is not to be found in an English ship after Charles II's reign. The frigates of the war of 1812 differ from English ships only by their greater size and armament, but not at all in form.

§ 2. THE BEAKHEAD-BULKHEAD

A certain degree of assumption seems necessary in order to find sure ground from which to start a consideration of this bulkhead. It seems to fit with the evidence, which for Elizabeth's reign is entirely pictorial, to assume that the floor of the beakhead was then at the level of the upper-deck under the forecastle, and that the beakhead-bulkhead was in consequence merely the fore bulkhead of the forecastle, the bows of the ship not being cut back. This did not always mean that the beakhead floor was level with the upper-deck in the waist, for commonly, perhaps almost always, there was a fall or rise of the upper-deck under the forecastle. The forecastle itself

might be two decks high;[2] but if the side of the ship was continued to the stem at the height of the upper-deck in the waist, then, owing to the fall of that deck under the forecastle, it followed that the beakhead-bulkhead was less than two decks high by the depth of the fall. The question is one of some difficulty, especially as the screen or berthing between the high Tudor upper rail and the main rail proper, obscures the junction of the head with the hull. Perhaps the position of the cathead is the best guide. It at least shows that the hull reaches so far forward, though not necessarily that it does not extend beyond it. In the ship with the fish,[3] it looks as though the forecastle reached a few feet before the cathead, to the beginning of the curved upper rail: in the *Ark Royal*[4] the position of the cathead, and of the upper-deck bow chaser, shows that the deck is carried to the stem.

In James I's time the berthing above the main rail was disused, and a half rail substituted, one result of which is that we can see the beakhead-bulkhead much more clearly. We can thus be certain that as late as 1623[5] there was considerable diversity of practice. The beakhead-bulkhead might be square down to the floor of the head; or it might be square above and rounded below, the rounding being shown sometimes as reaching to the stem, but more generally as stopping markedly short of it. What is this rounding? If it was always shown as going to the stem, it would be a natural inference that it was the bows of the ship built up above the head; and so it may be in a few cases, but not to its apparent

---

1. *Cp.* p. 34, fig, (c).   2. Plates 5 and 6.   3. Plate 5.   4. Plate 6.   5. M.M. III, 272, 305, 341; and VI, 365.

height, for the upper part of it is always an open gallery. Where the rounding stops far short of the stem, as in Vroom's painting of the *Prince Royal*, which seems to give the most trustworthy portrait of the ship, it certainly finishes above in an open gallery, and appears to be continued down to the deck below as a solid bulkhead.

There would be no occasion to raise any question about this bulkhead were it not that a somewhat mysterious reference turned up[1] to "galleries forward on" in the *Royal Charles* of 1673. There was nothing to explain what these galleries were, till fortunately a Van de Velde drawing of the ship came to light, showing the arrangement which is here reproduced.[2] The head is two decks deep, and the galleries, which are three in number, semi-circular, stretching the whole width of the bulkhead, are about level with the upper-deck. At first sight it seemed that there might be round houses under the lateral galleries, but on closer inspection this proved not to be the case.

As far as is known no other ship had the arrangement shown in the *Royal Charles*, but the *Prince Royal*'s round bulkhead seems to have been more or less normal practice in James I's reign. No instance of it is known in the next reign; but there seems to be a slight recollection of the round bulkhead of the *Prince* in the beakhead-bulkhead of the *Sovereign of the Seas*. This was two decks deep without a step, but instead of being flat, it was slightly convex throughout its height. This fashion too would appear to have been of no long continuance, and from

1640 to 1810 the bulkhead was flat, its surface being broken only by the round-houses which, from about 1705, were regularly fitted on it, one at each side. A model in the collection of Col. Rogers, formerly one of the Cuckfield models, and representing apparently a 54-gun ship on the gun establishment of 1703, is peculiar in having only one round-house. It may be that she shows the date of transition; but, though they are not represented either in draughts or models, there are mentions in the surveys of 1674-80[3] which seem to suggest that they may have been in use a good deal earlier.

The beakhead-bulkhead was not officially abolished till 1811,[4] after which date all line-of-battle ships were built with round bows, a change which did not affect the form of the head. It is perhaps one of the most surprising things in the history of naval architecture that the beakhead-bulkhead should have lasted so long. It was defensively weak, being a far lighter structure than the solid bow of the ship, and the deeper it was the more the ship stood to suffer when raked from ahead. The *Britannia* and the second rates of the Naval Defence Act of 1676 abandoned the very deep bulkhead, and from this date on the only English ships with a bulkhead more than one deck deep were the three-decked 80's of Anne's reign. But even so the upper-deck was almost entirely unprotected, as the *Victory* found to her cost at Trafalgar. The bulkhead also was otherwise objectionable, for it impeded the ship's sailing. Indeed, the only advantage which it was supposed to give was that it allowed guns to be mounted in chase;

1. Admy.; Navy Bd. Misc., 3118. f. 58. 2. P. 34, fig. (d). 3. Admy.; Navy Bd. 3118, 3119. 4. M.M. X, 183.

but as middle deck chase guns had been mounted in the round of the bow from the 17th century, it is the more strange that the same principle was not earlier applied also to the upper-deck.

It is not that there had been no experience of round bows, for probably there never was a time when many of the smaller ships of the navy were not so built. Certainly it was so quite early in the 17th century; and from 1760 all frigates had round bows. So had most merchant ships, including foreign East Indiamen, some of which found their way into the navy. So, too, thanks to Snodgrass, had our own East Indiamen of the 90's, including the *York*, which was bought into the navy in 1795; and so too had various foreign ships of the line long before Trafalgar. The first English line-of-battle ship, other than ex-Indiamen or prizes, to have round bows was a 90 razeed to a 74; but whether the *Blenheim* in 1801 or the *Namur* in 1804 is not quite certain.

The decoration of the beakhead-bulkhead was very elaborate. In the 17th century it was in important ships covered all over with carvings, of which the most important were six full-length human figures. In the *Sovereign of the Seas* these carvings represented the virtues. The main rail heads, which came at its upper corners, have already been mentioned; and so have the gun ports, which when on the forecastle had wreaths but no lids, and when on the upper-deck had their lids carved on the outside, sometimes as lions' masks.

The restricting order of 1703 abolished this profusion of carving, for which, however, a good deal of joinery work and elaborate painting was substituted. Commonly there were pillars instead of the figures, their tops joined to form a series of arches right across the round-houses and flat of the bulkhead alike; and for a long time, apparently till the order of 1773, the panels thus formed were painted in devices, sometimes with full-length figures, sometimes with trophies or the like. Above the arches and below the forecastle rail a balustrade was often placed as an ornament. This was perhaps a reminiscence of the galleries of the 17th century, though here there were no galleries unless the very small tops of the round-houses be considered as such. In the latter part of the century there seems to have been little or no orna-ment save the arcading, and even this was abolished by the reduction of 1796, leaving the bulkhead quite plain. The bow chase ports of the 18th century were unornamented, those on the forecastle being embowed into the fife-rail.

FOREIGN PRACTICE

There were two special peculiarities about early Dutch beakhead-bulkheads. In the first place they were not vertical, but raked considerably aft; secondly, they were commonly formed of "landed work", and consequently there was less orna-mentation than with us. Sometimes, as in the large Hohenzollern model there was a row of carved brackets serving appar-ently as stantions to the forecastle rail;

more rarely there were carved figures or terms at each side of the head doors.

An important difference between men-of-war of the early 18th century and East India ships, such as the *Padmos* class of 1722-5,[1] was that the men-of-war had the bulkhead a deck high with gun ports in it, while in the Indiamen the stem was raised, and a deck built from the forecastle to its head. This extension of deck was not quite on a level with the forecastle itself, but a foot or so below it, and was divided from it by a square thwartship rail. It will be noticed that the difference between this arrangement and the complete round bow is merely one foot of height. This arrangement seems to have eventually influenced man-of-war practice, the first example of it being in 1767. Thus the *Hercules*, 64, the *Vrijheid*, 74, the *Washington*, 74, and doubtless other ships,[2] had round bows with a low breastwork across the forecastle in the position of the old beakhead-bulkhead. It has been noticed that in their three-decked ships of the end of the 17th century the Dutch made the bulkhead two decks deep, as probably all nations did in their earliest three-deckers.

French treatment of the bulkhead seems to have been in general similar to English. Like us they adopted the round bow for frigates long before they did so for line-of-battle ships, into which it was not introduced until about the end of the Great Wars; and they had, from the mid-18th century, in some at least of their East Indiamen, such as the *Bertin*, the form of round bow which the Dutch had for long used in their India ships. It is probable that the many 74's razeed to 50-gun ships in and about 1793 became round-bowed in the process.

§ 3. TACK FAIRLEADS

Some late 15th century pictures show a large spike, slightly curved, projecting downwards from the stem at an angle of about 45 degrees under the overhanging carrack forecastle. This apparently was for boarding the fore tack; but as there is only pictorial evidence of it, it is a thing without a name. It may perhaps have had a continuous history in the 16th century: at any rate it, or something like it, still survived even after 1600, though by that date its use seems to have been confined to Dutch ships.[3] Whatever its name, it was in fact a standing fore tack bumkin, and its purpose was to give the tacks a lower lead than could be had on any part of the head. This bumkin is found as late as 1620 or so in Dutch ships, but seems to have been used little if at all in English ships with the gallion head.

The common lead for the tacks with this form of head was through a "serpent", so called because it was actually carved as a serpent, whose coils served as fairleads.[4] The "serpent" was under the stem, and each tack, after passing through it, was led up on the far side into the head. Apparently any carving in this position was called a serpent; but less important ships had merely a couple of holes in the stem.

1. Plate 15.   2. P. 44, figs. (B) and (C).   3. P. 34, fig. (a).   4. Plate 9.

The next stage was to put a "dead block" between the rails and timbers of the head on each side, a fashion which seems to have begun soon after the Restoration, and to have continued till about 1740. It is illustrated here from the *Prince* of 1670,[1] and the *Victory* of 1737.[2] The dead block seems to have been always an alternative fitting, for under the Restoration, as seen in the *Prince*, the stem was also commonly bored with holes for tack fairleads. From about 1700 these holes were discontinued in English ships, and a pair of bumkins began to be fitted instead. It is difficult to be very precise about these, for though the cleats on the main rail which served to secure them are often shown in models, they are not infrequently omitted from models, and still more frequently from draughts. The bumkins themselves are often omitted when the cleats are shown. These bumkins seem at first to have been square in section and to have been bent over the rail, being in fact both in form and position very like a pair of Dutch catheads, though on a smaller scale; but by 1720, or perhaps earlier, spars were used in the form which was kept to the end. Foreign nations do not seem to have used the dead block much, and their ships show the tacks led through the stem – as seen *e.g.* in the *Ary*[3] – till the middle of the 18th century, after which all alike adopted the spar bumkin, and kept it. The "*Royal Louis*" model shows that about the middle of the 18th century the dead block was sometimes found in a French ship,[4] but draughts contemporary with it show only the fair-leader holes in the head knee.

§ 4. ANCHOR GEAR

From the reign of Elizabeth English ships had a pair of catheads placed at the corners of the forecastle, their outboard ends having sheaves for the cat tackle morticed into them, and being finished off with a capping piece carved into a cat or lion face. Thus in all essentials the English cathead was the same for not far short of 300 years. There were, however, differences in the way of securing it. In Tudor ships a square bracket was used;[5] and under the early Stuarts this bracket became a decidedly ornamental feature. In the *Sovereign of the Seas* the brackets were whole figures of lions. As long as the head was flat it was necessary to end its rails short against the side; and the lower arm of the cathead bracket was found convenient for them to but against. Thus the bracket was parallel to the timbers of the head, and it reached down to the lower rail with which at first it made an angle of not much more than 90 degrees. This is well seen in the head of the *Antelope* of 1619,[6] though possibly the head may have been modified somewhat before 1648 when the drawing was made. It is, however, undoubtedly an early form, and perhaps original, as may be decided after a comparison with the Commonwealth head of the *Rainbow.*[7] In this latter the general arrangement is the same, but the angle between the rails and the cathead bracket is increased, so that from this stage of development it was but a small step to curve the end of a lower rail up a little more, and the lower end of the cathead bracket forward a little more, in order that the two might reconcile. This

---

1. P. 64, fig. (A).   2. P. 66.   3. Plate 15.   4. P. 42, fig. (A).   5. Plate 6.   6. M.M. IX, 59.   7. P. 34, fig, (c).

was done when heads were deepened after the Restoration: not all in one step, for some early models still show a slight angle, and a Van de Velde drawing of the *Old James*[1] in her Restoration form shows the bracket curved forward, but the lower rail not continued to meet it. But by 1670[2] the change was complete, and till the end of the 18th century one of the lower rails was always carried up to form the bracket.[3] It was always a mere matter of convenience which rail was chosen, and occasionally, about the time of George I, the upper cheek was used for this purpose instead of a rail.

Very occasionally late in the century the rails were allowed to end short, and the cathead was supported by a square bracket; and with the introduction of round bows this became the regular practice,[4] for the head was then placed so high that the old method was no longer possible. This was the last stage of development.

In the 17th century the cathead itself, as well as its bracket was often carved;[5] but after the order of 1703 the bracket had only a plain moulding, and the cathead itself was panelled on its sides and had an ornament on its outboard end. This was usually a cat face, but often a star, particularly after about 1750. Sometimes after the order of 1796 the end was merely carved in a "patera"; and very occasionally an anchor is found instead of a star or cat face. These, I think, exhaust the variants: I have, for instance, never met with a crown.

In the 17th century the hawse holes were often ornamented in important ships, *e.g.*, in the *Sovereign of the Seas*,[6] and the *Prince* of 1670;[7] but the wear and tear of carvings in such a position must have been prohibitive, and they seem to have died a natural death even before the order of 1703. They do not appear in the profusely decorated ships of William III's reign. In early Stuart

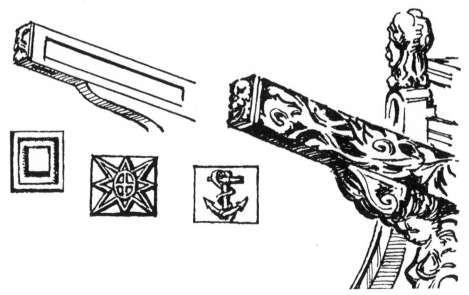

DETAILS OF ENGLISH CATHEADS

1. Plate 12.   2. P. 35, fig. (a).   3. P. 37.   4. P. 38.   5. P. 53. The carved cathead shown is from the *Prince* of 1670.   6. Plate 9.
7. P. 64, fig. (A).

times when there was only one cheek of the head the hawse holes were placed between the cheek and the lower rail; and when, towards the middle of the century, a second cheek was introduced, it was placed so low that the hawse holes still remained above the cheeks. A very few Restoration ships, such as the *Prince*, had the cheeks so high that the hawse holes came between them; but this was quite exceptional in the 17th century, and in the 18th was practically unknown until it was ordered in 1742[1] that three-deckers were to have their hawse between the cheeks. Two-deckers soon followed this example, but till about 1760 a few were still built with hawse and cheeks in the old positions.

FOREIGN PRACTICE

Dutch ships of the early 17th century show no cathead,[2] and it may be that in this they were not alone. When they did begin to fit catheads, which seems to have been about 1630, they placed them, not at the corner of the forecastle, but in the head itself and directly over the hawse holes.[3] Usually they came out over the main rail, but occasionally they were below it. This fashion lasted with them for about a century. In the East Indiamen of 1722-5 there is a slight modification. The cathead is still inside the head, but the building up of the bow before the forecastle has allowed it to be placed on top of this structure,[4] so that it is a few

DUTCH CATHEADS

(a) From an E. Indiaman, late 18th century. (*Rijks Museum*). (b) Head of the "Caravelle de guerre", probably an Ostend E. Indiaman, early 18th century. (*Musée de l'Armée, Brussels*).
(c) From *Prins Frederick der Nederlanden*, 44 guns. (*Rijks Museum*).
(d) From a line-of-battle ship, late 18th century. (*Rijks Museum*).

1. P. 35, fig. (e).   2. P. 34, fig. (a).   3. Plates 15 and 36.   4. Plate 15.

feet further aft than it used to be, and also some three feet higher, though not as high or as far aft as in an English ship. It is supported by a small carved bracket or strut, which spreads over the rails in the French manner and serves as a term for the lower rail.

It is of interest to notice that so very Dutch a ship as is represented by the "Caravelle de guerre" model at Brussels (fig. b, facing page) departs from contemporary Dutch practice in the fitting of her catheads. She has them at the corners of the forecastle, inside the main rail heads, and raking well forward. In this, and in the scroll carving under the main rail head, she is following the French fashion; but in almost every other detail she reflects Dutch usage, though, as has been already noticed, not in every respect contemporary Dutch usage.

In the second half of the 18th century the Dutch followed the English fashion.[1] That they had begun to adopt it in 1725 is seen in *'t Wickelo*,[2] a ship which had her cathead at the corner of the forecastle and its bracket formed by carrying up a rail; but her cathead, like that of the *Ary*, is still distinctly lower than in English practice. The arrangement seen in the head of the *Hercules*,[3] while corresponding in the main to English practice, differs from it in carrying up the main rail abaft the cathead. This seems to be a reversion to the method shown in the *Ary*;[4] but it is the more noticeable in the *Hercules* because in her the bow is built up round to its full height.

Man-of-war and East Indiaman fashions at the end of the century are illustrated in figs. (d) and (a).[5] The latter is the more remarkable. The main rail ends in a small spiral where it touches the round of the bow, and close abaft it a stout square bollard, from which the cathead springs, is fitted at the corner of the forecastle.

The northern nations did not follow Dutch fashion in this respect. The *Amaranthe* model, indeed, has the cathead in the head like a Dutch ship;[2] but probably this instance alone is not enough to show that this was regular Swedish fashion, especially as the few other examples collected show the English method prevalent in the Baltic. Thus a Bergen church ship[6] of about 1610 has a Dutch head but the cat English fashion; so has the *Norske Löve*[7] model; and so has the small Danish two-decker of the late Restoration period which is illustrated here,[8] though in her the cathead is lower than in English ships. The "Great Dane of 1600", engraved by Möller, shows a Dutch head and cathead, which seems to be an argument against the dating of the picture, seeing that the Dutch themselves did not adopt this fashion till some 30 years later. Apparently the Baltic powers early felt the need of standing catheads, and having no Dutch model to follow, borrowed from England.

When the French forsook Dutch fashions they placed the cathead at the corner of the forecastle, but raking forward more than in English ships, so that the bracket was on the beakhead-

1. P. 44, figs. (A) and (B).　2. Plate 14.　3. P. 44, fig. (C).　4. Plate 15.　5. P. 54.　6. Nance, Plate 14. (Ascribed to 1610, but probably later).
7. M.M. IV, 303.　8. Plate 36.

bulkhead and inside the head-rails.[1] In addition to this bracket, which was square, and being inconspicuous was little ornamented, they often fitted a flying bracket or spur, which came down to the ship's side outside the head-rails. This was elaborately ornamented, its upper part commonly being a bust. It is illustrated (p. 42) from the model of the *Soleil Royal* of 1692 at the Louvre. In the latter part of the 18th century this carved bracket was disused, but commonly the old square bracket was still fitted inside the head. From the latter part of the 18th century, however, a modification of the English method was adopted, especially in conjunction with the round bow, a rail being brought up to form the bracket.

Occasionally the main rail was used thus, a thing foreign to English practice, but found also in the Danish 74-gun ship *Norge*, captured in 1807.

There were other small differences between English and French or Dutch methods. Both the French and the Dutch, though seemingly not the Danes, kept the cheeks below the hawse holes till well into the 19th century; and they also did not often use a carving for the end of the cathead, because commonly, instead of morticing the sheave holes through the timber, they sawed them down into it from the end, sometimes adding a fair leader in a chock on the after side of the cat.

ORIGINAL CATHEAD OF H.M.S. TRINCOMALEE, 1817, NOW THE FOUDROYANT, TRAINING SHIP

1. P. 42.

CHAPTER V

FIGURE-HEADS

The figure-head takes pride of place among the carved works of ships ancient and modern; and when we remember the analogy between a ship and a living creature, which seems always to have presented itself to the minds of sailors, it will appear inevitable that it should do so. The consideration that religious symbolism had much to do with the choice of emblems by early nations hardly affects the present thesis, which is that the ship, having to find her way, needed eyes. The need was adequately supplied in different ways: in Egypt by drawing on the resources of an extensive pantheon; in Phœnicia by symbolising the ship as a swift horse; in many countries and in many ages, from ancient Greece to China,

by painting an eye on either bow; by the Northmen of the Middle Ages by likening their ships to snakes and dragons. In the particular case of the war-galleys of ancient Greece and Rome, the ram itself was fashioned into the head of a charging beast (fig. f), such as a ram, a boar, or even an elephant; but it is perhaps to stretch the meaning of the term unduly to speak of these utilitarian devices as figure-heads.

Under the Roman Empire there was considerable development, figures being carved in relief on the sides of the stem (fig. g), or a bust – and perhaps sometimes whole figures – mounted in a manner not differing perceptibly from that of the 19th century (fig. h).

EARLY FIGURE-HEADS

(a, b, c) Egyptian.   (d, e) Phoenician.   (f) Greek.   (g, h) Roman.   (i) Bayeux Tapestry.
(j) 11th century.   (k) 13th century.   (l) Seal of Dover.   (m) The *Jesus of Lubeck*.
(n) a 15th century carrack.   (o) The *Unicorn*.   (p) The *Salamander*.

The mediæval fashion in northern waters derived from the usage of the Vikings, and as long as ships built expressly for war followed the Viking model, their high stems afforded a conspicuous, and therefore natural, place for emblematical ornaments. Only one actual figure-head of this era has survived, that of the Oseberg ship of about 800 A.D.;[1] and in her, as probably in many other ships, the device was a serpent. Two centuries later Danish ships had their prows ornamented with figures of lions, bulls, dolphins, or men, made of copper gilt; and it is recorded that Sweyn's own ship in 1004 was in the form of a dragon, whose head formed the figure-head, while the stern post represented its tail.[2]

The ornamentation of both stems seems to have been not uncommon in important ships: thus the flagship (to use a convenient anachronism) of William the Conqueror had a lion head on her fore stem,[3] while on her stern post, as though for the guidance of the helmsman, there was perched the effigy of a boy blowing an ivory trumpet and pointing with outstretched hand to the promised land,[4] some of which details the Bayeux tapestry fails to reproduce. Representations of the figure-heads of the Middle Ages are not uncommon, and show that from the 11th to the 13th centuries they were carved on the high stems,[5] when such existed. The battle off Sandwich in 1217 is of interest in the story of the figure-head, for it showed that by then the pure sailing ship, the round ship, had become the capital ship. The high stemmed ships hitherto were the descendants of the Viking type

of the long ship, of which we know relatively much; but of the mediæval round ship we know almost nothing. She descended no doubt directly from the ships of the Veneti with which Cæsar tried conclusions. He found them horribly great and strong; and it can be calculated that they measured some 200 tons, *i.e.*, that they were as big as the ordinary run of ocean-going ships till well into the 19th century; but we can only guess what their form was and whether they had ornaments or not.

Among the king's ships in the 14th century there were both oared vessels and sailing ships. It would seem that the oared craft, whether great or small, whether galleys or barges, still retained the high stems. There is a direct mention of the ornamentation of the stems of one such ship, the galley *La Philippe* of 1336:[6] "For leopards, with painting of the same, placed upon the stampnes, – 21s." There seems to be no objection to deciding that the "stampnes" were the stems.

As long as the "stages" or "castles" which were erected in existing ships in order to convert them into men-of-war were temporary structures, they probably did not interfere with the traditional ornament of the ship, for apparently they stopped short of the stems. But when they became permanent they very soon began to grow in length, which they could easily do by extending themselves beyond the stems.[7] In this way the overhanging "carrack" forecastle[8] was developed, and, what concerns us more here, the old-established site of the

1. P. 10.   2. Nicolas, Hist. of R.N., I, 17.   3. P. 57, fig. (i).   4. P. 87, fig. (e).   5. P. 57, figs, (i), (j), (k).   6. Nicolas, Hist of R.N. II, 472. 7. P. 57, fig, (l).   8. P. 57, figs. (m), (n).

figure head ceased to exist, for the stem head itself was under the forecastle.

This change probably accounts for the almost complete absence of any reference to figure-heads in the 14th century, during which the forecastle was growing from a small to a large structure. Late in the 15th century the lower rail of the "carrack" forecastle was carried forward beyond the rest of the structure, and the distinct projection thus formed was frequently carved into the head of a beast, a greyhound being often chosen as being a badge of nobility. Such a figure was inconspicuous,[1] though sometimes an artist exaggerated it beyond anything that he is likely to have seen in an actual ship.[2] There is a reference in 1415 to the carving of a swan and an antelope, two of the royal devices, for the king's ship *Holigost* in 1415,[3] but there is nothing to show that they served as a figure-head; indeed from their relatively high cost, £4 13s. 4d., it seems improbable that space could have been found for such important carvings at the end of the forecastle, and it is more probable therefore that they ornamented the stern or quarters.

That the inconspicuous figure on the front of the forecastle did not satisfy all men is shown by the existence of an alternative arrangement, in which a device was placed on the stem itself directly under the forecastle. This is illustrated[4] from a carrack of Britanny which, about 1510, bore the crowned arms of the province in that position. This may have been distinctively a French arrangement, and have been followed in other ships of which we have no pictorial record:

in the *Grande Françoise* of 1527 for instance, which is stated to have had as a figure-head an effigy of St. Francis with the royal badge of the salamander under it.

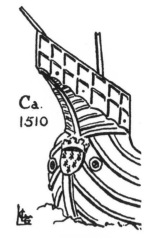

Ca. 1510

There was no further development until after the attempt had been made to combine some of the advantages of the galley with those of the sailing ship. The resulting beakhead offered a new and conspicuous position for a figure-head, which began to be introduced in that position even before the end of Henry VIII's reign. The earliest ships in which it is found are the *Salamander*[5] and *Unicorn*,[6] as represented in the Anthony Roll. These are the only ships of the navy which in 1546 had figure-heads, unless there were others in the old inconspicuous position of which the artist has taken no account, as from other evidence it appears certain that there were. Probably these two figure-heads were represented as being conspicuous and unusual; and incidentally they show that the origin of this form was not English, but probably French. Both the ships were prizes, the *Salamander* being French and named after the badge of Henry IV, while the *Unicorn* was taken from the Scots, whose royal device she bore both in her name and in her figure.[7]

For about a century, roughly from 1540 to 1640, the beakhead remained

1. P. 220, Original Frontispiece.   2. M.M. IX, 282.   3. M.M. V, 24.   4. P. 59, from M.M. III, 285.   5. P. 57, fig. (p).   6. P. 57, fig. (o).
7. Oppenheim, "Administration of R.N.", 61.

horizontal or nearly so, but there was some development in its construction which affected the position of the figure. At first there were no cheeks of the head; and when one was introduced, as seems to have happened towards the end of the 16th century, it either formed part of the head itself, or was hidden under its rails. A second cheek does not seem to have been introduced till 1620 or later, and even so did not become general at once: thus the *Sovereign of the Seas* shows only one. The state of development of the cheeks is of some importance in the history of the figure-head, both because their presence or absence affected its position, and because the trail-board, which lay between the cheeks, was very generally carved, in the 17th century in an independent design, but in the 18th in a continuation of the design of the figure-head.

Before the cheeks were developed the figure seems to have been placed on the fore end of the head itself, against the bracket in which the rails terminated. Then as the knee grew a little deeper, room was found for the figure between the single cheek and the lowest rail. It was thus rather under the head than in front of it, but as the fore end of the knee turned up a little, a beast thus placed seemed to be rushing from his lair.[1] This same method continued in use when the second cheek was fitted, the position of the beast being now between the cheeks, and the general effect much as before. One result of this arrangement was that the fore end of the main rail was a long way above the head of the figure, if the figure was a beast, and seemed to demand some ornamentation of its own.[2] This was frequently

given to it. The rail ended in a spiral, on top of which was placed something large and round, such as a rosette, a grotesque head, a helmet, or a crown. The *Prince Royal* of 1610 had in this position an enormous helmet surmounted by a crown much too big for it.[3]

But there was an alternative way of fitting the figure. Sometimes the knee of the head was continued several feet beyond the fore end of the rails, thus forming a little platform and giving the figure, so to say, level ground to stand on. This seems to have been common in English ships in the early Stuart period, and was particularly suitable for an equestrian figure or a group. Thus the *Prince Royal*[3] and the *Phœnix*,[4] each of which had a representation of St. George slaying the dragon, had the figure in this position; and so had the *Sovereign of the Seas*,[5] whose head showed "King Edgar on horseback trampling upon seven kings". In the Hampton Court painting of the return of the fleet from Spain in 1623 all the ships whose figure-heads can be made out have them in this position,[6] the *St. Andrew* having a lion passant, and the *"Benevolence"* (i.e., Bonaventure) having a lion salient. In other ships the arrangement is obscure owing to distance, but apparently the *Defiance*, which is well forward in the picture, has no figure whatever. Undoubtedly this method set the figure off well, but it seems open to the serious objection that it afforded very little support. Mr. Chucks no doubt would have described the position of the figure as "precarious and not at all permanent", and would have expected the ship to part company

1. P. 63, fig (a).　2. M.M. VIII, 289.　3. Plate 2.　4. Plate 1.　5. Plate 9.　6. M.M. III, 272; and *cp.* 321.

with it the first time she put her head into a sea.

It is a question whether late Tudor ships carried their figure-heads in this position. The engravings of the lost House of Lords' Armada tapestries can hardly be adduced as evidence on such a point; and it is unfortunately the case that "Ancient English Shipwrightry" does not treat its figure-heads very seriously.[1] It does, however, indicate that the figure was commonly placed against the end of the head rails, though in the one case of the *Ark Royal* a small projection of the knee may be suggested; but the devices shown do not correspond either in principle or in detail with what is known of the figure-heads of Elizabethan ships. It is true that a picture by Willærts, stated to represent an English ship of 1602, shows an equestrian figure standing clear before the head;[2] but it would be unsafe to trust much to this, for the picture was painted some 20 years later, and shows the features which we would expect to find in a ship of that date.

We have from Mr. Oppenheim a list of the figures of the queen's ships towards the end of her reign.[3] Five, the *Charles*, the *Defiance*, the *Garland*, the *Rainbow*, and the *Repulse* had a lion; five more had a dragon, the *Adventure*, the *Bonaventure*, the *Dreadnought*, the *Hope*, and the *Nonpareil*. The *Mary Rose* had a unicorn; the *Swiftsure* a tiger; and the *White Bear*, as rebuilt in 1598, had Jupiter seated on an eagle. The *Rainbow*'s lion is mentioned as having been gilt, which suggests that gilding was the exception. It may be that the single figures were in the old position against the end bracket of the rails, but probably the more ambitious design of Jupiter and his eagle needed to be treated as the equestrian figure-heads were in the next reign. It will be noticed that the lion, and the alternative supporter of the royal arms, the dragon, are in a great majority. This would appear to explain how it came about that the lion virtually had the field to himself in the 17th century, when the dragon had been relegated to a secondary position, and the unicorn had not yet made good.

It has been noticed that the device of St. George and the dragon formed the figure-head of at least two of the ships of James I, which had no particular connection with the saint. Doubtless the ship named *St. George* had a similar figure; but the case of the others suggests the consideration that the overthrow of the dragon may, at this time, have been considered as a national emblem, suitable for any ship.

The Dutch figure-head at this time seems to have always been the national lion, issuant from beneath the head rails, or from between the cheeks, and beginning his upward progress which was eventually to be checked by his contact with the spiral of the main rail. Sometimes he brandishes his sword, more often he is without it. The English lion was normally gilt from James I's time, but the Dutch lion seems to have been red as far back as he has been traced, and usually to have had a golden mane.[4] In their own ships the Dutch used no other figure-head until about 1720,

1. Plates 1, 5, 6.   2. M.M. III, 321.   3. "Administration of R.N.", 131.   4. Plate 2.

but with the alteration in the shape of the head, which has been described, the position of the lion became somewhat more upright. One peculiarity of the 17th century Dutch lion is that he was generally made pretty long in the waist, and that the carver, when he came to carve his ribs, seems to have taken one of the wooldings of the bowsprit for his model.

In ships built for their own use the Dutch did not adopt the platform for the figure, because there was no need for it; but when they built ships for foreigners who wanted fancy figure-heads, they placed the figure as in English ships. The "navire royale" of Hondius shows Jupiter on his eagle in this position; and a painting of another ship built for France in the same year, 1626, shows Neptune driving a pair of sea horses.[1] The only early model of a Spanish ship which we have belongs to 1592,[2] and strikes a very modern note by having only a scroll instead of a figure-head; but in general the Spaniards appear to have used a lion, as indeed in the 17th century most nations did, excepting the French, with whom it was comparatively rare. It should be understood that yachts are an exception to this, and indeed to almost every rule. Even Dutch yachts substituted some other device, such as a dragon, or a cockatrice, for the lion.

We know very little about the figure-heads of Commonwealth ships, with the exception of the *Naseby*, which is recorded by Evelyn to have had "Oliver on horseback trampling six nations under foot: a Scot, Irishman, Dutchman, Frenchman, Spaniard and English, as

was easily made out by their several habits. A Fame held a laurel over his insulting head: the word 'God with us'." Naturally this figure was removed at the Restoration: Pepys said that the new one was a Neptune, which, if true, seems to show that the fashion of portrait equestrian figures was not yet the rule; for as the ship was renamed the *Charles Royal*, a portrait of the king would be expected. It is a pity that the Van de Velde drawings of this ship both agree in showing the stern.[3] Paintings of the battles of the first Dutch war seem to show that the lion was already the figure-head in common use. There may have been other big ships besides the *Naseby* which had either groups or equestrian figures, but in such portraits of individual ships as survive, the stern, as the more decorative feature, has usually been preferred. In the *Lamport* we can see an indication of a lion, with the main rail forming a spiral over his head. There is also a Van de Velde drawing of the *Portsmouth* which shows the lion uncrowned, with the same fashion of rail; but it is not certain in this case that the drawing represents the ship in her original form. The head seems rather later in type than 1649, when the ship was built, and may have been renewed in or after the first Dutch war, or, perhaps less probably, after the second war. If that be so, we have the uncrowned lion after the Restoration. The Sheldon model at Stockholm has an equestrian figure-head;[4] and, though she does not represent an individual ship, yet she certainly does represent English practice of about 1656. The inference seems to be that probably some other Commonwealth ship, or possibly ships,

1. M.M. III, 376.   2. Nance, Plate 10.   3. M.M. II, 238; IV, 27.   4. M.M. X, 217.

ENGLISH LIONS
(a) to (d) are figure-heads; (e) a stern carving.
(a) From Vroom's painting of the Arrival of the Elector Palatine, 1613.
(b) From a Van de Velde drawing of the *Victory* of 1665.
(c) From a model of *c.* 1670 described as the "*Lion*". (*R.N. Museum, Greenwich.*)
(d) From a model of a 60-gun ship of *c.* 1750. (*Science Museum, South Kensington.*)
(e) Supporter of the royal arms on the stern of H.M.S. *Camperdown*, 1820. (*Messrs. Castle.*)

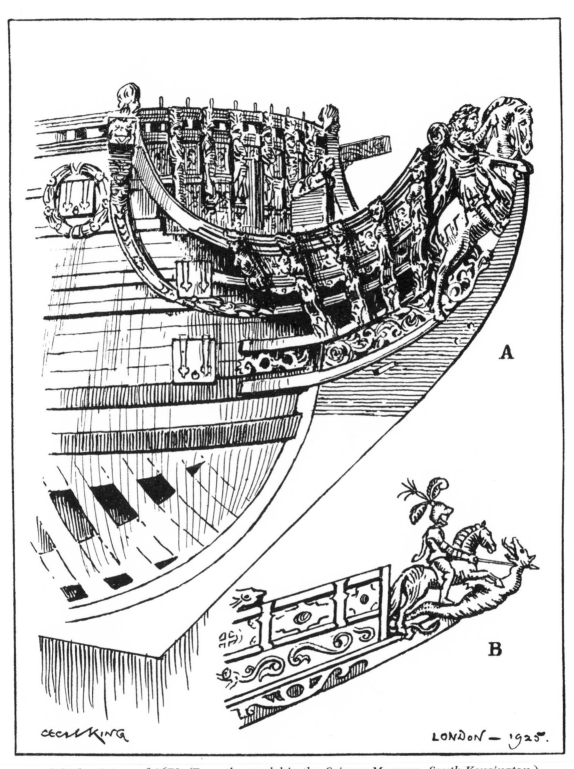

(A) The *Prince* of 1670. (From the model in the *Science Museum, South Kensington*.)
(B) The *Phœnix* of 1613. (From an Admiralty draught.)

besides the *Naseby* had an equestrian figure; though it is not likely that any other had such an elaboration of figures as she had.

After the Restoration there were very few ships which had a figure other than a lion. The exceptions were the first rates which were named after royal persons and had portrait equestrian figures. The *Prince* of 1670, which is illustrated from the model at South Kensington (facing page), may be taken as typical of this class. The rule, however, was not invariable, for the Earl of Sandwich possesses a model of a first rate, which is possibly the *Royal James* of 1675, but has a lion for a figure. The former ship of the name, burnt at Solebay, had an equestrian portrait of the Duke. With the second rates a lion was the rule, and only two exceptions have been noticed. The *St. Michael* of 1669 had Jupiter in a chariot drawn by a two-headed bird, presumably an eagle; and a model in Mr. R. C. Anderson's collection has a figure-head so far similar, that, as she cannot be the *St. Michael*, the temptation is strong to identify her with the *St. Andrew* of 1670.

Towards the end of Charles II's reign figure-heads became slightly less simple, the lion in some cases being mounted by a Cupid, as in the *Coronation* of 1685; and the *Britannia*, first rate, of 1682, having a man on horseback trampling on a reptile of the dragon order. Who is represented by the rider, and who or what by the reptile, is unexplained. The combination of lion and Cupid was not novel in 1685, for it is found as early as 1619, in the *Antelope*; but it is believed

that it was not common till late in the Restoration period. It is illustrated here from the so-called "*Lion*" model at Greenwich.[1] These figure-heads were simple and dignified: there was no crowding of the main figure with a host of supporters, nor was there as yet any extension of the figure down the trail board, which was carved in design of its own. It may be thought, however, that the general effect would have been better had the decoration of the timber and frieze of the head been less profuse; but as the figure was gilt, while the rest of the head was only painted in a substitute for gilding, it may be that the figure stood out better from its surroundings than pictures or drawings convey.

Though there are many models of the ships of William III's reign, unfortunately few of them have been identified, and it is not yet possible to be precise as to the exact course of development of the figure-head. The lion, or "beast" as he is frequently styled, was still the common wear for all ships from 80 guns downwards, and he was often "enriched" by the addition of a pair of Cupids; but for most three-decked ships elaborate figure-heads became the rule. Apparently it was at this time that the double equestrian figure was introduced, which had a long vogue in the 18th century; but it would seem that there were always variants of it. Two examples are given here of this type of figure, one from Balchen's *Victory* of 1737,[2] the other from Kempenfelt's *Royal George* of 1756,[3] and it will be seen that the difference of treatment is considerable. Even these figures, especially that of the *Victory*, are elaborate; but

1. P. 63, fig. (c).   2. P. 66.   3. P. 67.

they are simple when compared with the extremely rococo figures of about 1700. These earlier heads are so swamped with secondary figures and their attributes that without a written specification it is impossible to understand them, and the specifications have not yet been dug out from the Navy Board papers. Also it is extremely difficult to illustrate them. They are all either gilt, in the earlier ships, or varnished, and in either case the high lights on the mass of minute detail defeats the camera,[1] while to draw them is a tedious and difficult business. Early examples of this type of figure are shown by several models at Greenwich: by the so-called "Victory, 17th century", which probably represents the *Royal Anne* of 1704, and has an ox, a woman, and Cupids on each side; by the "100-gun ship" model, which seems to be of a 90-gun ship on the 1706 establishment, or perhaps before it, and has a most rococo figure consisting of a large crowned shield of the royal arms, supported by four Cupids, beneath which are two female figures, with further Cupids beneath them again.

The restrictive order of 1703 forbade the carving of fancy figure-heads without special order, but for first rates the special order was very often, or even usually, forthcoming. Indeed, of the surviving models of first rates of the next 20 years or so only one, so far as has yet been noticed, has a simple lion for a figure-head, this being the second of the so-called "*Royal Williams*" at Greenwich. This latter ship has not yet been identified; but as the *Britannia* of the same date, to which the ship may be assigned, had a lion, it may prove to be the case that she was the subject of the model.

Second rates of the William III and Anne periods at least sometimes had special figure-heads. We have one of William's time, the *St. George* of 1701, which shows the saint on foot fighting the dragon. The dragon is outside, his back following the contour of the head knee, and St. George, who is pinned against the head rails, looks to be in a decidedly tight place. The arrangement is no doubt ingenious, but unsatisfactory, for the design does not stand out well, and at a very short distance must have appeared to be a meaningless mass.[2] From the sums spent on their carved works it seems probable that most second rates of this reign had some more elaborate design than a lion;

BALCHEN'S "VICTORY" OF 1737

1. See *e.g.*, Plate 17; and M.M. IV, 69; and VII, 240.   2. Nance, Plates 58, 60.

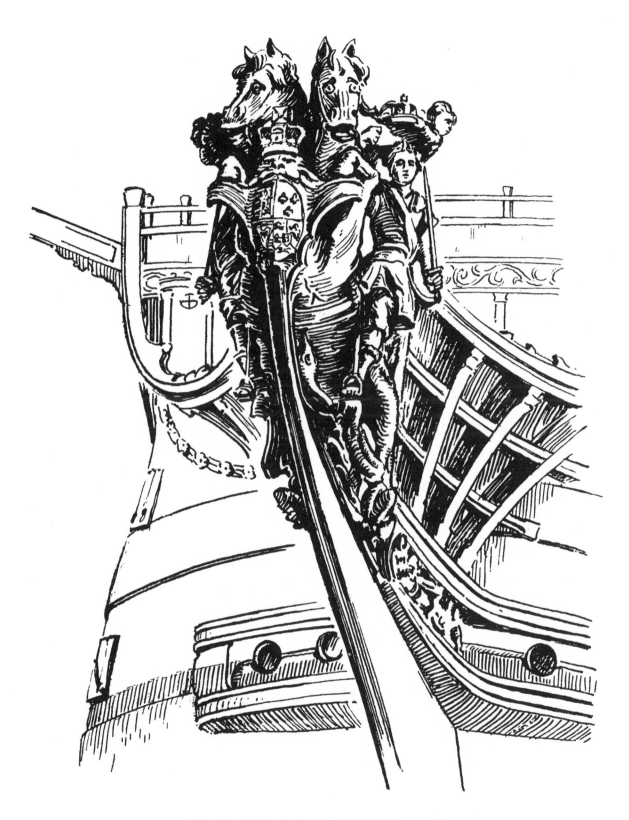

KEMPENFELT'S "ROYAL GEORGE" OF 1756

but under Anne the lion was probably departed from only in very special cases, such as the *Marlborough* of 1708, formerly in the London Museum, which has an equestrian figure of the duke, who, according to Narcissus Luttrell, is trampling Marshal Tallard under foot.

It was not till 1727 that the order of 1703 was relaxed somewhat. On 7th June of that year the Navy Board wrote to the Admiralty that "the officers of H.M. yards have lately represented to us that different figures for the head may be more properly adapted for ornament, and made lighter than the figure of a lion, especially for small ships, and be equally as cheap", and asked leave, which was granted, to carry the proposal into effect.[1] The immediate effect was that fancy figure-heads begin to appear in sixth rates and sloops, but, as far as has been noticed, not yet in larger ships. The earliest model illustrative of this is that described as the *Tartar* of 1734 in the Mercury Museum, which is, I think, of slightly earlier date. What is perhaps its chief interest is that it does not seem to have been "restored" in any way, and shows the figure painted in colours. Surviving models and draughts seem to show that in small craft, such as sloops, the figure chosen for the head was usually stumpy and grotesque. Thus the *Cruizer* sloop of 1732 had a very fat mer-boy, with wings, blowing a conch; a model of a sloop, now in New York, shows a little stout old woman of dignified port, with Cupid supporters, and snakes on the trail board; and a model, in Colonel Rogers's collection, of a 20-gun ship of before 1719 (and therefore before the date of the order), has a grotesque mannikin with a beard.[2]

By a schedule of prices issued in 1737[3] the price allowed for the lion of a 100-gun ship was £44 8s., and for the trail board £7 4s.; for a second rate £39, and £5 6s.; and so on down to £7 4s. and £1 4s. 8d. for a 20-gun ship. It was only the big ships that ever had the benefit of special orders; the third rates and below, when they had figures, were limited to the price of the lions. Yet about this time figures in line-of-battle ships seem to have begun. There is, for instance, in the South Kensington Museum a model of a 60-gun ship of about 1745, which has a coloured figure of a Roman warrior in a helmet which may have given the inspiration for the English "tin hat" of the late war.[4] It seems very probable that the ship represented is the *Centurion*, afterwards named the *Eagle*, which replaced Anson's famous ship. There are notices of coloured figures in other ships of about this time. The *Conqueror*, for instance, is stated by a contemporary journalist to have been named after Duke William, "whose image in golden armour forms the figure-head, brandishing the sword with which he overthrew our Saxon ancestors".

It must be admitted that the 18th century journalist sometimes, in default of exact information, drew on the bank of fancy. Thus one[5] who attended the launch of the third rate *Kent* in 1762 said that her figure was a "Man of Kent in Saxon costume"; while another[6] interpreted it as "King William the Conqueror dressed in armour, beautifully painted in the proper colours". That the

1. I am indebted to Maj. Evan Fyers for the text of this order.   2. Plate 13.   3. P.R.O. Ind. 10665, f. 559.   4. Plate 2.
5. London *Evening Post*, 27 Mar.   6. *St. James' Chronicle*, 27 Mar.

Navy Board should order the *Sphinx* of 1747, a 20-gun ship, to have "a carved image of that monster as her head" was perhaps inevitable; but it was hardly intelligent anticipation which decided that the *Prince of Wales*, 74, launched in 1765, should have for her figure a bust of the Prince with Liberty and Wisdom as supporters. This figure-head was entirely abnormal, for supporters were commonly confined to first and second rates, and no other instance has been met with of such a head in a third rate of this period. The exception may have been made in honour of so special an occasion as the birth of an heir to the throne; or it may perhaps have been suggested by the consideration that the ship was the descendant of several *Princes* and *Prince Royals*, all of them three-decked ships. Similarly when the Princess Royal was born a ship was named after her, but being a second rate had a double head, a grown-up princess seated with female figures as supporters and smaller figures and dogs down to the trail board.[1]

It is not to be supposed that the lion did not vary somewhat in appearance. We have seen that his angle depended on the form of the head;[2] that under James I he was nearly horizontal, in the Restoration period he began to ramp, and shortly acquired a crown. At the end of the century he became vertical, and from the time of Anne till he became virtually extinct about 1760 he tended to throw his chest out and his head well back. It also happened to him that he was seriously influenced by the curious epidemic of Chinese ornament which overtook the Navy towards 1720, and

lasted for perhaps 20 years. A carver's draught of the lion of 1720, reproduced here, illustrates this Chinese fashion:[3] so too does the figure-head of the *Augusta*, 60, of 1736, in which a dragon biting at the lion's heels has been added.[4] Apparently this combination of lion and dragon must have had something of a vogue, for it is still found some 40 years later in a Spanish frigate, the *Grana*. The lion of 1750[5] may be accepted as standard pattern. He is just such a lion as graced Anson's *Centurion*; or as Mr. Tucker, chaplain of the *Deptford*, referred to in 1740 as "awing the raging deep" in that famous petition of his which is often quoted but never reprinted. He still bears distinct traces of his Chinese relationship.

The lion of Anson's *Centurion* was set up in the yard of an inn near Goodwood Park, and on its base was carved –

> "Stay traveller awhile and view
> One who has travelled more than you.
> Quite round the globe through each degree,
> Anson and I have ploughed the sea,
> Torrid and frigid zone have passed,
> And, safe ashore arrived at last,
> In ease and dignity appear,
> He in the House of Lords, I here."

From Goodwood it was removed to Windsor Castle, and thence to Greenwich Hospital, where it stood in the Anson ward; but on the conversion of the Hospital into the College, it was turned out into the open, where it soon went to decay. One surviving leg of it has been mounted, and is preserved by the Earl of Lichfield at Shugborough.

1. Plate 13.   2. P. 63, figs. (a) to (d).   3. Plate 10.   4. Plate 25.   5. P. 63, fig. (d).

There is little need to follow English figure-heads of the 18th century in detail, for during about half a century practice did not vary appreciably. An order of 1742[1] enjoined that they were to be made as small and light as possible, but the effect of this is not very noticeable in models. Prices were regulated from time to time: apparently in or about 1756, when new classes of ships were introduced; and in 1773,[2] in which year the existing practice of giving "double heads" to three-decked ships was recognised. This schedule of prices allowed £100 for the "double heads" of 100-gun ships, and £85 for those of second rates; third rates of 74 guns were allowed £32 for "single figures enriched", and 64-gun ships £25. All ships were allowed whole figures, but for the smaller ships their price was still limited to the cost of lions. This was the regulation till 1796, when Lord Spencer's board decided "to explode carve work altogether on board H.M. ships that may be built or repaired in future, excepting what may be necessary for the mouldings about the scroll or billet head, and the stern and quarters".[3]

The "double head" of this period was less elaborate than in the middle of the century, as may be seen by contrasting the head of the *Queen Charlotte* of 1790[4] with that of the *Victory* of 1765. We have three records of the *Victory*'s original figure-head: the carver's specification; a copy, dated 1830, of an original draught showing the carved works;[5] and the more or less duplicate models in the Museum at Greenwich and in Portsmouth dock-yard.[6] It will be found that the draught, for the use of which I am indebted to the Director of Naval Construction, agrees very well with the specification for the starboard side; but that it is impossible to make out in the photograph from the model all the detail for the larboard side. The difficulty of obtaining good photographs of carved works of this nature has already been mentioned.

As not many of these specifications are accessible, it will be of interest to quote this one at length:[7] –

"A new large figure for her head cut in front at the upper part with the bust of His Majesty, the head adorned with laurels, and the body and shoulders worked in rich armour, and his George hanging before; under the breast is a rich shield partly supporting the bust and surrounded with four cherubs' heads and wings representing the four winds smiling, gently blowing our successes over the four quarters of the globe.

"On the Starboard side of the head piece the principal figure is a large drapery figure representing Britannia, properly crowned, sitting on a rich triumphal arch, and in one hand holding a spear enriched and the Union Flag hanging down from it, and with the other hand supporting the bust of His Majesty, with one foot trampling down Envy, Discord and Faction, represented by a fiend or hag: at the same side above and behind Britannia is a large flying figure representing Peace crowning the figure Britannia with laurels and holding a branch of palms denoting peace and the happy consequences resulting from victory. At the back of the arch is the British lion, trampling on very rich trophies of war, cut clear and open, and the arch on this side supported by two large figures, representing Europe and America properly dressed agreeable to the countries; and at the lower part of this side the head piece is cut a young Genius, holding in one hand a bunch of flowers, belonging to a rich cornucopia or horn of plenty filled with

1. Admy. Navy Bd. 2507, No. 342.   2. P.R.O., Ind. 10665, f. 559.   3. Admy. Navy Bd. 2511, No. 336.   4. P. 72, fig. (a).   5. Plate 16.
6. Plate 17.   7. M.M. VIII, 281.

fruit or flowers, cut clear, denoting abundance or plenty, which are the happy consequences arising from victory by bringing about a peace, and the Genius standing on contrast works and holding a branch of palms in the other hand is an emblem of peace, etc.

"On the larboard side of the head piece the principal figure is a large woman figure representing Victory, dressed in drapery and the head crowned with laurels proper, and with one hand holding a branch of laurels cut clear and through, and with the other hand supporting the bust of His Majesty; with one foot trampling down rebellion, represented by a Hydra with five heads, the whole scaled and the heads worked very clear resting on rich contrast scrolls and foliage leaves. At the upper part behind the figure Victory is a flying figure representing Fame, with one hand holding a trumpet as sounding forth our victories, and in the other hand holding a branch of palms denoting peace attending on victory; and behind this figure is a rich shield with the royal escutcheon worked in it proper, surrounded with laurels and crowned with an Imperial crown standing on rich trophies of war cut through and clear; and the arch on the side is supported by the figures Asia and Africa, dressed and decorated to the natives of the countries, worked very clear and round, with scarves of drapery flying about and hanging down; and at the bottom of the head piece is a Genius, representing the mathematics or navigation, in one hand holding a pair of compasses and pointing to a globe in the other, denoting our successes in all parts of the same, standing in a rich frame with brackets cut very clear and through, and worked quite round, with rich contrast works introduced in several other parts of the head piece, and other orna-ments with trusses, etc., 24ft. long, 18ft. broad, and 12ft. thick.

"A new large Trail board cut in two parts, each part cut (with) three Sea Anticks or Tritons, two of them holding of a shield enriched with the royal letters in it, enriched with foliage leaves; and the other boy on this side holding a

banner or flag with the Union Cross in it, etc.; and the end of each trail board is cut (with) a Sea Lion with wings tinned and scaled, and the tails cut through and clear, etc. Each 10ft. 3in. long, 3ft. 2in. broad, 1ft. 2in. thick."

The figure-head of the *Queen Charlotte* is much simpler, and therefore more effective, and the specification is correspondingly shorter. It is worth while to quote it, for soon afterwards, when figure-heads had fallen from their ancient glory, men regretted this one in particular, as being the most handsome that was ever put into a ship.

"In the head is Her Majesty in her robes with the orb and sceptre in her hands, standing erect under a canopy with two doves thereon, which is supported by two boys, the emblems of peace, one holding a dove, the other a palm branch; under which on the starboard side is Britannia sitting on a lion and presenting a laurel; on the larboard side is Plenty sitting on a sea-horse offering the produce of the sea and land; on the starboard trail board Justice and Prudence with their emblems; on the larboard trail board are two boys, Hope and Fortitude, with their emblems."

The figure-head as shown in the model[1] agrees very well, except for the omission of the doves on the canopy. It will be noticed that Plenty is decidedly sitting on her horse instead of being mounted on it, and that the horse, which is much too small for her, is looking round in protest. There is nothing exceptional about this curious treatment; it is found in ship carvings throughout the century.

After 1773 the figure-heads of second rates also grew very much simpler, being frequently a single figure with small

1. P. 72, fig. (a).

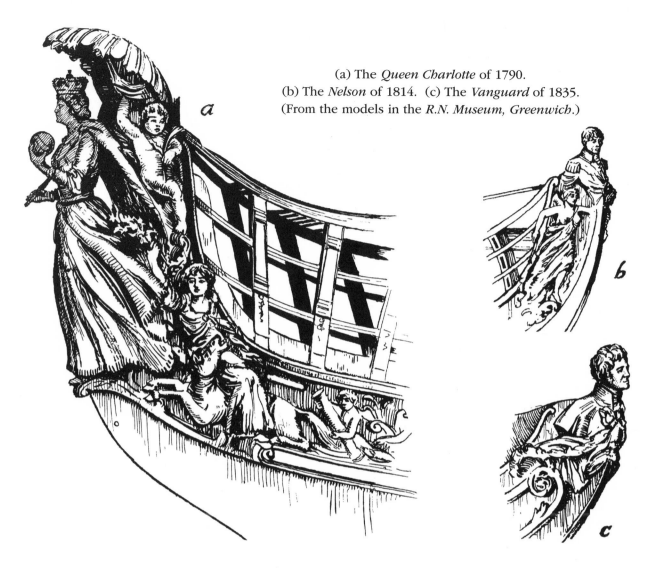

(a) The *Queen Charlotte* of 1790.
(b) The *Nelson* of 1814. (c) The *Vanguard* of 1835.
(From the models in the *R.N. Museum, Greenwich*.)

supporters below. That of the *Princess Royal*,[1] which is earlier than the new schedule of prices, is in marked contrast to the equestrian figure of the *Boyne* of 1790, or to that of the *Glory* of 1788, which had merely a single large figure, with a pair of Cupids on the trail board.

Much of our knowledge of the figure-heads of about 1773 is due to an order of that year;[2] "before any ship may be launched in future at your yard, send us a complete draught of her, with … the stern, head, and carved works sketched thereon, with the embellishments, such as

the finishing of the galleries, bannisters, or decorations of the stern". For a few years this order was in full force, and even seems to have been made slightly retrospective, but after 1790 it became dead letter. It serves well, however, to show what the figures were in the last days before the great reduction of 1796, for there are something like 80 of these draughts. Also it was then, and had been from at least 1747, and still was as late as 1815, the common practice to take off a draught of any prize that was added to the Navy. The Admiralty records thus include a considerable number of draughts of the carved

1. Plate 13.   2. Admy. Navy Bd. 2508, No. 642.

works of French, Spanish, Dutch, Danish, Russian and American ships, chiefly for the period of the French wars of the Revolution and Empire. Several of these have been photographed or traced to serve here as illustrations. It must be confessed that, when it came to freehand, the dockyard draughtsman, admirable in his own line, was out of his element; but as may be seen from his record of the carvings of the *Victory*,[1] he was very conscientious.

As long as the lion was the standard figure-head, it was usual to give ships carvings on their sterns to indicate their names, for until 1771 English ships had not their names painted on them. This practice survived the change to individual figures, and it is common in the second half of the 18th century to find both the figure-head and the tafferel carvings interpreting the name, even after the name was painted on the stern. The *Edgar,* for instance, of 1774, had King Edgar as a figure-head, her name on her counter, and on her tafferel Edgar in his boat rowed by the tributary kings. But this was not always the case, for sometimes the figure-head was non-committal, and it was left to the tafferel to disclose the ship's name: as in the *Cumberland* of 1774, which had a bust of the duke on the tafferel, but a whole figure of Neptune for the head. Neptune indeed was both then and long after a somewhat favourite figure. It may be that the designers considered that England had a certain proprietary right in the god, and that he should be regarded as being as much a national emblem as Britannia, or as St. George and the dragon seem to have been under the early Stuarts. According to a note by

Van de Velde, de Oude, a Neptune was sometimes used among the carvings of the tafferel in the 17th century, and was then indicative of a flagship.

A few typical figure-heads of this period are illustrated. That of the South Kensington model known as the *Triumph*, 74, of 1764,[2] shows a statesman in his robes, but seems to bear no resemblance to the elder Pitt who, if anyone, should have been the subject. It seems possible therefore that the model may represent another ship of the same class and nearly the same date, and that the figure is of a First Lord of the Admiralty, after whom both the *Egmont* of 1768 and the *Bedford* of 1775 were named.

The story of the *Brunswick*'s figure-head in the battle of the "Glorious First of June" is familiar. The figure represented the Duke in Highland costume, with a cocked hat; and during the *Brunswick*'s famous duel with the *Vengeur*, the hat was shot off: –

> "Then a solemn deputation from the
> *Brunswick*'s fo'c'sle came
> With the news to Captain Harvey:
> 'Sir! Your Honour! 'Tis for shame,
> And in no ways right or proper,
> for our Royal Duke to go
> With his noble head uncovered
> in the face of any foe.' "[3]

So the captain, himself wounded, gave the deputation a gold-laced hat, which the carpenter nailed in place,

> "And the noble Duke came through it,
> like a fighter born and bred,
> With his hand upon his sword hilt,
> and his hat upon his head."

1. Plate 16.   2. Plate 13.   3. R. Adm. Ronald Hopwood, "The Figure-heads".

It is said that the *Guadeloupe* frigate, when Cornwallis commanded her, which was from 1768-73, was the first ship to have her figure-head painted in natural colours. This is undoubtedly wrong, as we have seen; but it may mean that for some little time before 1770 the fashion of painting in colours had died out, and that yellow lions and figures had been the rule. Of this indeed there is some evidence in the Navy Board papers. It is probable that at this time, as later, a good deal of latitude was allowed, and that while the dockyards painted the heads yellow, captains frequently either repainted them after they got to sea, or persuaded the dockyard to do it for them. We do not need telling that there are ways and means, especially in the Navy.

As to such matters we get a little light from William Cathcart, who in 1802 was captain of the *Renard* sloop. He wrote[1] of the *Termagant*, another sloop, commanded by a friend of his: "Her head, which is a termagant, is painted in colours with a bloody nose and a real broomstick in her hand, in the attitude of making a blow. She has on her bows half a man on one side, and half a woman on the other fighting", an interesting survival of the double figure-head, for this *Termagant* was launched in 1796, and must have been one of the last ships to have a whole figure before the order of 1796 stopped such extravagances. The *Centaur*, 74, launched in 1797, is said to have been actually the last ship:[2] she had the whole figure of a Centaur, coming far down her cutwater, in imitation of the French prize captured in 1759.

The *Termagant* before this was built in 1780, and had a figure of a Fury, complete with sword, torch and snaky hair, and with more snakes on the trail board. This was very classical and in strict keeping with the fashion of the age, but we may believe that the younger officers, and no doubt the crew, preferred the more literal interpretation. Cathcart goes on to say that he thought that the figure of his own ship, the *Renard*, ought to have a whip in one hand and a fox in the other, and that he went to work to get them "by knocking off his arms in the night and stowing them away". So he succeeded in persuading the carver to make the desired alteration, and at the same time to make the arms to screw off and on, so that they might be unshipped in bad weather, as was not infrequently done with susceptible figure-heads. It was perhaps a little ungrateful of him after this to write home that "I have humbugged the yard out of a new arm for my head".

Lord Sandwich's penchant for classical antiquities was no doubt a boon to the carvers. It was so easy to personify Neptune with his trident, Hercules with his club, Diana with a crescent moon and a dog or two, and so on; and the secondary figures of the great heads were as a rule fairly easily recognised, for the carvers rang the changes on a small number of them. Such doubts as occur are when we come to

"those flatulent folks known in classical story as Aquilo, Libs, Notus, Auster and Boreas."

1. N.R.S., "Nav. Misc." I, 308.   2. M.M. X, 89.

But even here as a rule we get the "four winds" grouped together, and are not bound to recognise which is which.

But sometimes the figure-head seems entirely out of keeping with the name of the ship. As one instance of many it may be mentioned that for the frigate *Blonde*[1] of 1806 the dockyard officers suggested a bust of a bearded warrior, and that their design was approved. When a ship's name was changed her carvings remained, unless very unsuitable. Thus the *Waterloo*, launched in 1818, had an equestrian figure of the Duke of Wellington on her tafferel, and kept it after 1824 when her name was changed to *Bellerophon*. She was not broken up till 1892, and the watermen at Portsmouth used to point to the figure in her stern and tell visitors that she was "the ship that took Boney to St. Helena: and there he is on her stern"; plausible statements both, but neither of them strictly accurate. Similarly, just as Sir Robert Holmes's monument at Yarmouth, I.W., was altered from a captured statue of Louis XIV, so no doubt a touch or two of the chisel, or even of the paint brush, often did what was possible towards reconciling an old figure with a new name.

I believe it was Mr. Punch who once contemplated what might happen in such a case, and told how

> "There was an ancient carver,
> and he carved of a saint;
> But the parson wouldn't have it,
> so he took a pot of paint
> And changed his holy raiment
> to a dashing soldier rig,
> And said it was a figure-head,
> and sold it to a brig."

1. Admy. Navy Bd. 1820; 12 June 1806.

All went well till the brig met with a beautiful mermaid, who fell in love with the dashing soldier:

> "She had a voice like silver,
> and her lips were cherry red;
> She wriggled up the bobstay,
> and she kissed the figure-head."

a proceeding which distressed the gallant soldier,

> "for beneath his coat of paint,
> "The silly-headed noodle
> still thinks as he's a saint."

Again, no doubt there were figure-heads which might be claimed to be appropriate but yet were quite incongruous. The story of the *Vigilant*, a 64-gun ship of 1774, will serve to illustrate this point. The carver, being called on for a design, found himself somewhat at a loss, and took a friend's opinion on the matter. The friend said that dragons didn't sleep much, and might fairly be called vigilant, and that therefore he advised that the figure-head should be a dragon. The carver liked the idea well enough; but unfortunately he had a book of emblems, to which he turned for confirmation of his friend's suggestion, for he was one of those to whom the printed is of higher authority than the spoken word. The book of emblems said nothing about dragons, but considered that vigilance meant the observance of the precept to Watch and Pray, and accordingly symbolised it by a woman with a Bible in one hand and a lantern in the other. And this design, we are told, the carver adopted and transferred to the ship. As, however, there is among the official draughts no record of what carvings the *Vigilant* had, we are free to believe as much or as little of the story as we choose.

Lord Spencer took office as First Lord of the Admiralty in 1794 with a keen appreciation of the value of economy, and, as one step in this direction, decided to abolish figure-heads. Many draughts of 1795-6 show a scroll or billet-head, or, as Jack commonly called it, a "fiddle-head", instead of a block waiting to be carved into a figure. An order was issued in 1796 cutting down all carvings to a minimum, and directing that the scroll head should be the regulation pattern. It is common knowledge that this change was intensely unpopular in the Navy; it is perhaps less well known how immediate and complete was the success of the opposition to it. The draughts of the next two or three years show how the design for the fiddle-head was, in almost every instance, altered to a figure. In small craft, gun-brigs and the like, a billet-head seems in some cases to have been fitted till a much later date; but if we may believe Marryat's testimony, the officers or crew took immediate steps to replace it by a figure. Thus Swinburne had only one objection to the brig-sloop *Rattlesnake*, that she had a fiddle-head. "I hope the captain will take off her fiddle-head and get one carved", he grumbled. "I never knew a vessel do much with a fiddle-head … A coil of 4-inch will make the body of the snake; I can carve out the head; and as for a rattle, I'm blessed if I don't rob one of those beggars of watchmen this very night." However, the captain came to the rescue, and a handsomely carved snake

was fitted and gilded, But Swinburne, that is to say Marryat, was a little adrift in his history; for one ship certainly distinguished herself in spite of a fiddle-head. This was the famous *Téméraire*, which fought at Trafalgar behind one.

There was much to be said for the use of a standard pattern figure-head like the lion, and something even for the use of a fiddle-head, for it must be confessed that at the end of the century the designs put forward were often weak, and sometimes deplorable. Many rough sketches for the carved work of this period survive among the dockyard papers, though the finished large scale drawings in no case survive; and there is hardly a trace of art or inspiration about any of them. The Navy Board contented itself with seeing that the estimate did not exceed the allowed cost, and passed practically every design submitted, however bad it might be. Once in a way they returned one as unsatisfactory, not on the score of lack of art, but as a bad portrait. When the *Pitt* was built, naturally a bust of the statesman was called for, and the dock-yard sent a sketch accordingly. But the Navy Board, who had probably seen the Prime Minister a good deal more often than the dockyard draughtsman had, could see no likeness, and said so.

Early in the 19th century the "superior class of shipwright apprentices" was started at the R.N. College, Portsmouth, and freehand drawing was made part of their course. No doubt it was recognised from the first that these young men would design the figure-heads of the future. In 1811 J. C. Schetky succeeded

Robert Livesay as drawing master at the College, and one of his earliest official acts seems to have been the buying in London of a large number of plaster casts after the antique. In sending the bill to the Navy Board, he explained that their purpose was to train the apprentices for the designing of figure-heads; and it does seem to be the case that for a short period after this date the design of figure-heads improved somewhat. We have not indeed much evidence to go by, for almost all the actual figure-heads have disappeared, and there are few models of the period. That of one ship, however, the *Nelson* of 1814, is reproduced here from the model at Greenwich;[1] and parts of the figure-head of the *Howe*, another ship of the same class, still survive in the dockyard at Sheerness.[2]

It is not without interest that some years ago a number of plaster casts after antique statues were found in a garret in the R.N. College, Greenwich. No one knew how they had got there, or of what use they had been. The explanation probably is that they were Schetky's casts, and that, when the College moved from Portsmouth to Greenwich in January, 1873, they accompanied it.

The period after 1796 is, as far as the Royal Navy is concerned, perhaps the least interesting of all, for with the very small sums now allowed figure-heads dwindled sadly in all classes. First and second rates indeed still kept to the theory of a "double head"; but the new pattern double head was a very small thing when compared with such heads as that of the *Royal George* of 1756, the

Victory of 1765, or the *Queen Charlotte* of 1790. The change may be illustrated from the names of these last two ships. The *Victory* in her "large repair" of 1802-03 received a new figure-head, the old one presumably being rotten. There was some correspondence about what she should have, but the general principle had been settled by a decision of July, 1801,[3] that instead of whole figures "devices" were to be fitted in future. The "device" in the *Victory* took the form of the royal arms crowned, with a pair of Cupids as supporters. The cost of this figure-head was £50. In her next big repair, of 1814-15, she again received a new figure-head,[4] the cost this time being £65; and this is the figure-head which is still on the ship. It is believed that it differs from the Trafalgar head only in the attitude of the Cupids, which in the earlier head were standing sturdily on both feet, while in that which survives they are much at their ease with legs crossed. Even the royal arms are the same, though between the dates of the two heads the inescutcheon of Hanover should have changed its electoral bonnet for a crown. Apparently the change was not officially notified to the British Government, for the royal arms, wherever they appeared, continued to reproduce the bonnet for two years after its disuse.

The new *Queen Charlotte*, launched in 1810, was "similar to the old ship of the same name, except her head,[5] which is the most paltry production that ever disgraced so noble a ship. Those who ever saw the superb head which ornamented the old *Queen Charlotte* would naturally ask 'Could no line be drawn between grandeur and meanness?'" This

1. P. 72, fig. (b).   2. M.M. III, 289, figs. 2, 3, 4.   3. M.M. X, 197 *sq*.   4. Plate 17.   5. Nav. Chron. XXIV, 71.

figure-head has survived, being erected at Whale Island.[1] The ship was undoubtedly a sufferer, for in addition to the cutting down of heads, the *Queen Charlotte*, though of the same dimensions as the old ship, found herself left behind owing to the increase in the size of new first rates. So she was rated only as a second rate, and of course had only a second rate's figure-head. Such a figure-head at this time commonly meant a bust, with some small embellishment on each side: thus the *Union* of 1811 had a bust of the King "with a cornucopia on each side of a shield allusive to the union".

The Navy Board seems to have been particularly zealous in cutting down expenditure on figure-heads at this time, for they even succeeded in giving the *Caledonia* of 1808, a large first rate, a mere second rate's head at a cost of £35. This was "a bust of a female figure, emblematic of her name, with the plaid bonnet", and the only embellishments were a thistle on one side and a bagpipe on the other. But other first rates were not so scurvily treated, and the *Nelson* of 1814, and the *Howe* and *St. Vincent* of 1815, received busts with large sized supporters. The *Nelson* had a bust of the admiral, with 9ft. figures of Fame and Britannia as supporters, and a misquotation of the famous Trafalgar signal on the trail board. (See P. 72, fig. (b).)

It will be remembered that there used to be a story that the supporters of the *Victory's* figure-head at Trafalgar were a sailor and a marine. This was proved to be erroneous, but still the figures, or rather part of the figures of a bluejacket and marine exist in Sheerness dockyard to this day to give point to the story.[2] A search has proved that they belonged to the *Howe*, in which they stood as supporters to the bust. There was indeed a great deal of correspondence about this figure-head, because the Navy Board, disliking the carver's estimate, said he had better get on with the work and they would talk about the price afterwards. So the carver did as he pleased, making the supporters 10ft. 6in. high instead of 9ft. as in the *Nelson*, and adding other embellishments; and finally he brought in a bill which filled the Navy Board with horror. They cut the bill down drastically, as was their way; but the carver got over £100 for the figure-head, a most abnormal sum at that date. In 1835 this figure-head was reported rotten, and was replaced by a simple bust of Neptune, with the Howe arms on each side. The bust of Lord Howe was set up at the Queen's Head Inn at Bexley, Kent, and, from a journalistic account, "Hither on Saturdays and Sundays in the summer resort large numbers of soldiers, sailors and dockyardmen from Chatham. The figure-head of the old line-of-battle ship *Howe*, standing among the trees, is religiously decked with laurel and evergreen upon every anniversary of the Glorious First of June". About 1885 it was too rotten to stay longer on its pedestal, but fell off and broke up.

Few ships of this date demand particular mention, for other ships of the line, *i.e.*, the third rates, had only small figures, and frigates and sloops had only busts. The prices show that the work was no longer important, for though a third rate's allowance for the figure was nomi-

1. Plate 19.   2. M.M. III, 289.

nally £21, the Navy Board was always on the look-out to cut it down, and did succeed in some cases in reducing it to £16, and even to £10. A frigate's bust cost only £6, and a sloop's bust £3. Not very much could be expected at those figures. One somewhat notable exception was the *Victorious*, 74, which appears to have had what was really a first rate's head, *viz.*, a bust of Nelson, with "a large lion on each side trampling on the Gallic cock". When the ship was repaired in 1814,[1] she received instead of the lions a pair of weeping cherubs as supporters. Cherubs, after being in favour for a very long time, were by then pretty much out of fashion, and it would seem that the *Victorious* took them, like her name, from the *Victory*.

The lion was not quite out of fashion, but when he appeared now it was in a modified form. The *Dreadnought*, second rate, of 1801, had a lion standing on top of the knee of the head, where it was nearly hidden by the bowsprit; and the *Hogue* of 1811 had for a figure the same device that the *Victorious* at first had for the supporters, the lion crushing the Gallic cock under his paw.

Very few figure-heads of earlier date than 1815 survive. By association the most important of these is the head which belonged to what must originally have been a whole figure of Bellerophon, the figure-head of the famous 74-gun ship of 1786. Similarly, merely the head of the figure of the *Polyphemus*, 64, of 1782, has been preserved. Both these are in the Portsmouth Dockyard Museum. Most of the old figure-heads which had been

kept as relics perished by fire. That of the *Monarch* of 1765 formed part of the naval trophy in the armoury of the Tower of London, and was destroyed in the great fire of 1841. A large collection was made by Captain Ross at Devonport in the early 'thirties, but unfortunately they were all lost in the dockyard fire of 1840. Among them were those of many celebrated ships, including the *Brunswick*, 74;[2] the *Edgar*, 74, which led the line at Copenhagen; the *Amazon* frigate; Collingwood's *Royal Sovereign*; and, among the prizes, the *Malta* of 80 guns, formerly the *Guillaume Tell*.

There was no improvement after the peace. For a short time some few of the three-decked ships received whole figures, as, for instance, the *Royal Adelaide*,[3] launched in 1828; and the *Royal William* of 1833, and the *St. George* of 1840;[4] but busts or half figures were already the common practice, and became the rule from 1835. These busts and half-length figures tended to grow in size, and finally in large ships they were made three-quarter lengths of about 15ft. high. Several of these survive; three, of Anson, Duncan and Nelson are at Chatham, and that of the *Royal Albert* of 1854 – perhaps the first ship to have one of these gigantic figures – is at Portsmouth. Though an excellent likeness of the Prince Consort, it is a truly formidable production: the designer appears to have thought that mere bulk might serve as a substitute for art.[5] The Chatham figures of a few years later are by no means so stiff or unpleasing.

1. Admy. Navy Bd. 1887, 23 Sep.   2. P. 73.   3. Plate 13.   4. P. 38.   5. Plate 19.

The crude realism of the *Royal Albert* was in the spirit of the age, and was reflected in the figure-heads of many merchant ships. Thus we know that the celebrated *James Baines* had a portrait figure of her owner, buttoned up in a frock coat; the *Samuel Plimsoll* went even further lengths by adding the owner's top-hat; and there is a figure-head at Penzance, "featuring" what is presumably a British merchant, who might have sat to Gilbert as the original of the virtuous person whose whiskers curled so tight, "with cheeks so smug and muttony" and "coat so blue and buttony". It was, fortunately, no more than a passing phase.

What will probably be accepted as the most satisfactory of the post-1815 figure-heads is that of the *Royal George* yacht, launched in 1817, which shows a bust of the Prince Regent with two negroes as supporters, in reference to the movement for the emancipation of slaves. The original of this, which is finely carved and gilt, is preserved, with other carvings from the same yacht, in the museum of the Royal United Service Institution. The illustration given here shows King Edward on the S. railway jetty at Portsmouth superintending the removal of the carved works of the yacht, which was broken up in 1907.[1]

Several ships were built for the Navy in the Indian dock-yards, especially Bombay, in the early part of the 19th century, and it seems to have been the invariable practice to give them Indian figure-heads. One of them, now named the *Foudroyant*, but launched in 1817 at Bombay as the *Trincomalee*, still survives, and preserves

her original figure-head,[2] which like all frigate heads of the period is a bust. The brown face and white turban and tunic are set off by a little colour applied to the dress and to the "embellishments" which the carver was allowed to introduce. The belt, armlets, and collar are green edged with gold beads; the scroll over the shoulder and down the head rails is old gold, while that under the bust is crimson with an old gold fringe. The medallion bears a cross, red on green.

It seems always to have been more or less the fashion to give Oriental figure-heads and decorations to men-of-war built in the East; this is attested by a model, in a private collection, of a frigate of about 1807, perhaps of the *Salsette*, the first ship built at Bombay; by the figure-head of the *Seringapatam* of 1819, now at Devonport, which had an Indian riding an eagle; and by the figure-heads of the *Hindostan* and other ships of the line built in India after the peace of 1815. It appears to be the case that in these ships the regulations as to ornament were somewhat relaxed; for some of them had more carved works than homebuilt ships, and a few had whole figures when busts were the regulation wear.

How far British East Indiamen conformed to this practice is as yet undecided. In the 17th and the early part of the 18th centuries they had lions; in the 19th, after the days of John Company, they followed the common practice of the best class of merchant ships in having whole figures, symbolising their names. With the advent of the clipper ship the head knee again raked forward, so that

1. Plate 18.   2. Plate 22.

the figures necessarily followed suit and reverted to an attitude similar to that of the early Restoration period, or even of pre-Commonwealth ships. This will be noticed in the two figures, one of them Oriental, reproduced from a book of designs made about 1860 by Mr. A. P. Elder.[1] Another example of the Oriental figure-head is that of the ship *Bencoolen*,[2] set up in the churchyard at Bude beside the grave of men who perished in the wreck of that ship.

Another figure-head, from Morwenstow,[3] also illustrates this old West Country practice of erecting the figure as a memorial to a crew lost in a wreck. There is a story of a new curate who, in ignorance of this custom, passed through the churchyard in the dimpsy light, and there saw a white lady in the costume of Eve before the fall arising from a grave; whereupon he hurried off to report to the vicar that some of his parishioners were anticipating the resurrection. The large collection of figure-heads, made by Mr. Dorrien-Smith at Tresco,[4] testifies to the formidable reputation of the Scilly Islands as a trap for ships.

When men-of-war passed from sail to steam there was at first no change in the manner of fitting figure-heads, for the form of the ship was not altered. Even when the practice of armouring ships began, the old form, and consequently the old figure-head, was at first maintained, as seen in the *Warrior* of 1860[5] and her sister the *Black Prince*. But after this the change came very quickly, for though a ship without some kind of a figure-head was as yet inconceivable, yet with straight stemmed ironclads the old form was impossible. In the *Royal Sovereign*, as cut down to a turret ship in 1862, a lion on the stem was substituted for the old figure: in the ironclads the practice sprang up of fitting a shield or medallion with supporters or embellishments in relief. Thus the *Prince Consort* of 1862 had a medallion portrait of the Prince, with Art and Music as supporters, and similar figures were not uncommon. The aspiration after a proper figure-head, however, did not pass away, and even in the 'eighties some of the old Admiral class of battleships had portrait busts,[6] while the *Barfleur* of 1891 had a small lion; but devices were more common, as in the case of the *Warspite* of 1885, which had a Fury on each side of the stem, and of the *Hood*, which had Lord Hood's arms on one side of the stem and Lord Bridport's on the other. An Admiralty order of 1894 abolished figure-heads for large ships; but the small masted ships kept them a little longer. The sloops of the *Odin* and *Espiègle* class of 1901 were probably the last to have them, and indeed served with them still in place in the war of 1914.

FOREIGN PRACTICE

On this subject there is relatively little to be said. The Dutch took early to the lion, who in the 17th century sometimes brandished his sword; and apparently till after 1720 used no other figure-head. It has been noticed already that they continued the use of the spiral of the main rail over the lion's head later than we did, owing to the flatter form of head:

---

1. Plate 23.   2 to 4. Plate 24.   5. Plate 22.   6. So too in the royal yachts: *cp.*, Plate 19.

it has not been determined how early they modified the lion by the addition of secondary figures at his back. They did so certainly after 1700, and the form which this combination took with them is illustrated by the head of *'t Wickelo*,[1] which shows a small Neptune standing on each side behind the lion. Mermaids are sometimes introduced in the same position. The Dutch lion differed from the English in colour, being red with a gold mane.[2] It has often been suggested, but never proved, that the red lion of Martlesham, in Suffolk, may have come ashore from a Dutch ship. Rivals to the lion begin to appear after 1720, the earliest noticed being the Javanese women used as figure-heads of the East India ships *Ary*[3] and *Gertuida*. Twenty years afterwards the *Mercurius* had a Mercury; and other instances occur. But in general it seems accurate to say that until about the French Revolutionary war the lion was by far the most common figure:[4] in the closing years of the century, however, he fell into disuse, and the Dutch adopted the custom of using figures illustrative of the ship's name. About the same time they adopted in some cases the contemporary French fashion of cutting away the fore part of the knee of the head to the full height of the figure, which could therefore be "cut clear and through" (as the English carver's phrase went) and could stand on the step so formed.[5] This is shown by the *Washington* model in the "Mercury" Museum. Another point of difference is that the Dutch retained whole figures, even for frigates, to a much later date than we did. I have not enough instances to decide with certainty what was the practice, but have some half-dozen of

whole figures between 1800 and 1815, and none of a bust till about 1830. Also I am not clear how long the lion continued to be painted red, but have instances from models of lions gilt about 1780, while a draught of the figure-head of the *Vrijheid*, exhibited at Chelsea in 1891, showed the lion all red. Some models show the figure-heads of the early 19th century painted white. This suggests that the practice may have been the same as our own: white the regulation colour, but fancy colours used if or when the captain thought fit. One thing which seems certain is that neither the Dutch nor the French ever used the elaborate group, or "family", figure-heads which had so important a vogue in England.

The French differed from most, or perhaps all, other nations in that they never adopted the lion for common use. We have seen that from an early date, even in the time of the carrack forecastle, they were unconventional in the matter of figure-heads and tried to strike out a line of their own.[6] In the early part of the 17th century, when they had their ships built for them in Holland, they had fancy heads of their own devising fitted. Thus the "navire royale" of Hondius, 1626, shows Jupiter riding his eagle;[7] and another "navire royale faicte en Hollande" at the same date shows Neptune driving a pair of sea-horses.[8] In general, the French figure-head, even for the most important ships, was a single figure, which, it must be confessed, was both graceful and effective. This was because the French always took their ship decoration seriously: from the time of Puget onwards till the débacle of *c.* 1835 they had a regular school of carving

1. Plate 14.   2. Plate 2.   3. Plate 15.   4. P. 44.   5. Plate 52.   6. P. 59.   7. M.M. IV, 33.   8. M.M. III, 376.

in the dockyards, and were at pains to engage men who were artists, both for present use and that they might hand on the torch. An occasional figure such as that of the *Terrible* of 1692, in which the motif is the head of the Gorgon, approaches to the group form,[1] but even so the treatment is light. Decoration in other parts of the ship was at certain periods overdone and became decidedly rococo, but not in figure-heads.

In 1671 Louis XIV decided to rename his fleet, and names were chosen for all classes of ships and were established for future use. These names were, in fact, very well kept to under the monarchy, and no great inroad was made on the list until the Revolution. This must have been a decided boon to the carvers, who, in default of inspiration, would be free to adopt the design of the old ship for the figure-head of the new ship of the same name. But at the time of its issue the order caused a commotion in the dockyards,[2] for it was found that in many cases a name was transferred from one existing ship to another of a different rate, with the result that the carvings, including the figure of the head, which were to accompany the name, would not fit in the places assigned to them. The change seems not to have been complete for several years, probably in great measure owing to this difficulty.

The *St. Louis* of 1721[3] has an angel for a figure, with the main rail curved over as a canopy. The effect is particularly happy. The head of a first rate of the mid-18th century is illustrated from the *Royal Louis* model in the Louvre:[4] the "Pic"

model will stand for normal practice in two-decked ships about the middle of the century: the ungraceful eagle of the ship in the Colbert book[5] can be accepted merely as an indication, comparable to the "sketches" submitted from the English dockyards, in accordance with the order of 1773, by men whom regulation had forced outside their proper occupation.

Under Louis XVI French figure-heads reached their greatest degree of profusion, a few of the more important ships having something approaching to the English group figure. Thus the *Triomphant* showed Louis XIV in a triumphal car with shield and spear, and bowed captives on either side; and the *Conquérant* had the same monarch seated on his throne, sword in hand, with Victory holding a laurel wreath above his head. After this exuberance the pendulum swung the other way.

We have seen how in 1796 an English First Lord tried to abolish figure-heads, and did not succeed. Something of the same sort took place in France in 1785, but with a difference. Instead of enjoining the use of a mere fiddle head, the French ordonnance prescribed a scutcheon bearing the lilies, and with some slight ornament which differed according to the class of the ship. This is illustrated here from the model of a 40-gun frigate in the Louvre;[6] and is indicated for a line-of-battle ship on the diagram of the head of the *Pompée* of 1788.[7] After the Revolution the lilies gave place to the tri-colour in ships which kept this device; but in new ships, and apparently in the refit of old ships, new

1. Plate 14.   2. Rev. Marit., Feb., 1925, 183 *sq*.   3. Plate 14.   4. P. 42.   5. Plate 14.   6. P. 46 (2).   7. P. 47.

figure-heads were substituted. It seems worth mention that the scutcheon of lilies was in limited use before it was given this particular form in 1785: a few draughts of somewhat earlier date, that of the *Northumberland* of 1780, for example, show the scutcheon held by a lion. But the lion was always the exception; and that the *Northumberland* had one was very probably due to the fact that she was built to replace the former ship of the name, an English 70-gun ship captured in 1744, whose figure, as a matter of course, would be a lion. An uncrowned lion occurs in French East Indiamen.

If there was any one device which was more popular than others with French carvers it was that of a Fame or Renommée. This occurs in many ships, both as a figure-head and in other places, from the 17th century to the 19th, so that it cannot be taken as any sure indication of the name of the ship. She might be a *Renommée*, or a *Gloire*; but she might equally well be the *Rivoli*, the *Brillant*, or half a score of other names.

With the Revolution there came inevitably a change. It does not appear to have been decided what fashion should be adopted for general use, so that old and new were intermingled. It may be assumed that all emblems of the monarchy disappeared; but if any attempt was made to keep pace with the frequent renaming of the more important ships, the carvers must have been well employed. At least one of the first rates changed her name six times within ten years, and three or four renamings were not uncommon. In the circumstances a

figure-head which did not indicate the name of the ship must have been very welcome, and we find the lion appearing in a few cases, including the *Droits de l'homme*, 74, and the celebrated frigate *Muiron* of 1799. Whether the lion held a tri-coloured scutcheon is not determined; but it seems likely that he did.

Mr. Edward Fraser has been so kind as to give me notes collected from French books as to revolutionary figure-heads, concerning which I have no other evidence. The *Ça Ira* is credited with the lanterne of the Place de Grève: the *J. J. Rousseau* with a portrait full-length figure holding an open book inscribed "Droits de l'homme et du citoyen": the *Hautpoult* (which by capture became the *Abercrombie* in the Royal Navy) a figure of the general, with the English flag in his right hand, the Prussian eagle on his left, trampling on a lion: the *Carmagnole*, frigate, a model of the guillotine: and the *Marat*, a bust, with a towel for a turban.

Some time in the 1790's the fashion was introduced of forming a step for the figure at the top of the head knee,[1] so that it might stand "en clair"; but this was never universal practice. It is seen very commonly in "prisoner of war" bone models; perhaps in some cases, as may be suspected, because it was easier thus to fit in any little figure picked up at random than to carve one from a block. It is very rare to be able to identify one of these models from its figure-head.

The pseudo-classicism of the Consulate and the First Empire was represented in figure-heads: it was indeed no more than

1. Plate 52.

the continuation of a pre-existing vogue, for many earlier ships had "classical" figures whose costume would baffle a professed antiquary. Such were the *Spartiate* of 1796, and the *Guillaume Tell*, who carried his bow indeed, but was dressed in a Greek helmet and tunic. The series of designs for heads produced by P. Ozanne at the end of the century shows to what lengths men's fancies might run. The designs were quite impracticable, both because their adoption would in many cases have interfered with the working of the ship, and doubtless on the score of cost, and it would appear that not even the simplest of them were adopted. They are, however, of considerable interest in the history of figure-heads, and three of them are reproduced here.[1] These three represent Ozanne's three styles, the classical military, the amorous, and the grotesque.

After 1800 busts begin to occur in French ships, at first rarely and only in corvettes and smaller craft, but in 1810 in a line-of-battle ship, the *Achille*. Whole figures were still in a great majority, perhaps even for small ships; but after the peace the use of busts increased. It is interesting to notice that immediately after the restoration of the monarchy the scutcheon made its reappearance, crowned, as is shown by the model of a "bombarde", or bomb vessel, in the museum at the Louvre.

In the 'twenties whole figures and busts were used concurrently for large ships: thus while the *Didon*, frigate, and *Conquérant*, line-of-battle ship, of 1825 and 1827, had whole figures, the

Montebello of 1821 and *Suffren* of 1829, ships of the line, had busts. About 1835 there came an order comparable to the English order of 1796, "exploding carve work", which from this time on was reduced to a minimum, only a bust being allowed even in the largest ships, such as the *Valmy* of 1847.

Privateer figure-heads in the great wars appear to have followed the same course as those of men-of-war, perhaps with more latitude. When Surcouf returned to the Indian Ocean early in 1807 he named his privateer the *Revenant*, and, by punning reference to the secondary meaning of "ghost" which the word has, gave her for a figure-head the effigy of a corpse throwing off its shroud. It is unlikely that such a figure would have been found in a regular man-of-war.

Not enough examples have been collected to permit of any definite account of the practice of other nations. The Spaniards appear to have used lions to a considerable extent, but as early as 1730 the *Princesa*, 70, had a figure-head emblematic of her name. It was very large, with little lions added for embellishment.

Until the wars at the end of the century lions seem still to have been in the majority, but then large figures took their place. Many of the ships were named after saints, as the *San Josef* and *Sant' Ana*. As the latter was represented in a crimson robe, it may be that these figures were usually coloured. The four-decker *Santissima Trinidad* had a group figure representative of the Trinity, a subject which would have been unlikely

1. Plates 20, 21, 55.

to invite interpretation in wood save in the kingdom of His Most Catholic Majesty. This figure was painted white, as apparently was that of the *San Josef* when she had become an English ship.

The Baltic powers appear to have used lions in the 17th century, and perhaps till near the middle of the 18th, when portrait figures appear, to be replaced latterly, as in other navies, by busts.

From such instances as are available it appears that the Americans used whole figures both in the War of Independence and in that of 1812. One of the most celebrated of portrait whole figures was that of President Andrew Jackson which was borne by the frigate *Constitution*. This figure-head is still preserved in the Museum of the Naval Academy at Annapolis. There seems to be no record in England of the American figure-heads of the war of 1812: for the earlier war, in addition to casual mentions in intelligence reports, there are a few, *e.g.*, of the *Raleigh*, shown in the Admiralty draughts. But unfortunately the free-hand draughtsmanship is so poor that the results are not worth reproduction.

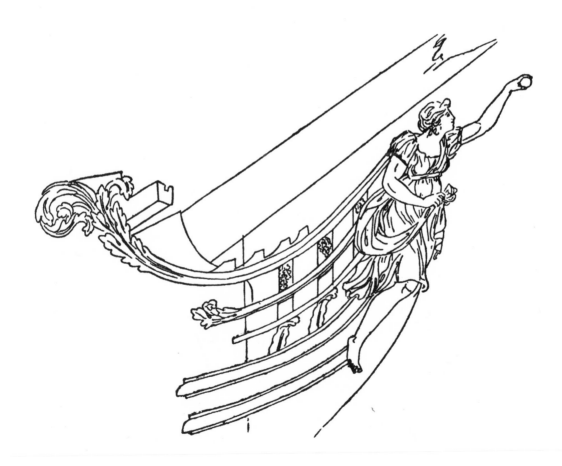

A FRENCH HEAD AND FIGURE OF THE FIRST EMPIRE

CHAPTER VI

THE STERN

§ 1. ITS FORM

Ships, whether descended from logs or from reed bundles, were naturally double ended, and continued to be so for countless centuries. There was a stem at either end, usually rising high above the planking, each of them commonly topped by some emblem or ornament. The present concern is rather with the position and form of these emblems than with their precise significance, and it is enough to notice that the Egyptians used a lotus or other simple device to decorate the after stem (figs. a, b), the Greeks elaborated this stem by the addition of the aphlaston (fig. c), and it was left to the Romans under the Empire to originate the practice of making structural additions to the after part of the sailing ship. Fig. (d) shows how about 200 A.D. the stern post was carried up in the form of a swan's head and neck, while the planking of the hull was continued abaft it to form a sort of stern gallery, at the extremity of which stood a god or goddess. At the same time the rounding of the stern was carved or painted with a representation of some mythological or religious subject.

The study of early mediæval shipping has not yet proceeded far enough to make it certain how much of this was lost in the dark ages, but there is some indication that among southern nations the swan-necked stern post, with the projecting deck or gallery abaft it, may have had a history of at least 1,000 years.[1] It seems certain, however, that

EARLY STERN DECORATIONS
(a, b) Egyptian.   (c) Greek.   (d) Roman.   (e) Bayeux Tapestry.   (f) 11th century.
(g) From a 13th century French MS.   (h) Seal of Winchelsea.   (i) 15th century.

1. Jal, "Archéologie navale", I, 21; Duro, "Marina de Castilla", 164.

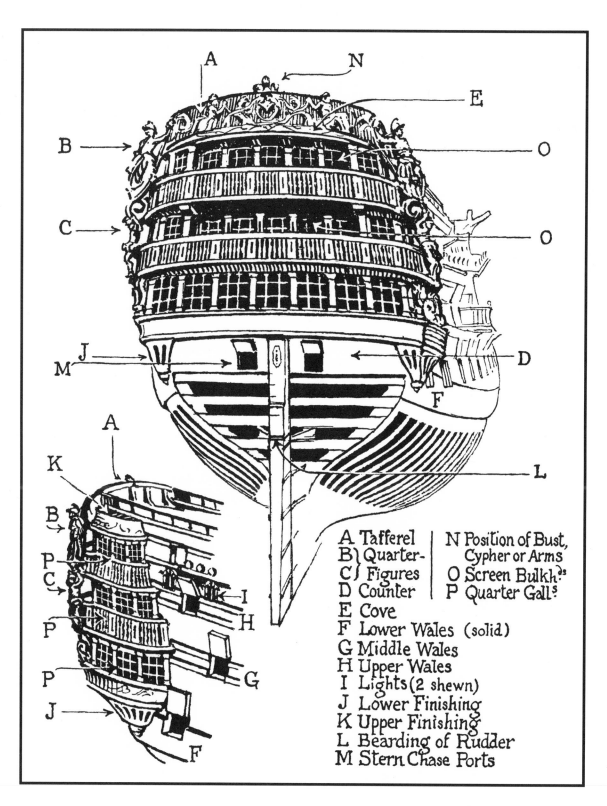

A Tafferel
B⎫ Quarter-
C⎭ Figures
D Counter
E Cove
F Lower Wales (solid)
G Middle Wales
H Upper Wales
I Lights (2 shewn)
J Lower Finishing
K Upper Finishing
L Bearding of Rudder
M Stern Chase Ports

N Position of Bust,
　Cypher or Arms
O Screen Bulkh.ᵈˢ
P Quarter Gall.ˢ

KEY DRAWING TO ILLUSTRATE DETAILS OF THE STERN AND QUARTER GALLERY

the ships of Northern Europe were not influenced, for the earliest dates at which we meet them show them, whether of the long ship or the round ship type, to have been high stemmed and double ended. The stems were often ornamented by carvings: in Viking ships the stern post sometimes ended as the tail of the beast with which the ship was identified, and the tradition of an ornament in this place continued until the growth of the after-castle left no room for it. Such an effigy as William the Conqueror had in the *Mora*[1] was probably quite exceptional: such representations as survive show sometimes a mere conventional ornament,[2] and at others a duplication of the figure-head.[3] But it seems probable that more often than not the after stem was left plain.

The after-castle, at first a temporary staging, was developing into a permanent structure in the 13th century, its ornamentation being the Gothic of contemporary architecture ashore.[4] In the 14th century in northern ships the stages or castles became parts of the hull, and grew in length till both projected beyond the ends of the ship. It is certain that Mediterranean ships had reached a further point of development than those of the north.[5] In them there were already two decks aft above the hull proper, a quarter-deck and poop as they would afterwards have been called;[6] with England and her neighbours in the 14th century even the quarter-deck was still a new thing. We have thus a round stern of the hull proper, a deck projecting abaft it and ending in a square vertical bulwark, and a counter to support the projecting

deck. The brackets of the counter were inside the planking, and the only stern ornamentation of these early ships was such as could be applied to the bulwark. This took the forms of trefoils, quatrefoils or diaper pattern.

The earliest mention of elaborate stern ornamentation dates from 1400, when the king's ship *Trinity*,[7] which was painted red, had four effigies standing in the stern, St. George, St. Anthony, St. Katherine, and St. Margaret, together with four shields of the king's arms within a collar of gold, and two of the arms of St. George within the garter. It is conjectural how these ornaments were disposed, but their importance seems to indicate that the *Trinity* must have had more flat surface aft than the rail of the poop; or, in other words, that she must have had two partial decks aft, which would give her a flat of the stern some ten feet high. There can be little doubt that this surface was all in one plane and vertical, as in the great ships of somewhat later date. From the number of the effigies it may be decided that two were placed on each side, perhaps two on what came later to be called the tafferel, and two as quarter pieces; or they may have been grouped in pairs as quarter pieces, one pair facing aft and the other to the sides. It is at least clear that there can have been no central device or figure on the tafferel. The arms would seem to have been small, and it is at least probable that a pair of them were on the quarters. It is also probable that a pair may have been placed on the counter, as are the crowns in the early 15th century ship picture in the Ashmolean.[8]

1. P. 87, fig. (e).   2. *Ibid*. fig. (f).   3. *Ibid*. fig. (g).   4. *Ibid*. fig. (h).   5. Jal. *Op. cit*., II, 355.
6. *Cp*., also the St. Peter Martyr ship of 1339, *ap*, M.M. I, 344.   7. Nicolas, Hist. of R.N., II, 445.   8. M.M. III, 200.

On artistic grounds the Ashmolean ship is believed to be Italian, but nautically speaking she shows little or nothing which might not equally well be found in a northern ship. There is, however, one decided peculiarity about her, which has not been noticed in any other ship. At the stern her tumblehome[1] begins suddenly some 3ft. above the water, making an angle of about 135 degrees with the bottom planking; and the treatment of light and shade in the picture makes it appear that this chime,[2] as it may be called, rises in a curve to meet the stern post at the level of the counter. It may even be the case that the stern planking above the chime may be meant to be flat; in which case we have an early and very curious variant of the flat tuck of the square-sterned ship. It is unnecessary to decide that the chime is un-English, for "Ancient English Shipwrightry" shows that in the royal ships of the 16th century there was sometimes a distinct chime where the tumblehome met the breadth.

The carrack stern shown from a late 15th century MS.[3] shows the lower wales brought up to the quarter instead of being carried aft to the stern post in normal fashion; and it may be thought that this suggests so near an approach to flatness in the stern that to continue the wales aft would have been difficult. The origin of the flat tuck has not yet been discovered; and it may be that these two ships show transitional forms between the round and the square. The date of its introduction is known within a little,[4] for the ships both of W.A. and of the Rous Roll show round sterns, while those of Henry VIII have the square tuck.

It will be well to make an end of this matter of the square tuck. This fashion of stern seems to have been general throughout the 16th century. It began to go out of use first in England; but owing to the difficulty of being sure what artists meant to show, there remains some doubt as to important instances. Thus it seems fairly certain that the *Constant Reformation*[5] of 1618 had a round stern; it is quite certain that the *Prince Royal* of 1610 had a square tuck; while in the case of the *Sovereign of the Seas* it seems probable, but by no means certain, that the artist meant to show a square tuck.[6] In the specifications of her dimensions the "height of the tuck" is distinctly mentioned;[7] but this supports no argument, for the old technicality continued in use. It is, however, safe to say that from about the date of the *Sovereign* the round stern became the rule in English ships, though an occasional instance of a square tuck occurs till the early 18th century, chiefly in small ships. By a throw-back the fir-built frigates of 1812-14 were given the square tuck.

Curiously enough a print, after Stoop, of the home-coming of Catharine of Braganza in 1662[8] shows all English ships with square tucks. These ships include the *Charles* and *York*, which we know from Van de Velde's drawings to have had round sterns. Stoop was an eye-witness, and by the rest of the detail in his picture is seen to have had a good eye for the details of ships; from which it should follow that he is right in this particular. That he is certainly wrong may have been due to his greater familiarity with Dutch ships, in which the square tuck

---

1. *I.e.*, the inward slope of the side.   2. Two surfaces meeting at a pronounced angle form a "chime".   3. P. 87, fig. (i).
4. *Cp*. Duro, Marina de Castilla, 296.   5. M.M. IX, 59.   6. Plate 26.   7. N.R.S., "Phineas Pett", Introd., 92, 94.   8. M.M. XI, 212-3.

was still universal. We have had a recent exemplification of this particular mistake in the "Sphere", which sent an artist to Portsmouth to draw the *Victory*; and he drew her with a square tuck.

The Dutch adhered to the square tuck for about a century later than we did. The earliest example of a round stern in a Dutch ship, other than fly boats, is of 1730; while the latest square tuck which has been noticed is of 1745. The French followed Dutch fashions till nearly 1670, but about that time began to pay more attention to English practice. As one result of this they began to build some of their ships with round sterns; the first ship to be so fitted being the *Souverain* of 1678; but the change was introduced gradually, the famous *Soleil Royal*[1] of 1690 was built with a square tuck, and the new fashion was not general till early in the next century. The Northern nations which followed Dutch fashions fairly closely, seem to have been even after the French in making the change: while the Spaniards, with whom in the early 18th century Dutch influence was strong, do not seem to have adopted the round stern till about 1720.

Above the counter 15th century ships ended flat and square, the profile from counter to rail being a vertical line. The next ship pictures we have are of about 1520, and show that by then a different type of stern was established. The new ships had a succession of counters, one to each deck, formed by the projection of each deck a little more aft than the one below it. There were as yet no external brackets, or mullions between the lights,

such as are so conspicuous in 17th century ships, the supports still being all internal. In the great ships the decks of the after-castle rose to a great height above the waist, so that in the stern there might well be three or four decks above the point where the tumblehome began. The towering stern, when seen end on, was thus both wall-sided and very narrow for a great part of its height. It may be that the men who designed it saw some beauty in this arrangement; but to us it looks ugly, our judgment doubtless being influenced by the knowledge that it was technically faulty. As was shown later, a superstructure half as high and twice as wide would have given the same living space while it wronged the ship far less.

The form of the stern itself, that is the stern to the fashion pieces, not including the galleries, changed slowly. The early Stuart stern, as seen in the *Prince Royal*[2] and the *Sovereign of the Seas*[3] was still very high and narrow. Commonwealth-built ships show an increase of width, which was further added to in the Restoration period. The *Sovereign* was rebuilt in 1659, and her stern presumably brought up to the standard of the time; but after the third Dutch war, when she was due for a "great repair", one of the proposals was to widen her main transom by no less than 6ft. to give her a better seat in the water. She had always been a crank ship. It may be assumed that this was done in the rebuilding completed in 1684, but it was first proposed 9 years earlier.[4] At the same time it was proposed to widen the stern of the *Old James* of 1633, a much smaller ship, by 2ft.[5] We thus

1. Plate 39.   2. Plate 8.   3. Plate 26.   4. Admy. Navy Bd. 3118, f. 56.   5. *Ibid*. f. 71.

have a measure of the increase of width given to the sterns of the thirty ships of the 1676 programme. As there was no corresponding increase of height, which had already passed its maximum, the difference of form is very noticeable. In later ships, from about 1700, the stern appears to have grown very greatly wider; but this was in great measure due to the increase of the width of the quarter galleries rather than of the hull proper. It has also to be remembered that increase of size, which was progressive throughout the 18th century, and rose by leaps and bounds in the 19th, added considerably to the beam, and consequently to the width of the stern, but not at all to its height.

The rough diagram herewith indicates the shape of the sterns of the *Sovereign*, 1637; a 90-gun ship of the 1676 programme; and the *Ossory*, 90, taken in hand for rebuilding in 1706. As far as the shape goes, the *Ossory* may

stand for any normal English flat-sterned three-decked ship for nearly a century. In the closing years of the 18th century the tumblehome was much reduced; and from 1817 a high proportion of new ships were both round-sterned and wall-sided. These last were entirely unlike anything of earlier date. A slight modification of the round stern was introduced after 1840, on Fincham's design; the difference being chiefly that while the early sterns in profile had little or no projection beyond the stern post, and no counter, as seen in the *Royal Adelaide*[1] and in the *Castor* frigate,[2] later ships, such as the *Royal Frederick*,[3] had about the same projection of counter as the square-sterned ships.

The elliptical stern introduced after 1827 differed little in appearance from a square stern. It was possible with it to apply the quarter galleries in the old manner, and to fit an open stern walk between them. When this was done the most noticeable difference from a square-sterned ship was that in profile the stern had a somewhat increased projection abaft the quarter galleries.

Apart from the longer retention of the square tuck abroad, the structural form of the sterns of foreign ships seems to have differed little from that of contemporary English ships. There were differences, of a very marked nature, between those of the principal shipbuilding nations, but they were due chiefly to the different treatment of the galleries and of the ornamentation.

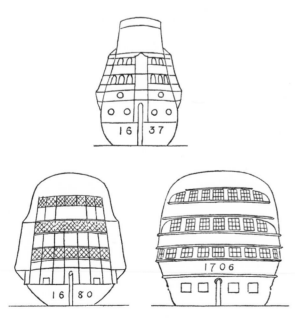

1. Plate 48.   2. P. 38.   3. P. 145, fig. (b).

FOREIGN PRACTICE

National variations in the shape of the stern and in the treatment of its galleries have been described together, and will be found at the end of § 2 of this chapter.

§ 2. THE GALLERIES

It is impossible to describe the galleries of the stern without mentioning also those of the quarters, which for long were directly connected with them. But as there were special ornamental features about the quarter galleries, which call for a good deal of illustration, it has seemed better to give them a chapter to themselves, even at the risk of a little overlapping.

There is a doubtful indication of a stern-gallery in one English ship of about 1460,[1] but in the comparatively numerous pictures of ships from that date to about 1540 there are certainly none. We first begin to get on sure ground with the ships of Le Testu and the Anthony Roll,[2] which show that about 1545 an open gallery, running across the stern and joining up with similar galleries on the quarters, was already common but still far from general. Of the king's ships the *Lion* of 160 tons, built in 1536; the *Jennett* of 200 tons, built in 1539; the *Dragon* of 140 tons, and the *Greyhound* of 200, built respectively in 1544 and 1545, have these galleries. Other ships, including the Scots built *Unicorn* and the French built *Salamander*, have none. The Le Testu drawings[3] show that at the

same time they were present in the larger class of private built ships. This form is shown in fig. (a):[4] it already occurs either without or with spurs for spreading an awning over it. Both these simple forms continued in use for about a century,[5] but from the end of the 16th century tended to become more elaborately decorated, by brackets below, by the carving of the spurs above, and by the ornamentation of the after face of the balcony.

In the earlier ships spurs though often fitted on the quarters are commonly absent from the stern gallery, probably because the projection of the stern overhead served as a canopy; but from about 1600, when the upper part of the stern was being built up flat in a tafferel, spurs begin to appear, and in some ships, especially Spanish and Dutch,[6] a standing roof. It is somewhat remarkable that the galleries are sometimes not shown when we know them to have been present. This is the case in "Ancient English Shipwrightry"; but here in some cases the door which gave access to the gallery is shown, though the gallery itself is not.

The Elizabethans seem to have been usually content with one gallery, which in a two-decked ship was fitted at the upper-deck level, but in a one-decked ship on that of the quarter-deck. Two galleries may occasionally have been used in high-sterned ships before 1600, after it certainly they were not uncommon;[7] but in the absence of a complete knowledge of the intermediate stages, it comes as something of a surprise to find three in the *Prince Royal* of 1601.[8] The *Prince* had the second gallery close, *i.e.*, it was built

---

1. M.M. V, 16.   2. Add. MS., 22047.   3. M.M. II, 65.   4. P. 134.   5. *Ibid.* figs. (e), (f), (h), (i), (j).   6. *Ibid.* figs. (b), (c), (g).
7. *Ibid.* fig. (j).   8. Plate 8.

up from the breast rail to the foot rail of the upper gallery, thus making the stern flat in that portion. A little later sterns are found with apparently no galleries, but flat from the lower counter to the top of the tafferel. The *Sovereign of the Seas* had such a stern in 1637;[1] so had the *Constant Reformation*[2] of 1618. The temptation naturally is to reckon them as ships without stern galleries, but that does not seem to have been how their builders regarded them. To them they were ships with closed galleries, the real stern of the ship being inside the galleries and unseen.

From 1637 to 1669 no example is known of an English ship built with an open stern gallery, and the question therefore arises how long men continued to build ships with sterns which were double to the level of the quarter-deck. As far as is at present known all the close-sterned ships of the middle 17th century[3] were so built, so that, when it was desired to reintroduce an open stern gallery, this could be done by the simple expedient of cutting away a strip of the outer covering of the stern. The earliest known example of this in an English ship is the *St. Michael* of 1669;[4] but the same thing is seen in a three-decked model belonging to Mr. R. C. Anderson, unidentified but undoubtedly of almost the same date.

Apart from differences in form between the new galleries and the old, there was an important difference as to their position. With the new galleries, unless with a very careless artist – and some artists were incredibly careless,

Sailmaker, for instance[5] – there could be no doubt as to the deck from which they were entered, for they were on the same level with it. Indeed, whatever may have been the case in the 17th century, in the 18th the floor of the gallery was formed by the projection of the deck. But in the ships before the *Sovereign of the Seas* it was not so. Most of those early ships had falls in their decks, especially abaft; and it is always necessary to allow for this when computing to which deck a gallery belongs. Even in the *Sovereign* herself things were not quite as they seemed. From a broadside view of her galleries it is easy to form the impression that they were on the middle and upper decks; but from the flat of the stern[6] it becomes apparent that they were in fact on the upper and quarter-decks. This point will be further discussed in the chapter on quarter galleries.[7]

The *St. Michael* of 1669 shows two forms of open galleries, both entirely different from anything that had gone before. The *Sovereign of the Seas* and later ships kept the fore end of the quarter gallery open, but that of the stern was entirely closed (fig. a).[8] The *St. Michael*, still having no windows on the quarter-deck, had her two open galleries on the middle and upper-decks. On the middle deck (fig. c)[8] it ran the width of the stern proper, and was narrow, its after side being flush with the after ends of the quarter galleries. On the upper-deck it ran the full width of the stern; and, as the quarter galleries here were small, and did not extend beyond the fashion pieces, it was carried round them on the quarters. It was also bowed out for about half its

---

1. Plate 26. 2. M.M. IX, 59. 3. Plate 46, fig. (E). 4. Plate 27. 5. M.M. IX, 1. 6. Plate 26. 7. P. 135. 8. P. 138.

length in the middle (fig. b).[1] This particular form did not become common, but from soon after this date until about 1710, or perhaps a little later, several instances are met with of ships which had, usually on the quarter-deck, a mere central dicky, instead of a gallery the width of the stern. The *Cumberland*, 80, of 1710 had such a dicky on the quarter-deck. As this feature occurs on two decks of the *Royal Louis* of 1668, it may be inferred that we borrowed it, with the open gallery itself, from the French.

The form shown in fig. (c)[1] was in common use during the later Stuart period, three-deckers usually having two such galleries, one on the upper-deck, the other at first more commonly on the middle deck, but after about 1680 on the quarter-deck. But some ships of later date than the *St. Michael, e.g.*, the *Prince* of 1670, had no open galleries whatever. It is probable that the early fashion of an open middle deck gallery was due simply to the fact that as yet there were no stern windows to the cabins on the quarter-deck, the carvings of the tafferel occupying all the space. When the height of the tafferel was reduced by placing a range of windows on the quarter-deck, an open gallery followed almost immediately. Another consideration, perhaps not without some weight in accounting for the middle deck gallery, is that at this time the great cabin of that deck was the abode of the reformadoes, who, though without command on board, were men of consideration in virtue of their social or service rank. But the position was not a good one, for a gallery placed so low cannot have been out of reach of the sea.

This brings us to the screen bulkhead. At first the inboard side of these galleries was the real stern of the ship, strongly framed; but when the idea of having a gallery on the middle deck had been abandoned, it seems to have occurred that for the upper-decks this strong framing was no longer necessary. Only a light glazed bulkhead was needed, and this could be made to take down so that it might be stowed away in action, and a considerable bill for broken glass saved thereby. Also it might be further forward than the old flat of the stern, thus giving a wider gallery; and it was in consequence placed some 4ft. in from the fashion pieces, thus making the gallery about 7ft. wide. This was the regular practice from about 1705, as shown in figs. (e) to (i).[1] There is little to add about the screen bulkhead: at first it was made with double sashes, and was in consequence awkward and heavy to shift; but by an order of 1757[2] it was made lighter, being constructed thereafter like carriage windows, with a single sash housing in the lower part. And so it continued till the introduction of close sterns about 1800 made it obsolete. There are indications that even with the close stern it may have been fitted in a few cases, but if so it certainly was not for long.

From the time of the first re-opening of the galleries it seems to have been always the rule, to which down to about 1750 there were some exceptions, that two-decked ships should have one open gallery, and one-decked ships none; but to about 1700 there were certainly many cases in which even large two-deckers had none. Even of William III's 80-gun ships

1. P. 138.   2. Admy. Navy Bd. 2508, No. 445.

some had close sterns, as shown by the model of the *Boyne* at Greenwich: others of the class, probably the later ships, had a gallery projecting square from the fashion pieces on the quarter-deck,[1] the windows being in the stern proper, not set in by a screen bulkhead. The quarter galleries on this deck hardly reach the stern, the width of which is spread out aloft by the carved quarter pieces.

There is in the Boyman's Museum an unidentified draught by Van de Velde of an English two-decked ship of about 60-guns. She has a closed gallery on the upper-deck, with mock balustrading under the windows, and on the quarter-deck has an open gallery, also balustraded, the full width of the stern, its floor forming the deck above the lower gallery. Except that this gallery has no central dicky, and ends at the fashion pieces, its arrangement is the same as that of the *St. Michael*. It seems to be an important piece of evidence, and it would be well that the ship should be identified. By a process of elimination and comparison I have formed the opinion that she may be the *Mountagu*, 62, of 1675; but this conclusion was reached from a photograph, and cannot be put forward categorically without further examination of the original. The *Mordaunt*, 46, of 1682, a fourth rate, has her one gallery on the upper-deck. It is in the fashion of fig. (c),[2] the windows being in the stern proper, which is carried up to the tafferel in a straight line. Thus the only projection of the stern is that of the gallery carried out on brackets from the counter. This ship has a tier of windows on the quarter-deck, but no gallery there.

The *St. George*, 90,[3] of 1701 has only one gallery, and like the *Mordaunt* has it on the upper-deck, but she differs from that ship by having a way through from it to the quarter gallery. She is therefore as shown in fig. (f),[2] except that she has the windows in the stern proper, instead of in a screen bulkhead.

In fig. (e)[2] a screen bulkhead is shown for the date 1700. This is perhaps a few years too early, the earliest certain instances yet noticed being of about 1705-6. The *Princess*, 90, designed in 1706 and launched in 1711, had it; so had the *Resolution*, launched in 1708, and other ships of the date. But the *Royal Sovereign* of 1701,[4] the "100-gun ship" model, and the "*Victory*, 17th century", both at Greenwich, both of them representing ships launched about 1704, still have the windows in the stern itself. Probably the earliest date that we can assign to this bulkhead is to say that we would expect to find it in any design prepared after 1700.

In figs. (f) to (i)[2] the dates are approximate, denoting common usage rather than first instances. It will be seen that for about half a century arrangements were made, differing slightly from time to time, whereby an officer in the stern gallery could get a clear view on the beam, and even nearly right ahead. When the galleries run round to the quarter in this way they usually pass under an arch, at first formed by the quarter piece,[5] later between the quarter piece and the side. Sometimes, as shown at A in fig. (h),[6] the after side of the stern gallery was glazed in wake of the quarter gallery, though

1. Nance, Plates 44 and 46; and P. 138, fig. (d).   2. P. 138.   3. Nance, Plates 58, 59.   4. M.M. IV, 71.   5. Plates 4, 47.   6. P. 138.

open to the side. This practice seems to have begun about 1715: it is seen in the *Royal William* of 1719,[1] and continued to occur till about the middle of the century. When it is present it is impossible, from a draught of the flat of the stern only, to determine whether the gallery ends at the fashion piece[2] or is continued to the quarter piece.

From about 1680 practice was approaching a standard, and there were few enough exceptions to make it worth while to state as follows the rules which were being observed. Thus: –

(1) There were as many tiers of windows as the ship had complete decks of guns; but the windows were one deck above the gun decks, being always absent from the lower deck, and always present on the quarter-deck.

An exception to this was made in the case of first rates from 1719 to 1737, which usually had a fourth tier of windows, to the cabins on the poop. This is shown in the *Royal William*,[1] in the earlier of the so-called *"Royal William"* models at Greenwich, and in Balchen's *Victory* of 1737. As cabins on the poop went out of fashion from this time, so too did the fourth tier of lights.

(2) Galleries were in number one less than the tiers of windows, not being fitted to the lowest tier. Thus in a ship with four tiers of lights, there might be three galleries, as there were in Balchen's *Victory.* But the other three-deckers, such as the *Royal William*, with cabin windows on the poop, had no gallery there.

With the wide open galleries the quarter pieces served to connect the galleries with each other and with the tafferel. Figs. (j) to (m)[3] show the different sections they had in the early 18th century, after the practice of cutting the figures clear had gone out. Fig. (l)[3] shows the form that was first abandoned: the other three were in use concurrently.

The ships built on the establishment of 1745 seem to have been the last in this country to have a way from the stern to the quarter galleries, or, in the contemporary phrase, to have "open quarters". Many small changes were introduced about 1756, and the general adoption of the form shown in fig. (i)[3] was one of them. This form indeed had been in occasional use long before: I have found it as early at 1710, and from 1710 to about 1756 have also noticed cases where there was this arrangement without any projection of the stern gallery. When the stern gallery did project in that period its width varied, being sometimes only about 2ft., sometimes 4ft., beyond the fashion pieces. From 1756 there was little variation, and till sterns were made close the normal projection of the gallery was about 3ft., which was about a foot or so more than that of the tafferel. Thus when the earliest ships were altered to close sterns between 1795 and 1797, what was done seems to have been to cut back the galleries till they ranged with the tafferel, and then glaze in the space between breast rail and tafferel, or, in a three-decker's upper-deck gallery, between breast rail and the projection of the deck overhead.[4] Thus the profile of the stern would be kept at its original angle.

1. Plate 28.   2. The "fashion pieces" from the side of the stern proper.   3. P. 138.   4. M.M. X, 184.

It is not very clear why a demand arose for close sterns, but such was certainly the case. Perhaps the winter service of the Revolutionary war, especially on the great blockades, made admirals think that the screen bulkhead was inclined to be draughty. At any rate, we find first Lord Bridport, then Nelson, asking to have the sterns of their flagships closed – the *Royal George* was the first, and the *Vanguard* was altered for the campaign of 1798 – whereupon the Navy Board reported to the Admiralty that the change had better be made general, for they could see plenty more similar requests in prospect. So it was made, but before the end of the war officers were regretting it. The celebrated *Téméraire* of 1798 was building when this change was introduced, and was a transitional ship. Her stern was closed on the quarter-deck, but not on the upper-deck, which had a normal open gallery.[1]

In 1813 the Admiralty asked the Navy Board which form of stern had proved stronger, and the Navy Board answered that the general opinion was that the close stern was stronger, besides that it allowed the stern chase guns to be worked with greater effect. But the Admiralty had clearly made up its mind to reintroduce galleries, and on 14th July the Secretary[2] wrote that "their Lordships are of opinion that the strength of the present mode of framing the sterns of line-of-battle ships, as well as the security of firing the stern chase guns may be preserved, and the beauty and convenience of the gallery be restored, by continuing the stern timbers from the wing transom to the tafferel, and projecting the decks as formerly beyond the transoms, applying the gallery rail as heretofore". The *Nelson*, 120 guns, launched in 1814, was the first ship so fitted. In their letter of 14th July the Admiralty said that they did not intend the rule to be general, and we do, in fact, find close sterns after this date; but in 1817 the whole question of the form of sterns entered on a new phase in consequence of the introduction of the round stern. This became very common in all classes down to frigates, but was never general. Before the introduction of steam 38 ships of the line, 57 large and 6 small frigates, and one corvette were either built or altered to this form, which was continued in the era of steam. When ships were so built they usually had three little projecting galleries like sponsons, one central and one on each quarter, with an open balcony beyond fitted with a light iron railing. This is illustrated here from the *Royal Adelaide*, 110, of 1828,[3] the *Castor*,[4] 36-gun frigate, of 1832, and the *Royal Frederick*,[5] 120, of 1841. The earlier round sterned ships went straight up from the water-line with practically no counter, but from about 1840 they were given a short counter, so that in profile they were similar to the square sterned ships.

It will be seen that the same cycle was twice repeated, with unessential differences. In 1610 the closing of the galleries began, as it did again in 1795. In 1669 they were re-opened, with the windows in the real stern of the ship, as was done in 1813. It is very doubtful whether, either in 1795 or 1813, the shipwrights knew that there was any precedent to guide them.

1. Plate 32.   2. Admy.; Sec., Public Offices, 677.   3. Plate 48.   4. P. 38.   5. P. 145, fig. (b).

FOREIGN PRACTICE

It has been seen that in the early part of the 17th century there was little difference between the stern galleries of different nations. One little point which has not been noticed is that the open gallery in Northern ships did not always run quite flat across the stern, but was bowed up and out a little in the middle, while its ends rose up to join the breast-rail of the quarter gallery. When galleries of this type were closed, they gave a stern slightly rounding, and if the old breast rail was kept below the lights, it had the form that we know in Dutch ships as the "slijngerlist". Dutch sterns were not closed till some little time after English, in the 1630's, and as there were among them no three-deckers, they at once assumed the form that is familiar from the many pictures of the English wars. All the great ships had only one tier of windows, ranging with the quarter gallery, which also was only one deck deep. In the few cases where the quarter gallery was more than one deck high, its upper part did not reach aft to the fashion piece, and therefore did not affect the form of the stern. This, as can be seen from the *Prins Willem* of 1651,[1] was wide at the level of the upper-deck, and then narrowed suddenly in a hard knuckle. The quarter pieces were at most seated figures, placed on this knuckle, and did nothing to detract from the narrowness of the stern aloft. The high tafferel above the single tier of windows gave room for a very large carving or painting, while the "slijngerlist" was retained as an ornament, and even exaggerated.[2] This form of stern was long retained in Holland, and was not in fact appreciably altered until about 1690. A second "slijngerlist" began to be introduced above the stern windows from 1666,[3] and at the time of the third war with England had become general.[4]

The alteration made in Dutch sterns at the end of the century consisted chiefly in a decrease of their height. The single tier of windows remained, without an open gallery, the upper "slijngerlist" was dropped, and with the decrease of height the space available for decoration on the tafferel was greatly reduced. As will be seen, the appearance of the ship was much altered.[5] Even the class of three-decked ships which were built after 1683 had only two tiers of windows, on the middle and upper-decks, and no open galleries; but by an alteration in the form of quarter galleries, now first introduced, the stern above the windows lost something of its former narrowness.

An interesting type of stern came in with the East Indiamen of 1717 to 1725. It is illustrated here from the *Padmos-Blydorp* model,[6] which shows it in its extreme form. A second, or quarter-deck, tier of windows is found, the double "slijngerlist" reasserts itself, and the old high tafferel has virtually disappeared. But what more than anything else makes the stern look unlike that of a Dutch ship is its extreme roundness. The square tuck, which has become less heavy, and as in the *Briel* of 1695[7] is now almost entirely above the swimming line, is almost semi-circular below, while the upper part of the stern, above the "slijngerlist", is a complete half circle.

1. Plate 3.   2. Plate 34.   3. M.M. VIII, 18.   4. Plates 34, 35, 37.   5. Plate 49.   6. Plate 38.   7. Plate 49.

The quarter pieces and tafferel form one continuous band round the circumference: the rails above and below the quarter-deck windows are themselves arcs of a circle, and meet on each side at the end of the upper "slijngerlist". This form of stern first appears in the *Valkenisse* of 1717. It had but a short vogue in Holland; but its general roundness of outline, and the horseshoe treatment of the tafferel and quarter pieces, were adopted by other nations, by which their use was continued into the 19th century. This "horseshoe stern" has often been spoken of as typically French. It is of interest, therefore, to be able to decide that it appears first in Holland, roughly some 40 years before it was adopted for French ships of war.

The stern of *'t Wickelo* of 1725[1] is interesting as showing a further development of that of the *Briel* of 1695. Owing to the form of the quarter gallery it is a little wider than it would otherwise be abreast the quarter-deck lights; and as its square tuck is extremely shallow, being lifted entirely from the water, the general effect is of squatness. Neither it, nor any other Dutch representation of as early date which is included here, shows any open stern gallery; but Mr. Cannenberg, director of the Scheepvaart Museum, has been so kind as to contribute some information. He says that, from a series of 25 examples covering the whole 18th century, it is quite evident that closed and open sterns were both in use during the whole period. The open gallery first appeared shortly after 1700; and, though it was never generally adopted, yet it never wholly went out of use. About 1800

one open gallery, very often projecting, was in pretty general use.

To the suggestion that in England a stern gallery had always been of value to an admiral, as allowing him to keep an eye on his command without the formality of appearing on deck, Mr. Cannenberg replied by calling attention to the Dutch East India ship *Gertruida* of 1717, which had an open gallery while others of her class had not, she being intended for a flag, and they not.

It is hardly necessary to follow Dutch practice in detail further, for from about 1730 English fashions were introduced and became general. The only noticeable difference of form between the stern of the *Boeken Roode* of 1732[2] and a contemporary English ship is that she has her open gallery on the upper, instead of on the quarter, deck; and that while her quarter-deck is close, it is balustraded, and has an open bay inside the quarter piece, communicating with the quarter gallery. This last feature is very rare in Dutch ships, and occurs for the last time in a ship of 1780. The draught of a two-decked ship of 1749[2] is still more like an English ship, having its open gallery on the quarter-deck, but without any projection which nearly all English ships then had. The other noticeable differences are the extreme lightness of the tafferel, and the central pillar to the gallery. A draught which is titled a "'s Lands schip" of 1767[3] shows the windows the whole height of the deck, and though there is no open gallery, has an open arch on each side between the fashion and quarter pieces. The general form of this stern is English,

1. Plate 49.   2. P. 44, figs. (D), (E).   3. Plate 41.

but the decoration is, on the stern, decidedly French. The stern of the *Washington*, 74, of 1797, as seen from the model in the "Mercury" Museum, appears to be in every way English; but the *Neptunus* of 1803[1] shows how in some at least of the smaller ships, the quarter pieces were made vertical, thus giving the stern a square and somewhat heavy appearance.

In 1669 the French Ministry of Marine was entrusted to Colbert, who had been virtually its chief since 1665. It is therefore probably a fair conclusion that the MS. treatise on shipbuilding, preserved in the Section Hydrographique, and cited here as Colbert's book, a work comparable in scope and importance with Deane's contemporary "Doctrine of Naval Architecture", may have been drawn up for him during these preliminary years.

This book shows a French ship whose stern is fully ornamented with galleries. This fact alone would raise the question whether stern galleries were found in French ships before the Colbert régime; but we have also a direct statement by Pepys that the *French Ruby*, a second rate captured by us in 1666, had "galleries quite round the stern, to walk in as a balcone, which will be taken down". It is quite certain therefore that the French set the fashion to the Northern nations in the introduction of these galleries, and reasonably certain that they had begun to use them before 1665. We know so little of the details of French shipbuilding during the 40 years or so when they were chiefly dependent on the Dutch for their men-of-war, that it can be only a conjecture that these galleries did not represent a sudden

inspiration, but may have been evolved by continuous development from the open galleries of the early part of the century. Alternatively it may have to be considered whether the fashion may not have come into the French navy from the South, the intermediate steps having perhaps been made by the Venetians. It is a point on which further evidence is needed.

It is of interest to compare the ship in the Colbert book[2] with the *St. Michael*;[3] for though the galleries in the *French Ruby* may in 1666 have seemed undesirable to English shipwrights, the fact remains that they were adopted immediately after. It will be seen that the stern galleries of the *St. Michael* are in arrangement exactly those of the ship in the Colbert book, differing from them only by the central projection added on the quarter-deck. It is therefore a pretty safe inference that the *French Ruby* also was similar. She may even have had the projection. I have seen in a private collection a Van de Velde draught of a French ship, apparently of about 1670, which had a dicky on the quarter-deck. It has been noticed that the *Royal Louis* of 1668 has two.

The French stern looks very different from the English, partly owing to its square tuck, but chiefly owing to the very different ornamentation, and especially the balustrading of the galleries. As has been seen, English ships began to balustrade their galleries by about 1675, apparently in imitation of the French practice. Apart from these features there is little difference between the sterns. The flat is the same shape, the greater apparent width of

1. Plate 37.   2. Plate 40.   3. Plate 27.

Name "Juste" on a panel of the national colours (red on dexter side).

FRENCH 18TH CENTURY STERNS

(a) *Ménagère*, 64, of *c.* 1775. (b) An English frigate, 1780 (*Cp.* with d.) (c) Name panel, 1794.
(d) A French frigate, 1780. (e) *Sanspareil*, 80, of 1788. (f) *Trident*, 64, of 1742.
(From prints in Mr. A. G. H. Macpherson's collection.)

the English above the upper windows being due to the use of a heavy arch surmounted by a seated figure instead of the mere spur which, in the French ship, parts the quarter from the stern gallery. The same general features are also shown by the *Paris*,[1] a contemporary of the *St. Michael*, in which however Puget's elaborate quarter pieces somewhat obscure the fact that the lower gallery has a way through to the quarter, which the upper gallery has not.

French ships of the end of the century, as seen by the *Soleil Royal*,[2] the *St. Philippe*,[3] and *Le Bon*,[3] which all served in the war against William III, continued to keep to the same form of stern, differing from English ships by the retention of the middle deck gallery, by the straight line given to the quarter pieces, and by the refusal to round off the angles of the tafferel, as was done in English ships.

In the early 18th century the French omitted the lower gallery, and like English ships continued to use only the quarter-deck gallery in two-decked ships. The same somewhat square, or rather truncated cone, form of stern persisted, as seen in the *Vénus*[3] and *Téméraire*,[4] and the chief differences from English ships of the same date were such as appear best from the profile of the stern. The projection of the gallery was greater than in English ships, and on the other hand there was no projection of the tafferel above it, the stern from the counter rising its whole height in one straight line. The first change that overtook this form was that in the 50's the tafferel was made to project over

the gallery, as seen in the "Pic" model of 1755 at the Louvre, at first without support, but shortly after with pillars from the gallery to the tafferel.[5]

But almost immediately this form of stern was abandoned in favour of a round model, in which the quarter pieces joined with the tafferel to form a continuous arch round the stern. This change seems to have begun about 1756, when corresponding changes were taking place in England. This form of stern, often referred to as the "horseshoe", remained in use, in small ships as well as in large, until the early years of the 19th century. It has commonly been considered as typically French, as indeed it was during the second half of the 18th century; but we have seen that the form was first used in Dutch ships some 40 years before the French adopted it. It can hardly have come to the French direct from Holland, for its vogue in Holland was over long before 1756. It seems that the course of transmission was that the Dutch introduced it into Spain, and that Spanish ships provided the direct inspiration for the French. It is illustrated here from the *Danae*,[6] frigate, of 1779; from the *Northumberland*, 74, of 1780, and from the *Spartiate*, 74, of 1796.[7] In both these 74's the gallery was open to the quarters, but the draught of the *Spartiate* shows it as closed by English shipwrights after the ship fell into our hands. Another small point which will be noticed is that by the slight projection of the tafferel, and the decreased projection of the gallery, the *Northumberland* has assumed very much the profile of an English ship. The resemblance was greatest about 1780,

1. Plate 33.   2. Plate 39.   3. Plate 40.   4. Plate 41.   5. Plate 52, No. 2.   6. Plate 25.   7. Plate 42; *cp*. p. 102 (e) and (d).

for in later ships the gallery was made almost flush, its rails from about 1800 commonly being vertical, thus following the line of the screen bulkhead instead of being parallel to the profile of the stern. Also from about 1780 the quarters were closed, leaving no outside passage between the stern and quarter galleries. From about 1825 the French followed the fashion of round sterns: the drawings, from models of a two-decked ship and a frigate,[1] show that, in the former at least, their treatment of the galleries did not then differ materially from our own.

Before we pass on to more important shipbuilding powers, a draught of a Maltese ship of about 60 guns[2] claims attention, because of its possible connection with French practice. Its date seems to be about 1670, and almost every feature of the ship seems strongly French. In particular, there is an open stern gallery to the quarter-deck. It is possible that this ship may give a hint of Mediterranean usage before 1665; but on the other hand it is at least equally possible that French builders may have been responsible for her design.

We have seen that the English, Dutch, and French all evolved forms of their own, but we come now to a nation which apparently never succeeded in doing so. A Spanish stern of 1670[3] shows a form which may best be described as Dutch with French influence. It is Dutch in outline; it has the Dutch single tier of windows, the seated quarter pieces, the heavy carving above the tafferel, and even a modification of the lower "slijngerlist". It differs from

Dutch chiefly in the reduced height of the tafferel, and in the straightening of most of the rails of the stern. Similarly a large Spanish two-decked ship of 1691[4] is very like the *Briel*,[5] having only a single tier of stern windows, no open gallery, and a squat tafferel; but she keeps the older Dutch fashion of heavy carvings on top of the tafferel.

From the beginning of the new century Spanish fashions begin to get somewhat complicated, and the reason for this appears in the list of line-of-battle ships published by Señor Artiñano.[6] Between 1700 and 1720 the Spaniards bought many ships of war abroad, chiefly in Genoa, which seems to have been a central mart for such goods. There they acquired a number of English men-of-war, taken by the French in Queen Anne's war and sold to the dealers. From this period English influence was strong in Spanish shipbuilding, but not yet paramount. In the first half of the century Dutch, English and French shipwrights were all employed in Spain, and the styles of the three countries can be traced. It was presumably due to Dutch influence that the Spaniards kept to the square tuck till after 1720; and almost certainly they adopted the horseshoe arch of the stern directly from the Dutch. It is illustrated here from the *Fenix*, 80, of 1749,[7] which became the *Gibraltar* in the English Royal Navy in 1780. A two-decker of rather earlier date shows French influence strongly, especially in the form of the gallery, but has the tafferel rounded off more in accordance with English practice. The *Real Carlos*[8], 112, of 1787,

1. P. 148, figs. (a) and (b).   2. In Mr. R. C. Anderson's collection.   3. M.M. VII, 44.   4. *Ibid*. VII, 178.   5. Plate 49.
6. Arquitectura Naval Española, Appx. XIV.   7. Plate 31.   8. Plate 43.

is strongly English in the shape and general treatment of her stern, but has French pattern galleries.[1] The famous *Santissima Trinidad*, of 1769, as would be expected seeing that she was built by an English, or rather Irish, shipwright, was hardly distinguishable from an English ship, save by having her quarter galleries open to the stern. This was an early English feature which was retained by those nations which copied English fashions for half a century after the English had given it up. The story of Spanish naval architecture virtually ends here, for from 1796 to 1853 they built no ships of the line.

Oliveira's illustrated catalogue of the models of Portuguese ships in the naval museum at Lisbon shows that Portugal, like Spain, followed foreign fashions. The earliest of them is the *Principe da Beira*, of about 60 guns, described as of the early 18th century. Probably she is of after 1725, for she has an exact reproduction of the *Padmos* stern,[2] square tuck and all, but with the addition of a small gallery on the quarter-deck. *N.S. do Bom Successo*, a 64-gun ship of 1764, has a stern in the main English, with close quarters, and no heavy quarter pieces, but with a French gallery. A second *Principe da Beira*, described as of the end of the 18th century, a 74-gun ship, has a decidedly French stern of the horse-shoe type, with open quarters; but her tafferel is as high as that of an English ship. Two other line-of-battle ships of the end of the century have sterns hardly differing at all from English; a third, unnamed, has a stern generally English in manner, but with so wide a projection of the quarter galleries that the sides of the stern are vertical.

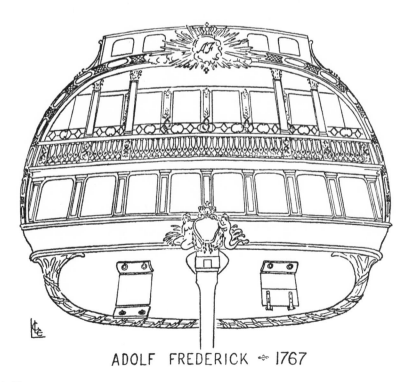

ADOLF FREDERICK ⚓ 1767

1. Plate 43.   2. Plate 38.

Sweden in the 17th century followed Dutch fashions. The *Amaranthe* of 1654 is not distinguishable from a Dutch ship, though about this date there were other ships which grafted some national peculiarities on to the Dutch stock. One of these is seen here in a ship named *Victoria* on her stern. This is taken from a contemporary print of the battle of the Sound in 1658, and shows a stern generally Dutch in shape, but with two heavy turrets coming to the stern at the after ends of the quarter galleries and crowding out the quarter pieces.[1] The same feature is shown in other Swedish ships in the same picture. Towards the middle of the 18th century the Baltic powers evolved a handsome composite stern unlike any met with elsewhere. The Danish *Tre Kroner* shows it in 1742.[2] It is somewhat round, recalling recent Dutch practice, but in most of its ornamental features it is nearer to the English fashion, except for the width of the gallery, and the treatment of the upper edge of the tafferel, which are as in a French ship. The ships of Chapman's time, such as the *Adolf Frederick* of 1767[3] and the *Gustaf* of 1776, were in most respects very strongly English, but further improved the new Baltic type of stern. They had the horseshoe arch, very narrow, round the stern, a French gallery on the quarter-deck running right across and open to the quarters, and two pairs of pillars a side from the breast rail of the gallery to the tafferel; but above the tafferel they showed the after bulkhead of the poop, with windows in it. This last feature is found also in some French ships. As would be expected of Chapman's great reputation,

the whole effect of these sterns is exceptionally graceful.

What we know of Danish and Norwegian sterns suggests that during the greater part of the 17th century they, like the other features of the ship, followed Dutch fashions. What is perhaps the earliest Danish ship of which we have any particular record is the so-called "Great Dane of 1600".[4] A great Dane she undoubtedly is, but there seems to be no real evidence that she is much more than a fancy picture, and from various details of the ship herself it seems likely that she should be placed considerably later than 1600, perhaps by 30 years. An important feature of her is that she has high turrets in lieu of quarter pieces, or rather above her quarter pieces, not dissimilar in principle to those shown by Swedish ships in 1658; and she has an exaggeration of the high poop that was common in Dutch and Northern ships in the second quarter of the century, in the *Norske Löve* for example.[5]

We get to sure ground with a Van de Velde drawing of a little Dane,[6] which may probably safely be placed between 1670 and 1680. This ship is very strongly Dutch in form, and in her stern, save for the Danish royal arms in the tafferel, could only be told from a Dutch ship by the fact that she has straight rails instead of "slijngerlists". In view of the extreme Dutchness of this ship, the stern of the modern model of the *Christianus V*,[7] a 100-gun ship of 1673, may reasonably be termed surprising. Like other features of the ship it is essentially French, with three tiers of windows and three galleries,

1. P. 134, fig. (k).   2. Chatterton, Plate 81.   3. P. 105.   4. M.M. IV, 225.   5. Nance, Plate 19.   6. Plate 36.   7. Nance, Plate 34.

of which the two lower are open to the quarters; and it shows a narrow tafferel square in the French manner. It is difficult to believe that a navy would follow, at one and the same time, two fashions so widely different as those shown by this model and by the small two-decker; and it is also a difficulty that even in a French ship such simplicity as is shown by the *Christianus V* model would not be expected till some twenty years later than the date assigned.

In the 18th century the Danes were apparently adopting such details from other nations as commended themselves, and were combining them after a distinctive manner of their own. Thus they replaced the square tuck by the round stern in the first years of the century. The stern of the *Fyen*, 50, of 1746,[1] has a light horseshoe arch, which at that date can only indicate a Dutch ancestry; the galleries in general suggest French practice, and yet the stern, if the pillars between the galleries were omitted, would have almost an English look. This type of stern, though composite, may be accepted as a definite contribution by the Baltic powers. We have already

seen it, slightly modified and improved, in Swedish ships of from 20 to 30 years later. It would be of interest to know how long it persisted.

After 1800 other fashions prevailed. The sterns of the 74-gun ships *Norge* and *Princess Carolina*, taken at Copenhagen in 1807, had one very marked peculiarity. They retained the horseshoe arch, the tafferel being wider than formerly, but they were almost frigate sterns. Instead of having a poop these ships had merely a light awning above the quarter-deck, and this awning stopped some 15ft. short of the tafferel. The aftermost quarter-deck guns were thus mounted in the open, and had ports in the tafferel for firing in chase. The sterns were close, with only the upper-deck tier of windows, so that it is only from the great height of the windows as compared with those of a frigate that it can be recognised from astern that the ships are two-deckers.

The curious and simple Hohlenberg stern of the *Christian VII*, also taken in 1807, is illustrated.[2] Its peculiarities are its extreme narrowness aloft, a reversion seemingly to 17th century fashion, and

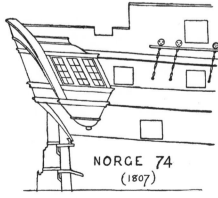

NORGE 74
(1807)

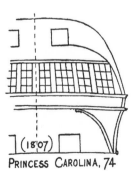

(15'07)
PRINCESS CAROLINA, 74

1. Nance, Plate 83.   2. P. 108.

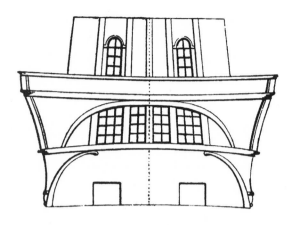

THE CHRISTIAN VII, 1807

A SHIP OF HENRY VIII

its very wide open quarter galleries reaching to the stern. This ship was very highly thought of, and her lines were copied in England. One at least of the ships built after them, the *Cambridge* of 1815, was equally successful: she had the same narrow stern but without the curious galleries. Whatever chance this model may have had of exercising a permanent influence was destroyed by the introduction of round sterns in 1817.

The Russians seem to have kept the square tuck in their Baltic fleet at least till 1725, though by 1700 it had been abandoned in some, if not all, of their Black Sea ships. The Baltic ships naturally followed the Northern fashions learnt by Peter the Great, and the stern of the *Poltava* of 1712[1] in outline was generally similar to contemporary English ships. So far as a very inadequate portrait of her can be trusted she was rather a clumsy-looking ship: she had a dicky stern gallery on the upper-deck with a deep cove in the centre of the stern before it, and had no gallery to her quarter-deck lights. A Black Sea ship of

1700 shows very heavy quarter galleries reaching to the stern, and a wide and heavy tafferel, but no quarter-deck windows. There is little evidence for the 18th century, but, from a half model at the Royal United Service Institution, it would seem that even in the Black Sea English fashions were in the ascendant: the model is undated, but belongs perhaps to the 1770's, showing English fashions of some 30 years earlier. From some draughts preserved it may be seen that the *Ratvisan*, 64, had in 1796 a stern such as has been described above for the Danish *Norge*; and the *Pobiedonosetz*, also a 64, built in 1806 at Archangel from designs by Le Brun, had the same frigate stern. Like all other nations the Russians adopted the round stern: in 1839 Sir W. Symonds noted that about half of their ships were so fitted.

The Americans in the revolutionary war had at least some ships built after French fashions. The *Raleigh* was such, as may be seen from her stern.[2] But in the war of 1812 there was no appreciable difference in the fashion of building between

1. M.M. VII, 313.   2. Plate 50.

American and English frigates. Both the *Constitution*, the *Chesapeake* and the *President* might easily be mistaken for English ships from their appearance.

§ 3. ORNAMENTS

It has been shown that before about 1400 the only ornamentation of the stern can have been the railings of the aftercastle, with perhaps the occasional introduction of badges on the counter; and that, though there is from the year 1400 a mention of carved figures, yet there is no clear knowledge of how they were applied. In the late part of this century the stern appears to have been very plain, undecorated except by paint work; and this seems also to have been the case with Henry VIII's ships. The royal arms or badges on the counter, a light painted frieze of geometrical pattern, and some pavesses aloft completed the adornment.[1] To this from about 1540, or a little earlier, might be added a gallery, which, though at first a very simple structure, soon became decorative with carved brackets and spurs and some ornamentation of the railings.

From 1598 the decorative period may fairly be said to have begun. From this time it seems to have been an almost invariable practice to put either the royal arms with their supporters, or some device indicative of the name of the ship, into the tafferel. In English men-of-war the royal arms were preferred, which served indeed to show that the ship belonged to the Crown, but did not reveal her identity. Of early 17th century ships there seem to have been relatively few in which the ornamentation suggested the name. It did so in the *Prince Royal*,[2] which had the ostrich feathers and the Prince's letters in various places, especially on the stern galleries. It was only their prominence that made them indicative of the name, just as the royal arms repeated and accompanied by the King's badges declared the identity of the *Sovereign of the Seas*; for the arms were common to all, and the ostrich feathers to many ships throughout the 17th century.

With the introduction of quarter-deck windows and open galleries about 1670 the width of the tafferel became much reduced, and the representation of the royal arms decreased in size. It continued, however, to be common practice, but with the progressive narrowing of the tafferel there ceased to be room for it, and from soon after 1700 it is rarely found there.

The Commonwealth substituted the twin scutcheons of the red cross and the harp for the royal arms, and these might be prominent and provided with supporters,[3] but were often inconspicuous, the greater part of the tafferel being covered with miscellaneous carvings which no doubt had their significance, at least to those who held the key to them. This treatment is well shown by the *Naseby* of 1655 and the *London* of 1657.[4] Also there were ships which, like some few contemporary Dutch ships, had a great figure in their stern. A Van de Velde drawing which is believed to represent the *Henry* shows this. The same

1. P. 108.   2. Plate 8.   3. P. 134, fig. (I).   4. M.M. IV, 27.

fashion continued in occasional use after the Restoration: in the *Royal Katherine* of 1664,[1] and in the *St. Michael* of 1669,[2] but it cannot be assumed that it was common in men-of-war. A Van de Velde drawing of a number of ships of about the end of the third Dutch war laid up in ordinary in the Medway shows the royal arms uniformly in all the tafferels. In merchant ships the "picture in the stern" did indicate the name, and it would not be surprising to discover that the *Kingfisher* of 1675, which was built like a fly-boat and was our first Q ship, had a great bird instead of the arms on her tafferel.

An exception seems regularly to have been made in the case of yachts, which usually had a large central figure which, both in the 17th and in the first half of the 18th century, was often painted white, and thus stood out very conspicuously against the gilding or yellow of the stern. This figure rose from the sills of the windows, taking the place of the central light, and also extended the whole height of the tafferel. In most cases it must have been a portrait, but in a picture of 1672 an angel, with wings spread out to the quarters, is found in one yacht. In the early 18th century the figure usually stood in a recessed cove.

When the tafferel had become narrow, the royal arms were at first shifted to the galleries, but did not remain long in that position. They were placed there in some at least of Charles II's and William III's ships, even when there was better room for them above;[3] but in the early years of the next century the royal cypher was used instead of the arms, instead of as

hitherto in conjunction with them. This might be placed in several positions, but when on the stern was either in the centre of the tafferel or on the gallery railings. But the use even of this soon became comparatively rare on the stern, for it was often placed instead on the finishing of the quarter gallery.

Perhaps the Naval Defence Act of 1676 may have marked the turning point, for two or three of the ships of that Act which have been identified have elaborate carvings on the tafferel instead of the arms. These are all three-decked ships, however: none of the third rates have yet been identified, so that it is possible that they may have kept to the older fashion. The *Coronation*'s carving was representative of a coronation; but it shows that it is difficult to be sure of the meaning of such emblems when it is mentioned that a model of another 90-gun ship of this class, in the possession of the New York Yacht Club, shows a very similar carving, which – had not the other model been identified – would have suggested that she was the *Coronation*. There does not seem to be another name in the class to which such a scene is appropriate.

In the large ships of William III the same practice was continued. The same difficulty of identification also continues. There is for example a model of a three-decker of the very end of the century which is generally described as the "*Britannia*, 1700". It is by no means certain even that there was such a ship, but *adhuc sub judice lis est*. This point, however, deserves attention, that the figure-head is a mounted man trampling

1. Plate 11.   2. Plate 27.   3. Nance, Plate 44.

on the heads of enemies, while on the tafferel two horsemen are engaged in combat. Taking this consideration apart from all others the indication would seem to be that the ship represented is the *Namur*, 90, of 1697. If she is not, how then do tafferel carvings help us?

In the 18th century the shallowness of the tafferel made it no longer possible to include full length figures. Seated figures had been introduced in ships of less than three decks from about 1680, but from the *St. George* of 1701 they became universal also in first and second rates. The most general arrangement was that there should be a central device, a bust if the name of the ship suggested it, or sometimes the royal cypher crowned, with a pair of seated or reclining supporters, beyond whom to the quarters were Cupids, mermaids, sea-horses and so forth, their number varying according to the size of the ship.[1] The treatment usually was conventional; but once in a way, if we may believe what a contemporary journalist tells us of the *Revenge* of 1742, it might be topical. By his account the *Revenge* had in her stern Captain Jenkins in the hands of the Spaniards, with his ear cut off. It will be noticed that in models the central stern lantern often masks the bust or device. This form of tafferel lasted, with some reduction of its exuberance after 1742, until the virtual abolition of carved work in 1796. From that date a central medallion or trophy and some simple scroll work became the general practice.[2]

The slight arching formed under the tafferel and over the quarter-deck gallery

was called the cove. It was carved or otherwise ornamented throughout the century. A little feature distinctive of English ships, and of such foreign ships as followed English fashions, was that from about 1730 the continuation of the tafferel over the stern lights of the quarter gallery was arched on its under side between the fashion and quarter pieces,[3] thus forming secondary arches in continuation of the low central arch of the cove. In earlier ships the lower edge of the tafferel ran in an even curve right across the stern. The older fashion is found in small ships several years later than in large.

Quarter pieces formed the sides of the tafferel, and till late in the 17th century did not reach below the upper tier of windows. They may have been introduced earlier than is recorded, but if so probably only in a few cases. The *Prince Royal* of 1610[4] shows none, unless perhaps the pair of figures on the tafferel itself and outside the arms may be accounted such; the *Constant Reformation* of 1618[5] shows rather heavy pieces, on each of which two terms or half human figures are carved, one pair facing to the sides, the other pair nearly aft. This was more ornament than most ships had in that position. The *Sovereign of the Seas* had relatively little, being limited to some ornamental brackets; but by Commonwealth times usage seems to have settled down, and a pair of full length figures to have become the rule. This is shown in the *Naseby* and *London*,[6] and also in other ships of the period.[7] Restoration practice was, allowing for some characteristic difference of treatment, virtually the same,

1. Plates 28 to 31, 50. 2. Plate 32. 3. P. 113, figs. (a), (b), (c). 4. Plate 8. 5. M.M. IX, 58. 6. M.M. VII, 27.
7. Plate 46, figs. (A), (D), (E).

but the figures generally were small and inconspicuous. The Naval Defence Act of 1676 introduced a period of change, for in the ships built under it a tier of stern windows was introduced on the quarter-deck, thus greatly lessening the depth of the tafferel. If the quarter figures remained in their old position they could therefore only serve as pillars or brackets to the ends of the tafferel, and they were converted to this use. Also as the vertical space available for them was less than before, the practice seems to have been then introduced of making them seated instead of standing figures, rising only to the lower edge of the tafferel. The earliest ship to show this is the *St. Michael* of 1669,[1] which has a pair of figures seated on the arches which lead through from her stern to her quarter galleries. Little is yet known of the details of the smaller ships of this period, and it is possible that many of them may have had quite perfunctory carvings in this position, the use of whole figures being confined to third rates and above.

In William III's reign the figures were cut clear, instead of, as usually hitherto, in high relief. They were placed seated or kneeling on the end of the upper quarter gallery where it met the stern, and as in that position they did not rise to the lower edge of the tafferel, a second figure on each side was added above them.[2] This rose to the full height of the tafferel, and ceased therefore to serve as a bracket. It became a mere ornament, not even of an existing structure, for its only purpose seems to have been to complete the fulness of the stern by filling the gap

left on each side where the quarter gallery, or its finishing, did not reach aft to the plane of the stern. Towards the end of this reign it became the regular practice to open a way through from the stern gallery to that on the quarter; and as the lower quarter piece figure was in the way, the remedy which suggested itself was to make the figure seated, facing to the broadside, so that an arch might be formed under its knees.[3] The *Britannia* of 1682 is the first known example of this method. The idea that the quarter piece belonged to the tafferel had clearly been forgotten, for in the ships of about 1700 the figures reached down to the level of the upper-deck, and there for the future they remained, usually two a side in a three-decker, one to each deck,[4] and one a side in a two-decker.[5]

When the quarter gallery of the quarter-deck came aft to the stern, as it did early in Anne's reign, the quarter figures were transferred from the fashion piece to the outside of the gallery, and the widening of the stern aloft was complete. There was thus no longer any need to form an arch of the figure, but the tradition of a seated figure in this place continued for a little time. In the *Royal George* of 1715[6] both the upper and lower quarter-figures are seated: in the ships of 1719[7] they have resumed the standing position which they kept till the end. In the period before 1742 there was a distinct tendency to increase the size of the quarter pieces, and in large ships to put two figures side by side on each level, but from the date of the restrictive order of that year single figures of about 6ft. high were usual.

1. Plate 27.   2. Nance, Plate 44.   3. *Ibid*. Plate 57.   4. Plates 28 to 31.   5. Plates 4, 48.   6. Nance, Plate 68.   7. Plate 28.

After the further order of 1796 these figures, or "strong men" as they are sometimes familiarly called, became merely vestigial. A single pair might be carved in low relief, or even painted, on the after side of the quarter piece in a three-decker;[1] frequently there was no figure, but merely a little conventional ornament of foliage.

Of the brackets and mullions of the stern not much need be said. The 17th century practice was to carve the brackets of the counter heavily, often as figures or half figures, of which the heads served as corbels to support the carved mullions which rose between the stern windows to the lower edge of the tafferel. From these mullions the first impression of a middle 17th century stern is of a series of verticals.[2] The introduction of open galleries broke in upon this system, though it did not cause its abandonment.[3] The mullions continued in use until abolished by the order of 1703. They could not however have been continued longer in anything approaching to their old form, owing to the introduction about the same time of screen bulkheads, to which they were not applicable. In the 18th century pilaster work, often highly ornamental, took the place of the old carved brackets and mullions.[4]

The earlier galleries commonly had their gallery rails planked up and carved, at first by compartments, or with strap ornamentation, but sometimes arcaded. When the galleries were reopened both panelling and balustrading were used, and in the 18th century the panels were sometimes elaborately perforated, as in

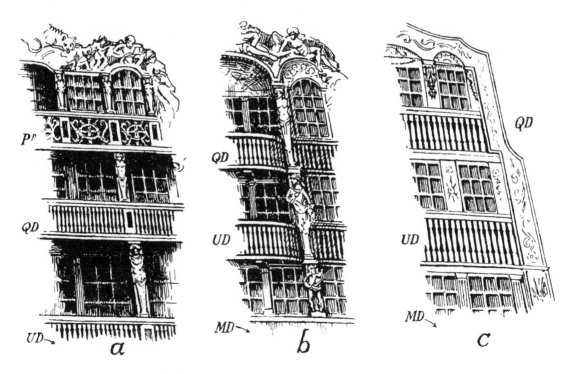

ENGLISH GALLERY TERMS, 1737 TO 1802

1. Plate 32.   2. Plate 11.   3. Plate 27.   4. Plates 28 to 31.

the *Royal George* of 1715.[1] From very shortly after this date two methods alone survived in general use: balustrading, either plain or interspersed with pilaster work, and light open carvings.[2] Often one gallery was carved and the other balustraded, but towards the end of the century balustrading became the rule. When sterns were made close about 1800 the tradition of this was maintained by sawing the balusters down the middle, and nailing them on to the stern where the galleries had been.[3] In the 1820's iron railings were introduced.[4]

In conjunction with gallery rails, their general connection with the stern must be considered. In the early 18th century it was customary to support the ends of the galleries by running up a pair of pilasters between them and to the tafferel in the wake of the fashion pieces.[5] A second pair were sometimes fitted a little nearer the centre line, but not often in English ships, these pilasters being merely the extension of those used for the gallery rail. But in 1737[6] the use of terms, that is of half carved figures, is first found in this position. It did not become general till the middle of the century, but in the second half it passed through certain recognisable phases. The *Royal Sovereign* of 1701 had a pair of small figures to the breast-rail in wake of the fashion piece on the upper-deck, and three flowered pillars on the quarter-deck, but there is no continuous history of this feature from so early a date.

In Balchen's *Victory* there were poop galleries, a unique feature. Above the breast-rail of the stern gallery were six small terms,[6] three a side, of which one was in wake of the fashion piece, one close against the quarter figure, and the third at the end of the cove, which was in this ship, as in others of the same date, separated from the stern arch of the quarter gallery by one light. The quarter-deck and upper-deck each had a single pair of terms in wake of the fashion pieces, which became thereafter the normal position. All these terms were small, their pedestals only reaching to the breast rails. This again seems to have been a unique feature.

I have at present only one example between 1737 and 1746, the date of the design of Kempenfelt's *Royal George*.[7] In her there was a pair each on the quarter-deck and upper-deck galleries, and a pair of whole figures as brackets on the middle deck. The terms were increased in size, their pedestals going down to the foot rail of the gallery in each case. In the *Victory*, designed in 1759, launched in 1765, the draught[8] shows one pair on the quarter-deck gallery and two pairs on that of the upper-deck: strictly these are hardly terms, for they have no pilaster finishing of their own, the breast rail remaining uninterrupted; but doubtless they were considered as terms ending in the pilaster of the gallery rails. The model at Portsmouth,[9] however, shows only one pair, on the quarter-deck, true terms of quite different design from those in the draughts; and has only brackets in lieu of terms on the upper-deck. The specification[10] mentions eight terms, from which it may be decided that the word was not used strictly in its architectural

1. *Cp*. Plate 28.   2. Plates 29, 30.   3. *E.g.*, in the *Victory*.   4. Plate 48.   5. Plate 28.   6. P. 113, fig. (a).   7. P. 113, fig. (b).
8. Plate 16.   9. Plate 29.   10. M.M. VIII, 281.

sense, and implied any figure or bracket in the appropriate position, the brackets against the quarter pieces counting as two pairs, the terms or brackets in wake of the fashion pieces as the other four.

The *Princess Royal* of 1773[1] had two on the quarter-deck, with no brackets against the quarter pieces, and four on the upper-deck. These were true terms, larger than those of the *Royal George*, and with their pedestals carved. Three 74-gun ships of 1770-4 show a pair on the quarter-deck, true terms, reaching to the foot rail; but in one of them, the *Conqueror* of 1773, instead of human figures, secretary birds, each with a snake in his beak, have been introduced.

The *Atlas* of 1782 shows the next stage.[2] Instead of true terms she has whole figures to the breast-rail, one pair each on the upper-deck and quarter-deck. On each deck against the quarter piece, and on the middle deck in wake of the fashion piece, she has flowered brackets. An unidentified 74-gun ship of about 1785 in Colonel Rogers's collection shows two whole figures of boys to the breast-rail on the quarter-deck, with four whole figures as brackets under the gallery. The *Boyne*, 98, of 1790, has merely flowered brackets; but the *Queen Charlotte*, first rate, also of 1790, has whole figures of boys above the breast-rail on the quarter-deck, and large whole figures, representing Justice and Fortitude, to the foot rail on the upper-deck.

Latterly the whole figure of an Atlas, supporting the balcony overhead, was not uncommonly used for these terms. Two

of these figures are preserved at Chatham and three at Portsmouth, one of which is here illustrated.[3] Probably one of the last ships to have them was the famous *Téméraire* of 1798: her Atlas terms are in the possession of Messrs. Castle, who have mounted them as the jambs of a mantel-piece in their office.

With the cutting down of ornament in 1796 these things vanished. The *Victory* model of 1802 at the Royal United Service Institution[4] shows only small floral ornaments in place of the quarter-deck terms, and nothing below. With the slight increase of decoration towards the end of the war some ornament was restored to this position. Thus the *Nelson* of 1814 had flowered pilasters on the upper and quarter-decks, and a pair of large spread eagles as brackets on the middle deck. This seems to end the history of terms.

From the above description it will be seen that this feature alone will afford valuable evidence towards dating an unknown model or drawing.

In the early part of the 17th century the counter was left plain,[5] or very slightly ornamented. The *Constant Reformation* of 1618[6] shows only one bracket on each side of the rudder, and three discs, which perhaps bore badges. The upper counter has a trophy on each side and an arch in the middle between brackets which are not, as soon after, a continuation of those of the lower counter. The *Sovereign of the Seas*[7] was much more elaborate, but, like the ships of the Commonwealth, was still short of the Restoration fashion,[8] in which each

1. Plate 30.   2. Plate 31.   3. Plate 52, No. 1.   4. P. 113, fig. (c).   5. P. 134.   6. M.M. IX, 58.   7. Plate 26.   8. Plates 11, 27.

of the mullions of the stern windows was carried right down to the counter by a continuation of brackets. In all important ships from the *Sovereign*, however, the upper counter bore a carved frieze.

The same fashion continued under William III, but by the order of 1703 ornament in this position was greatly reduced. More or less plain pilasters, sometimes joined by arches, were the most usual form of carving that remained, with painted figures or trophies sometimes introduced between them.[1] The upper counter continued to be friezed, but usually only with paint work, except in great ships, in some of which it was elaborately carved, apparently till the order of 1737; after which it had a painted frieze, which from models would seem to have been handsomely coloured. Sea-horses, nymphs, mermaids and tritons were common subjects in these friezes.

In 1771 an order was issued that henceforth ships should have their names painted on their second counters, in letters a foot high, and enclosed in a compartment. This left room for a trophy or the like on each side of the name, and designs of this year show trophies accordingly. But in 1772 the order was amended, and the name ordered to be painted without a compartment in letters as large as the counter would admit. So the trophies were crowded out. It has long been thought that in 1778 these names were "rubbed out" again on Keppel's initiative. This is only very partly true.[2] They were rubbed out only from the ships in Keppel's fleet, and only for that

one campaign of 1778. The large letters continued in use until after Trafalgar; but in the closing years of the war apparently the name was painted small in a little compartment; and not long after the peace it was entirely omitted.

It has till lately been supposed that the rudder was first hung on the sternpost about 1300; but recent discoveries suggest a date more than a century earlier. In this new fashion the rudder-head rose above the stern post, and therefore, in small craft which had no superstructure aft, was the highest part of the vessel. It was therefore pitched upon as a feature naturally demanding ornamentation, and it is found that from its first introduction it was sometimes carved. The stern post ornament in that part of the ship was traditional; and men probably thought, as it could be no longer placed in its proper position, because the stern post had to be shortened to allow the new-fangled tiller to come inboard, that they had better transfer it to the usurping rudder.

As ships grew bigger and a counter was formed over the rudder-head, means had to be taken to bring the tiller inboard, and this was done by cutting a hole low down in the counter for the tiller. The head of the rudder remained outside, with the counter curving close over it. It resulted from this that the rudder-head carving had to be transferred from its top to its after side. As long as the tiller embraced the rudder-head it must have made it difficult to find room for an ornament; but from about 1600 the tiller was morticed into

1. Plate 4.   2. M.M. X, 203.

the rudder-head, thus leaving a flat after surface. The opportunity was taken to apply an ornament, the design most commonly used throughout the century being a lion's mask.[1] The order of 1703 put a stop to this practice; and this is a pity, for within a very few years after this date the rudder-head was taken in through the counter. Had the carving still been in use when the change was made, its disappearance would have given an exact indication of the date, which hitherto has escaped determination.

Only the lanterns of the stern remain to be mentioned, and the first thing to notice is that they were probably already in use before 1500 though shown in no picture. Jehan Bytharne,[2] who wrote in 1543, but reflected the usage of some 50 or more years earlier, advised his admiral to hang out a flaming cresset so that everyone might know him and follow him.

"Aussy il vous est besoing d'avoir en ungne naviere ungne grande lanterne, où il y ait trois ou quatres grosses lampes à tous grosses lumières pour faire grosses lumillions; car quant il fait grant vent et que le vent vient par derrière, forche vous seroit de mettre ladite lanterne en lieu de l'aultre feu, car aultrement souvent ladite naviere seroit en danger de brusler."

The chief point of interest concerning the lanterns of early Stuart ships was as to their position. The centre one, which was always the largest, was placed on the poop and rose high above the tafferel: the difficulty was to find a suitable position for the two others. They were not placed at the corners of the tafferel, then nearly square on top, presumably because the stern was so narrow that

they would have been too close together to allow their number to be distinguished at any distance. The common practice therefore was to place one at the after end of each quarter gallery. This is illustrated[3] from an Spanish ship, but the practice seems to have been universal. An objection to this method was that from before the beam only two could be seen. It seems probable that one use of the turrets which occur in early ships at the after ends of the quarter galleries – and earlier still occasionally at the corners of the stern, before there was a quarter gallery – may have been that they might serve as lighthouses. In the case of the *Sovereign of the Seas* contemporaries were chiefly impressed by the magnificence and size of her great stern lantern, wherein a man might stand upright. To us it is of greater interest that she had a very ingenious arrangement for showing her regulation three lights. Of the three domes which surmounted each of her quarter galleries, the first and third bore lanterns;[4] and as the aftermost of these was some feet before the stern, it followed that the light from it could not be seen on the off-side of the ship. Thus from any position except almost directly ahead three lights and three only could be seen. It is not known how far this method was repeated in other ships; but by the time of the Commonwealth, when sterns had begun to get a little wider, the side lanterns were transferred to the corners of the tafferel. It is interesting to notice that in a drawing of the *Sovereign*, which may represent her at the time of the first Dutch war, or as rebuilt in 1659, Van de Velde was in great doubt as to

1. Plate 26.   2. N.R.S., Nav. Misc. I, 16.   3. P. 134, fig. (j).   4. Plate 9.

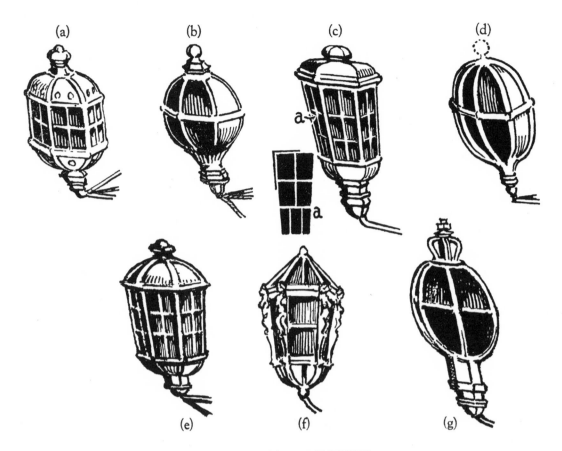

ENGLISH STERN LANTERNS

where to place the lanterns, and finally kept a pair on top of the central turrets of the quarter galleries.[1]

We have some interesting details of one of the early stern lanterns in 1622:[2] -

"Thomas Bostock, joiner ... for making the great lanthorne to stand on the poope of the *Merehonora*, finding all manner of stuffe except glasing barrs and plating   £4 11 6.

"Garrett Christmas, carver, for carving seven tearmes, seaven cartrooses, seven fishes and one lyon for the lanthorne in the *Merehonora*   £2 0 0.

"Thomas Rocke, painter, for duble pryming and painting into oyle colours and guilding with fine gold a greate new lanthorne with a carved lyon upon the topp thereof for the use of His Majesty's shipp the *Merhonour*   £5 6 8."

The details may be compared with the illustrations. It will be noticed that the section was a heptagon, instead of the more usual hexagon, or occasional octagon; also that it was the fine gold that ran away with the money.

The early pattern lantern seems to have been of the street-lamp type; but from Van de Velde's drawings of the *Lamport* of 1654,[3] with the twin scutcheons on her stern, and of the *Antelope* and *Constant Reformation*, made presumably in 1648, it is seen that the globe type was already

1. Plate 46, fig. (B).   2. Declared Accounts, 2659-2661.   3. M.M. VII, 129.

in use, as well as an intermediate pattern, conoid in the lantern itself, with a high ornamental top.[1]

The transitional period lasted till shortly after the Restoration, when the globe lantern became very general. Three slight variants of it are shown here; but there were other forms a little different, the globe sometimes becoming flattened, onion-shaped in fact, as in the model of the *London* at the Trinity House; and more commonly pear-shaped, in continuation apparently of the form shown in the *Constant Reformation* and the *Royal Katherine*. A carved pentagon straight-sided lantern affixed to Mr. R. C. Anderson's three-decked model of a Restoration ship cannot be taken as evidence for the use of that form in the Royal Navy at this date: the lantern appears to be Dutch (fig. f, facing page).

The globe lanterns came to an end under William III, and for some fifteen years there was no one pattern in general use, but many lanterns of that time were squat and parallel-sided,[2] being in general similar to the one illustrated. But about 1707, the exact date being as yet undetermined, a standard pattern[3] was introduced, which continued in use for more than a century. It was hexagonal in section; but as a few octagonal lanterns of the same type survive, the presumption is either that there may have been some occasional latitude permitted, or more probably that the survivals are of somewhat later date than 1815.

FOREIGN PRACTICE

The name as well as the idea of the tafferel came from the Dutch, who, because their men-of-war were not all built by one central department, but by the admiralties of the several provinces, had the opportunity of using many armorial designs. In the great majority of cases the tafferel from early in the 17th century bore either the Dutch lion, or one or other of the provincial coats of arms. The treatment of the lion varied: sometimes he was armed with sword and darts, sometimes not; occasionally he was in his park, but more often not. There seems to have been no rule as to what supplementary figures should accompany him. One of the most decorative of Dutch sterns, that of the *Hollandia* of 1664 as restored by Mr. Crone,[4] shows the lion on a scutcheon, above which is a crown, and at the sides two seated female figures symbolising Justice and Peace. Above the tafferel there are the heavy carvings, cut clear, which were characteristic of Dutch ships from before 1650 to 1690. A Cupid kneels on each side of a seated central female figure, and towards the corners are two large crouching lions. The lions often occur in this position, nearly always with their heads outwards and their haunches raised well up on the arch of the stern.

A model of the same period in the Musée d'Archéologie at Ghent[5] has a similar decorative scheme, and is typically Dutch in every feature except the Imperial eagle on the scutcheon, which discloses her ownership. Frequently a pair of lions was introduced as

---

1. *Cp*. Plate 11.   2. P. 118, fig. (a).   3. *Ibid*. fig. (c).   4. Plate 35.   5. Plate 37.

supporters to the scutcheon, as in the famous *Zeven Provincien* of 1666; but she, in honour of her name, had the central scutcheon surrounded by seven smaller ones of the provincial arms. The lion supporters may be seen also in the *Briel* of 1695.[1]

The drawing of the *Eendracht* of about 1664 which is reproduced here[2] does not show the tafferel carving, but has the peculiarity of having the lions on the arch of the stern with their heads inboard. The *Gouda* of about 1670[2] has dolphins instead of lions in the uppermost position, and instead of a coat of arms has in the tafferel a picture of the town of Gouda. This fashion of decoration, though very well known, was not common in men-of-war. The *Dom van Utrecht* affords another example of it, but in general the fashion was that of merchant ships which used the tafferel as a sign-board. It seems likely that before the middle of the 17th century the merchant ships of all nations did the like: there are constant references to the pictures in the sterns of ships met at sea, and the names seem generally to have been chosen with a view to illustration. In the list of Dutch merchantmen captured between 1665 and 1673 there occur, among other names, the *Milkmaid, Hare, Golden Hand, Blue Boar, Bull, Spread Eagle, Horseman* and *Lamb*, whose tafferels can hardly have been ambiguous; though there may have been some doubt about the *Patriarch Isaac* and the *Land of Promise*. There was a distinct virtue in the method, for such a language is cosmopolitan. No one, for example, ever had any difficulty in

reading the names of the ships of the Barbary corsairs, which were invariably *Date Tree, Orange Tree, Two Lions, Jumping Tiger* and so on; and it was doubtless a great help to a captain bidden to look out for a particular Dunkirk privateer to be told that she had a stump head and a flower-pot in her stern.

East Indiamen appear to have allowed themselves more latitude than the States' ships, and sometimes to have had a portrait statue in the stern, corresponding of course to the ship's name. This is shown here by the coloured plate of the *Prins Willem*[3] of 1651.

From the *Briel* it is easy to notice that by the end of the century there was a considerable reduction of ornament. The tafferel is much lower and admits no more than the shield and its supporting lions. The upper carving is still deep and elaborate, but is greatly less heavy than formerly, scroll work being substituted for the lions or dolphins. The beginning of the next century saw a much greater reduction: it will be seen that *'t Wickelo* of 1725,[4] a large two-decker, is as plain as an English ship of 1800, having nothing but the lightest ornament. This extreme simplicity, however, did not last long, for in adopting a modified English form of stern, the Dutch adopted also the English disposition of ornament, as may be seen from the *Boeken Roode* of 1732,[5] and from the Scheepvaart draught of an unnamed 64-gun ship of 1749.[6] The fashion of these ships does not seem to have been universal, for till after the mid-century some men-of-war had tafferel and quarter piece carvings similar to the

1. Plate 49.   2. Plate 34.   3. Plate 3.   4. Plate 49.   5. P. 44, fig. (E).   6. P. 44, fig. (F).

East Indiamen of the 'twenties. Towards the end of the 18th and early in the 19th century Dutch ships in their fashions were even more like English ships, but naturally with some appreciable lag. The curious draught in the Scheepvaart Museum, entitled a *'s Lands schip*, of 1767,[1] shows a distinct mixture of styles. The form in the main is English, including the breaking of the arch of the cove at the fashion pieces; but the height of the arched windows, and the deep indentation of the upper edge of the tafferel are an exaggeration of anything seen in English practice. The ornament in detail, though not in disposition, is very strongly Louis XV.

The history of the ornamentation of French sterns is relatively short. The symbolical tafferel carving remained much in the Dutch fashion till towards the end of the 17th century, when, as in England, it was greatly limited by the introduction of quarter-deck windows. Puget and other great artists had the old-fashioned tafferel to work upon, and made full use of it. The design in this position was commonly in low relief, as illustrated from the *Paris* of 1670,[2] one of Puget's ships. It would seem probable that, as this ship was one of the many renamed in 1671, this design was never carried out. Puget retained the Dutch heavy carving above the tafferel, but for national emblems substituted miscellaneous classical features. The two little corner pieces at the top of the stern were much in favour with him – after all his heavy quarter piece pillars had to have something to support – but the idea was not new, and probably had a continuous

history. It will be remembered that the *Sovereign of the Seas* had a lion and a unicorn in this position.[3]

After 1678 there was a very great simplification of French ornament, as may be seen by comparing the *St. Philippe* and *Le Bon* with the pre-Puget ship from the Colbert book,[4] and with Puget's own work. The tafferel, now a deck narrower, had nothing but small figures symbolising the name; and the heavy work above it vanished, almost without leaving a trace. But the little corner ornaments remained in ships which did not need their positions for an admiral's lanterns. The same fashion went on into the middle of the next century, as seen from the *Vénus*,[4] an early ship with a really handsome tafferel carving, and the *Téméraire*,[5] in which decoration has become perfunctory. Indeed in the 1740's the French economised in decorations to a high degree, as shown by the tafferel carving of the *Trident*;[6] while a 60-gun ship, captured by the *Augusta*, proved to have no stern carving whatever, but merely painted canvas. The "horseshoe" tafferel of the second half of the century left little room for carved work. The slight difference of treatment between 1780 and the revolutionary period will appear from a comparison of the *Northumberland* and *Oiseau*[7] on the one hand with the *Spartiate* on the other. The *Oiseau* shows that with little ornament this type of stern could be made distinctly handsome. The increased severity of the *Spartiate* when compared with the *Northumberland*, corresponding to the difference of date, is very noticeable.

1. Plate 41.   2. Plate 33.   3. Plate 26.   4. Plate 40.   5. Plate 41.   6. P. 102, fig. (f).   7. Plates 25, 42; and *cp.* P. 102.

The example given of the stern of a galley of Louis XIV's reign,[1] shows that it was possible to adapt the ship type of ornamentation to this very different pattern of stern. The after panel of the carosse, corresponding to the tafferel, was carved in relief, and like that of the ship, was surmounted by figures cut clear. The small scutcheon bearing the fleur-de-lys, which is raised higher still, here occupies a position which it never had in a ship; but the royal ships from at least Louis XIV's time always bore a similar scutcheon, sometimes two or three, the position of which varied between the tafferel, the galleries, the counter and the quarters.

Perhaps the finest example of Puget's marine work, certainly the finest which survives, is the series of panels carved for the galley *La Réale*. Although two of these were for the quarters, they may be mentioned together, for the treatment was the same in all, and the four were combined as chapters of one narrative. The theme was elaborate, each panel having a threefold significance. The first, on the port quarter, illustrated the East, Morning and Spring. The second, on the tafferel, the South, Noon and Summer. The third, on the starboard side of the carosse, the West, Evening and Autumn; and the fourth, on the counter, the North, Night and Winter, The whole story is represented by the progress of the sun god, symbolising Louis XIV.

These carvings, which are in high relief, are not reproduced, as they are already easily available in standard books;[2] it will be enough here to give a detailed description of one of them.[3] The tafferel carving shows Apollo seated in his chariot, laurel-crowned, his lyre in his left hand, the right hand raised. Cupids display a scroll bearing Louis XIV's motto, "Nec pluribus impar". To the right is Jupiter with his thunderbolt and eagle; below him Cybele, with crenelated crown, holding a cornucopia, and reclining against her lion. To the left is Juno with her peacock; beneath whom is Neptune, a trident and a laurel crown in his hands, emblematic of the glories of Louis's navy. The three summer signs of the Zodiac are introduced, and below them is the globe encompassed by two genii, who hold in their hands the palms of victory.

The earliest Spanish ship shown is a two-decker described as of the early 18th century. I have no exact history of this form, and cannot date it at all closely, but would assume it to belong to the 1730's. In decoration, as in form, it is reminiscent of French practice, but not wholly so, for the shape and decorative treatment of the tafferel, and the ornamentation of the brackets between the lights, recall rather a form which occurs in Holland earlier in the century.

It has been mentioned already that Spanish shipwrights adopted the horseshoe arch earlier than the French. The *Fenix*[4] of 1749 affords an early and good example; and it is interesting to see that even in this form, which was quite foreign to English practice, the established English system of ornamentation was followed. The arch is slightly interrupted by scrolls where the tafferel

1. Plate 45. 2. Auquier, "Pierre Puget, mariniste"; and Pâris, "Souvenirs de Marine". 3. Rossi, "L'Art naval (1919), 34 *sq*. 4. Plate 31.

should end. The tafferel bears the central device indicative of the ship's name, with seated supporters and minor figures beyond them, exactly as in an English ship. The *Grana* frigate, of some 30 years later, has the same type of stern, but has the ornament reduced to formal designs in low relief.[1] The *Real Carlos*, three-decker, of 1787, has a heavy tafferel, which both in shape and in ornamentation is purely English.[2] Such other examples of Spanish line-of-battle ships of the latter part of the century as have been noticed seem to show that this was then the accepted mode in Spain.

The little Danish ship of about 1680[3] belongs to the period of Dutch influence, and the tafferel decoration of the national surrounded by the provincial arms recalls that of the *Seven Provinces*. The carvings of the stern above the tafferel are relatively light, as are the quarter pieces, an indication probably of a comparatively late date. It is interesting to recall that the "Great Dane" of early in the century, probably a fancy picture,[4] also uses the provincial arms for decorative purposes. Apparently in the 18th century both Swedes and Danes alike used only the lightest of tafferel ornaments, and this was especially the case in the Baltic form of stern which seems to have been evolved soon after 1740, and is illustrated here by the *Adolf Frederick*,[5] a Swedish ship of the Chapman period. The reconstructed *Christianus V* model affords another example of the Baltic fashion of using provincial arms as a stern decoration. The *Tre Kroner*[6] of 1742 is an interesting ship, showing in her stern the combination of features from different

styles into one distinctive whole. The large angels cut clear above the tafferel suggest 17th century Dutch practice: the form of the tafferel itself and the heavy terms as gallery supporters can only be paralleled from French ships of the same period: the deep cove with the secondary arches towards the quarters is an exaggeration of the fashion established for English ships about 1730. At the same time the general roundness of the stern can hardly have been devised without some thought towards the *Padmos* and her sisters, the more so as the immediate successors of the *Tre Kroner* proceeded directly to that form of stern.[7]

The tafferel carvings of the American frigate *Raleigh* of 1775[1] follow the English practice of a central bust with seated supporters, though the form of the stern itself is entirely French. The cutting of the tafferel ports, done presumably when the ship was taken into the Royal Navy, interferes sadly with the decoration. In the war of 1812 American fashions went even beyond English in the economy of ornament.

In the matter of quarter pieces Dutch fashion soon after 1600 seems to have been to place a pair of small upright figures at the sides of the tafferel.[8] These, or a substitute for them, remained in that position as long as the high tafferel endured, tending to become heavier and more elaborate. Thus the *Eendracht*[9] has terms, about 6ft. high; the *Gouda*[9] has whole figures half as high again; while the *Prins Willem* has only carved brackets. The size and elaboration seem to be in direct ratio to the date; and this

---

1. Plate 50.   2. Plate 43.   3. Plate 36.   4. M.M. IV, 225.   5. P. 105.   6. Chatterton, Plate 81.   7. Nance, Plate 83.   8. P. 134, fig. (g).
9. Plate 34.

view is supported by the other relatively late ships, the *Hollandia*[1] and the Ghent model,[2] each of which has large whole figures cut clear. Perhaps the heaviest of these upper quarter pieces ever put into a ship are those shown by the so-called "caravelle de guerre" in the Musée de l'Armée at Brussels,[3] which is believed to represent an Ostend East Indiaman of about 1720. Her general fashions are Dutch, but with a curious combination of the form of stern which went out of use in Holland about 1690, with the form of quarter gallery which was only then beginning to come in. As an exaggeration of decorative fashions is to be expected in yachts, it is not surprising to find that the Dutch yacht of about 1680 has these figures most abnormally developed.[4] With the reduction of the tafferel from about 1690 these figures fell into disuse, there being no longer room for them. Only the lower pair of "hoek mannen" (literally cornermen, though the phrase means something quite different in English) survived.

This lower pair began its history later than the upper. It could not exist with the open gallery; but when the closed quarter gallery was formed by building a permanent roof over the spurs, a pair of figures was introduced seated on it at the angle made with the stern, these figures thus being under those standing by the tafferel. These seated figures were most characteristic of Dutch designs, and helped to increase the hard knuckle already formed by the projection of the gallery. They grew steadily in size. Relatively small in the *Prins Willem*,[5] the *Eendracht*,[6] and the *Gouda*, they have become much more

prominent in the *Hollandia*,[7] while in the Ghent model they are doubled, the Cupids who sit at the angles being alarmed by a pair of lions which climb up from under the gallery.[8]

The *Briel* and her sisters, having what is essentially the old type of quarter gallery, retain these figures, their treatment being particularly dainty.[9] The theme of a girl riding a dolphin is repeated in more than one ship, the variants showing the lady either clothed or not, and riding sometimes side-saddle, sometimes astride. Mr. R. C. Anderson's model of one of the Dutch three-deckers of 1683-1695[10] shows a curious phase of this corner figure. The quarter gallery has taken a new form to which such a figure is quite unsuited; but it is retained, sprawling over the gallery and holding on apparently for dear life, as considering the angle of the gallery it might well do. From the end of the century this form fell out of use; but it may be thought that the huge dolphin quarter pieces of the Admiralty yacht of about 1750[11] are reminiscent of it. They must presumably be accounted as quarter pieces, though they run forward against the yacht's side instead of athwartships.

In ships with the *Padmos* type of stern the quarter piece is merged in the horseshoe arch; in *'t Wickelo*[12] there is a little light scroll work as a derisory substitute. There appears to have been for a matter of some 30 years a distinct hiatus, till the gradual adoption of English fashions introduced the standing figures at the corners of the gallery. These are seen in the *Boeken Roode* of 1732,[13] and in

1. Plate 35.　　2. Plate 37.　　3. P. 143, fig. (c).　　4. Plate 44.　　5. Plate 3.　　6. Plate 34.　　7. Plate 35.　　8. Plate 37.　　9. Plate 49.
10. Nance, Plate 39.　　11. Plate 44.　　12. Plate 49　　13. P. 44, figs. (D), (E).

other 18th century ships,[1] down to the *Washington* model in the "Mercury" Museum, which has very large figures. But from about 1800 carvings became much reduced: the *Neptunus* model of 1803, for example, is ornamentally on a par with '*t Wickelo* of 1725, and with English ships of its own date.

The quarter piece in French ships had a somewhat curious history, and for certain periods is most useful as an indication of date. The Colbert ship[2] may be taken as marking the transition from Dutch to national fashions. She shows the upper quarter figures, standing by the tafferel, then (*i.e.*, 1665 or so) common throughout Northern Europe, but by the reintroduction of open galleries on three decks she has made the retention of the Dutch "hoek mannen" impossible. Instead of them she has a pair of scutcheons with the fleur-de-lys, fitting close to the gallery. The critics of the luxuriant classicism of Puget and his contemporaries objected especially to the very heavy quarter pieces which were introduced. In the *Paris*[3] there were two enormous pillars a side, against the stern inside the galleries; and, as the ship in her form still retained a good deal of the Dutch manner, it was possible also to give her the lower pair of quarter pieces; for these a very handsome pair of Sphinxes was used, their wings forming arches through to the quarter gallery.

The revolt against these superfluities resulted in an almost total abolition of quarter pieces. The *Soleil Royal*,[4] the most ornate ship in the war with William III, had large figures seated at the quarter-deck, and terms above them; but the *St. Philippe*[5] had light pillars supporting the corners of the galleries from the middle deck upwards, and a term above the quarter-deck as the only carved quarter figure. The use even of this seems to have been reserved for the largest classes of ships, but it persisted as long as did the straight-sided type of stern. In the *Téméraire* of 1755,[6] one of the last ships of this period, there is a pair of small Cupids perched on the arches of the quarter-deck gallery; but in the *Royal Louis* of 1758, perhaps the very last ship built before the fashions changed, the only quarter figures are those which serve as brackets to the lowest gallery.

The adoption of the horseshoe stern at this date merged the quarter pieces in the tafferel design, to which apparently there might be some exceptions. Thus the *Oiseau*, frigate, built about 1770,[7] in addition to the horseshoe arch, has a pair of eagles cut clear in the position of the old "hoek-mannen". But in general during the half century or so for which the horseshoe lasted there were in French ships no distinctive quarter piece carvings.

Under the Empire a squarer type of stern, in the main based on English practice, came into use; and though at first the fashion of a statue for a quarter piece, which had by then been abandoned in England, was not introduced, yet from about 1807 it became common. The earliest example of it which I have identified with any approach to probability is in a "prisoner-of-war" model which I believe to represent the *Thésée*, 74, of 1807; but in "Souvenirs de Marine"

---

1. P. 44, figs. (F), (G).   2. Plate 40.   3. Plate 33.   4. Plate 39.   5. Plate 40.   6. Plate 41   7. Plate 25.

Admiral Pâris gives several examples, which show that in square-sterned ships these figures went on till the middle of the century. Among his instances are the *Ville de Marseille*, 74 of 1812; the *Suffren*, 90, of 1829; and the *Valmy*, 120, of 1847.

Few examples are available to illustrate Spanish practice; but as Spanish fashions were borrowed in turn from the French, Dutch and English, it may be that those offered are representative. Thus we have the two-decker of about 1730,[1] French in the main, with no quarter pieces, but with scutcheon shaped ornaments in the place of the lily-bearing shields of the Colbert ship. We have the *Fenix* of 1749,[2] with the horseshoe arch which afterwards became French; but the carvings on the arch are definitely English in fashion and include figures in high relief in the position of the English quarter pieces. In the *Grana*, frigate,[3] taken at the same time but a later ship, the carvings of the arch are as in contemporary French ships. A little later, as seen in the *Real Carlos*, 112, of 1787,[1] the adoption of an English type of stern was accompanied by the introduction of quarter piece figures cut clear, as in English ships, two a side in a three-decker, one to each of the open galleries.

I have nothing approaching to a complete history of this feature in Baltic ships. That unconvincing ship the "Great Dane" has at the corner of the open upper-deck gallery a carved figure which does not seem to differ from the other brackets of that gallery. Above this she has, even with the half deck, some large and elaborate carving which may perhaps be a dragon: above this again is a turret. But in the main it is probably true that both Danish and Swedish ships of the first half of the 17th century reflected Dutch practice tolerably closely, though with less ornament. The quarter pieces of the *Norske Löve*,[4] for example, are little more than small pillars carved in low relief, and even the *Amaranthe* of 1654[5] has only floral brackets instead of "hoek mannen". On the other hand the Swedish stern, from a contemporary print of the battle of the Sound in 1658,[6] shows a pair of standing figures at the sides of the tafferel. She is a curious ship, with her galleries terminated abaft by turrets and a deck higher than usual, but she has as lower finishings to her turrets, and nearly in the position where the "hoek mannen" would normally come, a pair of heavy carvings which seem to represent figures.

The small Danish ship of about 1680,[7] though very Dutch in her general appearance, has neither upper nor lower quarter figures, but merely a long straight piece from the gallery to the top of the tafferel carved with foliage. The *Christianus V* model, to which reference has already been made, a very French-looking ship, has terms level with the tafferel as in French ships of 1690.

That interesting transitional ship the *Tre Kroner* of 1742 has, among her English features, a pair of very large "strong men" cut clear, each with an arm raised to support a crown placed on the corner of a very French tafferel; and below, level with the upper-deck, is a second pair of quarter figures some 6ft. high. The Northern ships with the

1. Plate 43.   2. Plates 31, 48.   3. Plate 50.   4. M.M. IV, 302.   5. *Ibid*. VI, 196.   6. P. 134, fig. (k).   7. Plate 36.

horseshoe stern show no quarter pieces whatever; but the turama *Lodbrok*, of 1771,[1] in a stern slightly recalling by the form of its tafferel early French practice, has a pair of medallions placed where in French ships the quarter terms used to be. No source to which I have had access has given any information as to Baltic stern carvings of later date beyond that afforded by such models as are illustrated by Mr. Nance. The largest of these, a corvette of a little after 1800,[2] shows the quarter pieces quite plain.

It has been mentioned that the American frigate *Raleigh*,[3] though she had the French horseshoe type of stern, had English fashion carvings on her tafferel. The English fashion, however, did not extend to the quarter pieces, for where they should come the arch was carved with scroll work.

The illustrations serve to show that, allowing for national variations of ornament, the method of decorating gallery rails by the several powers did not differ in principle from contemporary English practice.

As to the ornamentation of the upper counter, it seems to have been the common rule with all nations to treat this part with carved brackets and a frieze until late in the 17th century, and in the 18th to retain the frieze, whether carved or painted, after the heavy brackets had gone out of use. The *Padmos* is one of the latest ships to show these brackets. Only Dutch ships besides English appear to have ornamented the lower counter: the arrangement shown in the *Gouda*,[4]

which has the Dutch lion and the Amsterdam Admiralty badge there on scutcheons, may be regarded as typical. As will be seen from the *Spartiate* of 1796[5] and other ships, foreign nations were able to continue the ornamentation of the upper counter much later than English ships, because they did not adopt our fashion of painting the name large the whole width of the stern.

The French are supposed to have been the first to put the name on the stern. In 1678 Seignelay issued orders to the dock-yards that the king wished the names to be painted or gilded there; "and if foreigners do not do so he will set them an example", his navy being the finest and most perfect in the world. And considering the state of the English navy in that year, there was a good deal of justification for Louis XIV's opinion. It may be accepted that the French were the first to name their ships thus as a regular practice, but it appears to have been the case that a few Dutch ships bore their names much earlier. Of these the *Amilia*, Tromp's flagship in 1639, was one, and the *Eendracht* of the second war with England another.[6] It will be noticed that the latter has a scroll for the name on her counter. Also a Swedish ship of 1658 shows a name in plain letters across her stern,[7] whether rightly I do not know.

After the French, apparently all nations but the English took up the practice, the Dutch from about 1690 putting the name under the arms in the tafferel.[8] The French method was to put the name in a decorative compartment, and it is still shown thus in the Admiralty draughts

1. M.M. III, 49.   2. Nance, Plate 112.   3. Plate 50.   4. Plate 34.   5. Plate 42.   6. Plate 34.   7. P. 134, fig. (k).   8. Plate 49.

of prizes taken in 1747 and 1759.[1] When names were first put on English sterns in 1771 it was objected that this was Frenchifying the navy, for a compartment was then used; and it may have been to meet this objection that the method was changed in the following year. The Baltic nations, including Russia, seem to have used the compartment;[2] but the Dutch to have continued to do without it. Many draughts and models show no names, so that without knowledge of orders issued it cannot be said how far the practice was general in Holland; but instances for Dutch ships occur at intervals from 1564[3] at least until 1821. From the models in the naval museum at Lisbon it would appear that at the end of the 18th century Portuguese ships painted their names in English fashion right across the upper counter. They had to space the letters much closer than in an English ship to get them all in.

Most of the later draughts and models of French ships, from about 1760, show no names; but this does not mean that they were dropped, as may be seen from the *Danae*,[4] in which a Cupid displays the name on a ribband, and from the *Northumberland* of 1780.[5] It is, however, worth attention that this omission is in great part responsible for the serious doubts which exist as to the identity of many of the French official ship models which survive.

In the profuse period of French orna-mentation large terms on the galleries were lavishly introduced. The *Royal Louis* of 1668 had enormous terms and whole figures, some of them two decks high,

closely spaced along all her galleries. Even after the great reduction some few large ships had them. This is seen in the *Soleil Royal*,[6] which has two large half figures a side on the lower gallery, the inner female, the outer male, and a single small pair on the upper-deck. But from this time they do not again occur in French ships, and very few instances are available of the use either of them, or of corresponding brackets under the gallery, in the ships of other nations. The Danish *Tre Kroner* of 1742[7] had a pair of large terms as gallery brackets, but only pillars above. The figures represented were two-tailed mermen, their tails being cable-laid. Incidentally it may be noticed that the French commonly, and the Dutch and other nations not infrequently, gave their mermen and mermaids two tails, whereas the English variety had but one. It will be seen that the *Fenix*,[8] Spanish ship of 1749, has a pair of whole figures of boys on her quarter-deck gallery in place of the contemporary English terms. I have no later example, but think it probable that in some cases foreign ships which copied English fashions may have had this feature.

Foreign practice with regard to the carving of the rudder-heads of large ships seems to have been less generous than English. None of the Dutch 17th century ships represented show it; and the French ships of the end of the century show only spirals or other conventional ornament. But in Dutch, and probably other Northern, merchantmen with outside rudder-heads the practice was common in the 18th century, and by no means unknown in

1. Plate 41.   2. P. 106.   3. M.M. IV, 157.   4. Plate 25.   5. Plate 42.   6. Plate 39.   7. Chatterton, Plate 81.   8. Plate 31.

the 19th. There is a story that Captain William Montagu, commonly known from his eccentricities as "Mad Montagu", having brought to a Dutch convoy, sawed off the rudder-heads of a dozen galliots and other such craft. He is represented to have set these up round his cabin and to have introduced them to his visitors as the twelve Cæsars. Whether the story be true or not – and the probability is in favour of its being true – it at least shows that this type of rudder-head was common enough at the middle of 18th century. Another type was found in yachts, which from these heads are styled "kop jacht". In this the head was surmounted by a cap or helmet fashioned like the head of a dog or other animal, so that on a horizontal view the human face appears, and from above the head of an animal. An example of this is given from a photograph of a model lent by Mme. Enthoven. A similar head is also illustrated from an undated model of a "hek jacht" (fig. b) in the Rijks Museum. The 18th century rudder-head (fig. a), which is picked out in white, red and blue, may be taken as representative of normal practice.

Two ornamented tillers are shown from models in the Rijks Museum. In one (fig. d) the decoration is painted in chevrons of different colours. The other, from a "boeier" of 1757, named "Het is niet anders" and belonging to North Holland or Zeeland, has the end carved to represent a sea-serpent swallowing a mermaid.

DUTCH RUDDER-HEADS AND TILLERS

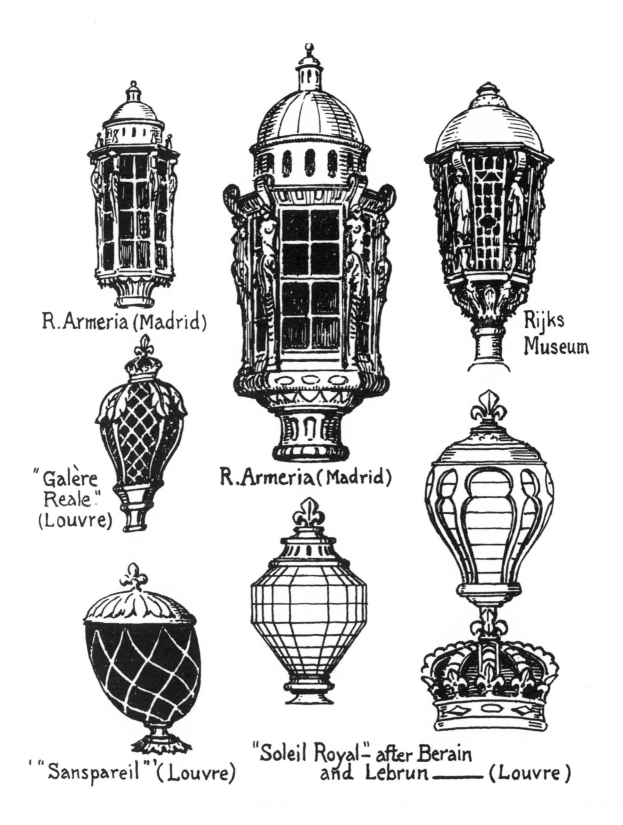

R.Armeria (Madrid)

Rijks
Museum

"Galère
Reale"
(Louvre)

R.Armeria (Madrid)

' "Sanspareil" '(Louvre)

"Soleil Royal"- after Berain
and Lebrun _____ (Louvre)

STERN LANTERNS (CHIEFLY FRENCH)

Of the stern lanterns illustrated the oldest, and it may be thought the most handsome, is the large one from the Real Armeria at Madrid.[1] This was the fanal of Strozzi's galley, which was captured when he himself was killed in the action with Santa Cruz at the Azores in 1582. The smaller lantern with the same dome is so similar to the fanal that it may safely be decided also to be French and of about the same date.

Apparently the form shown below in figs. (a), (c) and (d) had a very long vogue in Holland. Fig. (c) is from the Prince of Orange's yacht in 1613: (a) occurs in the *Zeelandia* of 1653, and as late as the Dutch Admiralty yacht of about 1750.[2] Fig. (d) with its thorn-like ventilators is the most usual form of this type: it will be seen that the lanterns of the *Hollandia* model,[3] one of which is original, are of this pattern. Fig. (b), which is from a 17th century merchant ship, occurs also in the beginning of the next century, but does not appear to

have been a naval form. Fig. (e) is from an early 18th century draught in the Scheepvaart Museum. No other lantern of this very peculiar form has been found: the only example here at all like it is shown by a Swedish ship of 1658.[4] It is to be feared that lanterns sometimes get adrift from models, and are reattached where they do not belong.

Another example of a doubtful lantern is one in the Rijks Museum, said to be from the *Royal Charles*.[1] This is impossible: we even have the bill for the *Royal Charles*'s lanterns, which distinctly states that they were globes. The three of them cost £36.[5] It would seem possible, therefore, as the lantern is neither Dutch nor English, that it may very likely be French. The Colbert ship shows a tall lantern of somewhat similar type[6] as being in use before 1670; but from the *Paris*[7] it appears that at about this same date another pattern was coming into use in French ships, and the illustrations of the "Galère Reale",[1] the *Soleil Royal*,[8]

a b c d e

DUTCH STERN LANTERNS

1. P. 130.   2. Plate 44.   3. Plate 35.   4. P. 134, fig. (k).   5. Cal. S.P. Dom. 21 Jan., 1665.   6. Plate 40.   7. Plate 33.   8. Plate 39.

the *St. Philippe* and *Le Bon*[1] show that it had a long vogue and was still in use at the end of the century. Presumably the older form was borrowed from Holland, and this form was devised in France to supersede it.

The *Vénus*[2] of the early part, and the *Royal Louis*[2] of the middle, of the 18th century, revert to the form of lantern which is found in the Colbert ship, but without its exaggerated height. So far as may be judged from these few examples, it would almost seem that alternative patterns may have been in use concurrently in the French navy. The *"Sanspareil"* model,[3] attributed to 1760, shows an entirely different form, of which no other example has been found.

Excepting the *Norske Löve* and *Christianus V* models, all Baltic ships appear to show the Dutch form of lantern.[4] Of the ships named the one has a parallel-sided lantern with very heavy stiles; the other has hers pear-shaped, with no concavity in vertical section, and therefore differing from any French 17th century practice.

1. Plate 40.   2. Plate 51.   3. P. 130.   4. *E.g.* Plate 36.

CHAPTER VII

——— QUARTER GALLERIES ———

§ 1. THEIR FORM

Quarter galleries when first introduced in the 1530's[1] were all of a piece with the stern gallery, and so continued till about the end of the century, forming a mere open walk round the stern. As the counter above afforded some shelter to the stern gallery, that of the quarters in compensation was early fitted with bails or spurs on which to spread an awning.[2] There is very little trustworthy evidence as to how these galleries developed during the Queen's reign. To be sure there is Visscher's series of engravings, which it has been the custom to accept literally; but those representations differ in so many respects from what we know from other sources, that I hesitate to believe, on their authority alone, that "about 1588" any English ship had either an upper gallery longer than the lower, or an upper gallery with a house in it built square to the side and flat-roofed, or still less that any of them had a large turret there with a domed roof. I have never succeeded in finding a precise statement as to when or where this series was engraved; and, so far from accepting it as of contemporary English authority, I would be inclined, on internal evidence, to suppose that it was produced twenty years or more later and in Holland, by a man more familiar with Dutch than with English ships, and not very careful how he represented either. The Armada tapestries of the House of Lords were no doubt of much higher value, for we know that they were contemporary, by a most able artist, and that they passed the scrutiny of the Lord Admiral; but as all that we have of

them now is a set of engravings, made in the 18th century by a man who, apart from the tapestries before him, knew nothing of Tudor ships, it is a question how far they too are to be accepted as evidence on points of detail. In the matter of a turret at the after end of a quarter gallery, for instance, it seems quite possible that this may have been the engraver's interpretation of a partly spread tilt.

On the whole it seems safer to leave the question of Tudor developments for future solution, though with an inclination to the belief that till after 1600 quarter galleries were, if not always, at least very nearly always entirely open. Such definite evidence as we have of their progress comes from Dutch artists of the early 17th century, many sketches after whom are given here. From these it can be seen that development was in two or three directions: by covering with a permanent roof the upper part of the spurs, thus converting the balcony into a verandah;[3] by completely roofing in the spurs for a short space either at or near the after ends of the galleries;[4] or by adding a little house at the fore end of the gallery.[5] It seems likely that the second of these methods may have been tried first, and that conceivably it may have been something of this kind that was imperfectly represented in the Armada tapestries and by Visscher.

It may be accepted that the galleries of the *Prince Royal* of 1610[6] represented the extreme development reached at that time. In her there were three; and though by this date two were not

---

1. P. 93, and p. 134, figs. (a), (e), (i).   2. P. 134, fig. (a).   3. *Ibid.* fig. (g).   4. P. 134, fig. (d); and Plate 1, the *Phœnix.*
5. P. 134, fig. (b).   6. Plate 8.

EARLY STERN AND QUARTER GALLERIES
(a) From Le Testu.   (b) to (l) After Dutch artists.

uncommon, there is no other example of three for about 70 years, by which time the fashion of the galleries was very different. In the portrait of her builder the ship is shown with the lower gallery, which is above the middle deck stern chase guns, entirely open. The second, or half deck gallery, is close, being built up to the foot rail of the upper, or quarter-deck gallery. Each is considerably longer than that above it, so that the fore end of the second remains open. It would thus appear that it was the original intention to leave the lower gallery open, but by 1613, as seen from a painting by Vroom,[1] it was roofed in from about the middle nearly to the stern, and is still shown so in later pictures of the ship. The Hampton Court and Hinchinbroke paintings of the return of the fleet from Spain in 1623 show the gallery of only one other ship, the *Bonaventure*, which was built in 1621. In her there is a close structure crowned by a dome rising from the open gallery near the stern, much such a feature as Visscher put into one of the gallions of his series.

It has been mentioned that in early ships it is sometimes difficult to be sure to which deck a gallery belongs. This is particularly so with the quarter galleries, which roughly followed the line of the wales. The anonymous author of a treatise on shipwrightry, of about 1625,[2] laid it down that the gallery should be in length one-sixth of the gun deck, "and the depth in the steeving line one-fifth thereof", *i.e.*, of the length of the gallery, not of the gun deck. In his typical ship of 550 tons this gave a gallery 22ft. long, steeving up 4ft. 4in.; and I have assumed 3ft. as the height of the breast rail. The diagrams annexed are not exact, for they show the decks laid horizontal, though in fact they rose aft to some degree as yet undetermined. One of the changes which was made during the survey and overhauling of the navy in 1626-7 was the lowering of the sheer of the decks and getting rid of the falls. Diagram (a) shows that, with flush decks, an upper-deck gallery at its fore end would drop so much that it could only be entered there from the lower deck; and in (b) it is seen that when the decks had falls, the fore

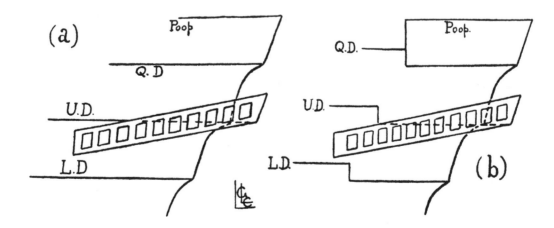

1. M.M. VI, 365.   2. Admy. Library, M.S. No. 44.

end of the gallery was almost level with the lower deck. The diagrams are drawn to scale, allowing 6ft. 4in. for the height of the decks, but the position and height of the falls is conjectural. A height of only 2ft. is shown for them, but this may have been exceeded at times.

The Royal Commission of 1618 recommended that the King's ships should be "somewhat snug-built, without double galleries and too lofty upper works, which overcharge many ships and make them loom fair but not work well at sea".[1] It may be supposed that the *Constant Reformation*[2] was fitted to accord with the report of the Commission, and it is interesting therefore to notice what her fashion was. Though a three-decked ship, she had only one pair of galleries; and, with the single exception of the *Sovereign of the Seas*, this seems to have been the rule in English ships till the time of the Commonwealth. Her galleries were closed from the middle point to the stern, the fore half being left open. This was essentially the same arrangement as is seen in the *Phoenix*, but in this case the gallery at its fore end carried a small plain house such as is shown in fig. (b).[3] Some 20 years later the open fore ends of the galleries had been removed, and then the little house was shifted into the main chains, where for the rest of the century it remained conveniently hidden.

In the 17th century there was in England very great latitude in the fitting of these galleries; so much so indeed that it would be hardly an exaggeration to say that no two ships were alike in this respect, and that at any rate

down to 1670, or perhaps later, the quarter gallery was the most distinctive feature. But in spite of the diversity, a comparison of their forms shows that the galleries can be grouped into four main types, and that these types succeeded each other without more than the usual degree of overlapping.

(1) The oldest form was the flat gallery, whether on one deck, as in the *Constant Reformation* of 1618, and in the ship in Blankhof's picture,[4] or on two as in the *Sovereign of the Seas*.[5] The oldest examples of this type show a lean-to roof, which went out of fashion in England from about 1640; later instances, beginning with the *Sovereign*, and including the *Bristol* of 1653,[6] show the roof finished with three domes or turrets of nearly equal size.

(2) This gave way under the Commonwealth to the so-called five-sided type, in which the central portion projected in a bay further outboard than the wings. The wings were relatively small, so that when the ship was seen from an angle, one was commonly hidden by the central bay.[7] Earlier ships with this type of gallery sometimes had the triple dome finishing, the lateral domes being very small; but in later ships the wings ended above as a small shelf which supported an ornament, such as a beast, a plume, or even a shell. When the wing itself was very small the quarter piece crowded out the after ornament, thus leaving only one as a vestige of the former lateral turrets. All the ships in Deane's "Doctrine" show these vestigial ornaments. The latest

1. *Ap.* Oppenheim, "Administration of R.N.", 205.   2. M.M. IX, 58.   3. P. 134.   4. *Ibid.* fig. (l).   5. Plate 9.   6. Plate 46, fig (C).
7. *Ibid.* figs. (A) and (E).

example of them noticed is in a model of the *Bonaventure* of 1682, in Mr. R. C. Anderson's collection, which has a shell on the fore wing, the after being crowded into the quarter piece. The *Naseby* of 1655[1] had one dome to finish the wings as well as the central bay. In later ships it seems to have been more usual to make only the gallery of the upper-deck five-sided, that of the quarter-deck being without the wings.

(3) The form thus reached may be called the bottle; for, as seen from the *Prince* of 1670,[2] it is bottle shaped in side elevation. This type seems to have had a double origin, in the five-sided gallery, as in the *Prince*, and in the flat parallel galleries, as seen in the London of 1657,[3] which however had a tumblehome between the upper and lower tiers of windows such as is not found in the *Sovereign*. The *London* model at the Trinity House[4] – it matters little for the present purpose whether she represents the *Loyal London* of 1666, or the first rate of 1670 – shows what is probably better classified as a flat gallery, with vestiges of the lateral turrets, than as a bottle.

(4) Each of these forms represented the progressive shortening of the gallery in a fore and aft direction. The limit of development along these lines came when the after edge of the galleries on all decks reached aft to the fashion piece. Few English 17th century ships show this feature, even of the two-deckers, none of which, as far as is at present known, had their galleries more than one deck deep until William III's reign; for though the gallery itself reached to

the stern, the upper finishing did not. In this reign the largest of the two-decked ships had double quarter galleries, but the smaller still had only single. The *Mordaunt* of 1682,[5] a ship not built in a royal dockyard, seems to be the only exception. In her the finishing as well as the gallery comes aft to the fashion piece, thus producing a one-sided look, as if the after half of a normal bottle-shaped gallery had been cut off. It will be convenient therefore to call this form the half-bottle; for though it was little used in England, it had, as will be seen, a considerable vogue in Holland.

These distinctions are arbitrary, and, owing to the intermingling of types, not altogether satisfactory; but they will at least serve as a point of departure.

Towards the end of the century two changes of importance were introduced. In the first place, with the building of open stern galleries, it began to be the practice also to have open galleries on the quarters. These, however, were not in the least like the Tudor or early Stuart open quarter galleries, which ran along the solid side of the ship: they were built curving round a close projecting gallery, and were commonly so narrow that it is difficult to see that they can have been of much use. The open space was normally about 2ft. wide at most, though sometimes with a little more room on the fore side of the bay of the windows, and always with enough room abaft to afford a passage into the open stern gallery. The *St. Michael* of 1669,[6] the first English ship in which the galleries were re-opened, shows this

1. Plate 46, fig. (E).   2. *Ibid*, fig. (F).   3. M.M. IV, 27.   4. *Ibid*. II, 194.   5. *Ibid*. II, 164.   6. Plate 27.

arrangement on the upper-deck, there being no galleries to her quarter-deck. The *Britannia* of the 1676 programme was similarly fitted, though in her for the first time the quarter galleries were three decks deep; but the gallery of the quarter-deck was still rudimentary, being little more than a badge. The second rates of the same date had three tiers of quarter galleries like the first rate, but these were still all close, with no opening to the stern gallery.

Seventeenth century correspondence does not appear to have very much to say on the subject of quarter galleries. In the Duke of York's letter books, for the whole period of his tenure of office as Lord High Admiral, there are only two mentions of them, both from 1670,[1] but they are of some little interest. On 12th July the Duke wrote to the Navy Board that Captain Cox of the *Greenwich*, a fourth rate, complained that the galleries were dangerous for fire and hindered her sailing, and asked that they should

be taken down. This was ordered to be done. Conversely on 29th October the Duke wrote: "In regard H.M. ship the *Assistance* is bound into a hot country, where it will be convenient for the health of her company that she be as open and airy as may be, I think it fitting that she have a pair of galleries built on her". She was an old fourth rate, of 555 tons, built in 1650, and the form of the order suggests that probably hitherto she had merely quarter badges like the *Tiger*. Complaints that the galleries caught the wind and made the ship leewardly when close hauled are found occasionally in the 18th century, and no doubt had much to do with their reduction to the standard pattern which may be said to have been established by 1750.

The accompanying diagrams will give some idea of the development of quarter galleries in plan, and their relationship to the stern galleries. The diagrams are rudimentary, and do not distinguish between flat and five-sided galleries,

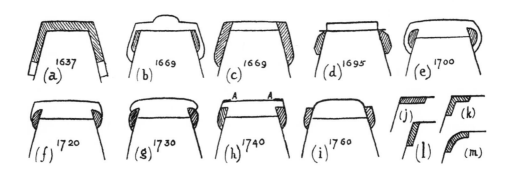

(a) is from the *Sovereign of the Seas*.   (b) & (c) from the *St. Michael*.
(d) from one of the two-and-a-half-decked 80-gun ships.
(e) is probably placed about 5 years too early. This form is found in the large ships of George I's reign.
In figs. (f) to (i) the dates are approximate.
Figs. (j) to (m) represent cross sections of quarter pieces.

1. Admy. Sec.: Out Letters, 1746.

their purpose being rather to show how until a fairly recent date arrangements were made whereby some part of the open gallery might extend to the quarter. The hatched lines show what parts were close.

An illustration is given here of the quarter galleries of the model known as the *"Britannia, 1700"*,[1] which shows the fashion that had been in use since 1669. The way through to the stern from the upper-deck gallery is well seen, but the gallery of the quarter-deck is small and close. It does not reach to the fashion piece by some 5ft., and has no opening to the stern. The *Royal Sovereign* of 1701 differs from this ship in having the quarter piece carried up at full width to join the tafferel;[2] but though there was an open space inside it on the quarter-deck level, by which the stern and quarter galleries might have been joined up, this does not appear to have been done. Nor was it done in the second rates of the same date, if we may judge of them all by the *St. George* of 1701[3] for, like the *Association* of 1696,[4] they had quarter galleries on only two decks.

In Anne's reign usage at once began to settle down. The model known as the *"Victory*; 17th century"*, at Greenwich, which probably represents the *Royal Anne* of 1704, shows the upper-deck gallery carried to the quarter piece and made close, while that on the quarter-deck is open to the stern; that known as a "100-gun ship", which seems to be of a second rate on the 1706 establishment, has openings to the stern from both the upper-deck and quarter-deck

galleries. From this time for nearly 50 years the same system went on, both for three and two-deckers: either one or two galleries might have the opening inside the quarter piece, the common arrangement being that one was open in a two-decked ship[5] and two in a three-decker. But occasionally, early in the period, a two-decker might have two such openings, as is shown from a 70-gun ship on the gun establishment of 1716.[6]

By about 1710 the uppermost quarter gallery was made to reach to the fashion piece in three-deckers. Admiralty draughts of the *Ossory*, 90, and *Cumberland*, 80, launched respectively in 1711 and 1710, show this. The *Ossory* shows an opening through the quarter piece to the stern on both decks, but the *Cumberland*, which has only a central dicky instead of a complete quarter-deck stern gallery, only one on the upper-deck. In contemporary two-deckers the upper quarter gallery did not reach to the fashion piece and there was no opening; but in a 60-gun ship, the *Ripon*, there was an opening on the upper-deck. These examples, together with those illustrated, will serve to show that in the early 18th century there was some latitude. The latest model in which these openings have been found is of the *Royal George*, 100, designed in 1746. She was not launched till 1756, and probably was completed without them, for no other instance of them has been found after 1745. For 20 years before this date the practice was growing of making the quarter galleries close: of ten ships, of 60 and 80 guns, plotted between 1726 and 1745, only four, including Anson's

---

1. Plate 48.   2. M.M. IV, 71; but *cp. id*. VIII, 31, 91.   3. Nance, Plates 58, 59.   4. M.M. IX, 157.   5. Plate 47, No. 2.   6. *Ibid*. No. 3.

Centurion, show an opening from the quarter to the stern.

The form of these closed galleries was as shown by the *Augusta*, 60, of 1736,[1] and the *Victory*, 100, of 1765;[2] and this form was used without exception in all square-sterned ships down to the 19th century. With the round stern naturally this shape of quarter gallery could no longer be used, but a structure, semicircular in plan, was sponsored out on each quarter, and joined up to a similar gallery in the centre of the stern. Open balconies with iron railings were fitted round the stern and quarters.[3]

After 1827 some ships had elliptical sterns, and it was found possible in them to fit the quarter galleries very much as in square-sterned ships.

Commonly there was a quarter piece at the middle deck level, not so important as the whole figures on the upper-decks, but enough to make a distinct break between the windows of the quarter gallery and those of the stern. Frequently, however, in three-decked ships, from about 1704 to 1740, there was no such interruption, and a tier of windows ran right round the stern and quarters, the sharp angle at the quarter being rounded off in such cases.

It has been noticed that the first rates of George I's reign had a fourth tier of stern windows[4] to light the cabins on the poop; but they had no corresponding quarter galleries. The only English ship so fitted was Balchen's *Victory* of 1737, as shown by the model at Greenwich, which is believed to have been made after the ship was built.[5]

It must always have been a question how big a ship had to be to deserve a pair of quarter galleries. Small ships had none; but as some light was wanted in the cabin space a window was necessary on each quarter, and because to eyes accustomed to the splendours of the galleries of great ships a quarter entirely bare of ornament must have seemed an

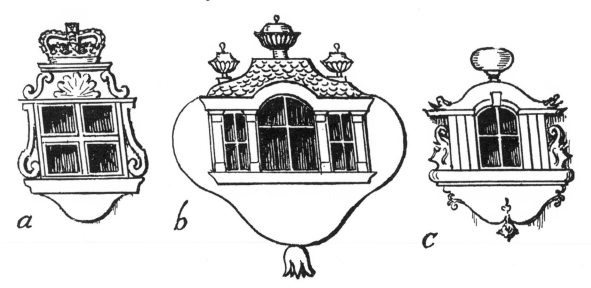

1. Plate 48, No. 2.   2. Plate 16.   3. P. 145, fig. (b).   4. Plate 28.   5. Nance, Plate 77.

absurdity, this window was put into an elaborate frame. This substitute for a gallery is known as a quarter badge, a term which still survives in the Navy to describe the fender fitted on the quarter of a ship's boat.

Small two-deckers were the largest ships which ever had these badges, and even in them galleries were more usual. An early example is here given from the *Tiger*[1] of 44 guns, built in 1647. It will be seen that the badge is merely an elaborate frame, such as was fitted to the windows on the quarters of the Restoration yachts. In the 17th century it was usually square; in the 18th it was often made round or oval, but beyond this there was little room for variation. The limit of size below which galleries were not fitted seems to have been roughly 500 tons. Thus in the Commonwealth time while the *Tiger* of 453 tons had badges, the *Jersey* of 556 tons had galleries: and so too at the end of the 18th century, when frigates commonly had galleries but sloops not. There were some exceptions. Thus the *Termagant* of 1780, a large sloop with a quarter-deck, was fitted as a small frigate;[2] but the *Renard*, a similar ship, was fitted as a sloop, and in 1802 her captain built a pair of dummy galleries upon her, which, with other unofficial improvements, he thought would "make her beautiful beyond description".[3] The order of 1815 fixing the cost of ornaments recognised ship-sloops with quarter-decks, which by then were over 500 tons, as the smallest class to be allowed quarter galleries. The 18th century badges illustrated (facing page)

are (a) from the *Royal Escape*; hoy; (b) from the *Plymouth* yacht of 1754; and (c) from the *Senegal* sloop of 1760.

FOREIGN PRACTICE

From a very early date there were decided differences between English and foreign methods of fitting quarter galleries. The evidence as to those of Spanish ships is neither full nor clear enough to admit of a very definite statement; but it seems to be the case that in Spain the galleries were left open, and joined up to open stern galleries, to a much later date than in England. Thus fig. (j) shows a Spaniard in 1639[4] with open galleries on two decks exactly as they are represented in 1607. This form might have been possible in England in 1607, but certainly not at the later date.

Dutch practice also diverged from English. We have no example to show that the fashion shown in fig. (g)[4] was ever introduced into an English ship. The galleries are verandahs throughout their length, open-sided between the spurs. In English ships only a half of the length was covered over, and the front was closed by windows. The Dutch do not appear ever to have left the fore ends of the galleries open, either before or after they began glazing in the space between the roof and the breast rail, as they seem to have done from about 1625, or perhaps earlier. The well-known Hondius "navire royal",[5] and another ship built in Holland for France,[6] both in 1626, show the same form of galleries. They have one pair, on

1. Plate 46, fig. (D).   2. Plate 50, No. 2.   3. N.R.S., Nav. Misc.: I, 310.   4. P. 134.   5. M.M. IV, 33.   6. *Ibid*. III, 376.

the upper-deck, of the form shown in fig. (g)[1] but with the front glazed in, and with a small turret at each end of the gallery. Turrets in those positions have not been found in ships built by the Dutch for themselves, but the form adopted for the gallery itself became the regular practice, and remained in use, always on only one deck, till the end of the century. From the Dutch it found its way into the ships of all the Baltic powers.

Sometimes, but rarely, a turret is found rising out of it in Dutch ships a little before the stern. Tromp's *Amilia* had such a turret; so some 30 years later had the *Eendracht*.[2] But in general the gallery was plain rather than ornamental, its roof often being of weather-boarding without ornament, of the form shown in an English ship in fig. (l).[1] In the second half of the century ornaments were introduced on the roof, and these, perhaps in imitation of the English fashion of triple turrets, were more often than not three in number, whether they were spikes,[2] or figures, or floral brackets. Not infrequently there was a door in the middle of the gallery, surrounded by a decorated arch rising well above the windows. There was often a somewhat similar feature in English quarter galleries of the Restoration period; but what exactly was its use either in English or in Dutch ships has not been determined.

At the end of the century the Dutch altered the form of the roof of this gallery, not raising it, but gathering it up into a kind of domed finishing, as is seen in the *Briel*.[3] It may be that earlier examples of this form will be noticed in

Dutch ships, for exactly the same thing existed in England more than 50 years earlier.[4] It will be interesting too to have a more exact date for the little Danish ship, which I have assigned at a guess to about 1680, for she has the same gallery and finishing.

The "half-bottle" form of gallery began to grow common in Dutch ships from about 1700, but at least one instance occurs several years earlier. This is in Mr. R. C. Anderson's model of a three-decked ship, which possibly represents the *Westfriesland* of 1685.[5] The form is illustrated here from the "Caravelle de guerre" at Brussels (fig. c), which is presumably an Ostend East Indiaman; and from the models of *'t Wickelo* of 1725,[6] and of the *Mercurius* (fig. d). It will be seen that its form did not appreciably vary, and that it had windows only on the upper-deck. East India ships and men-of-war alike used it in the first half of the 18th century, after which it gave way to English influence, though not immediately or entirely. It would probably be approximately true to say that before 1750 Dutch two-deckers had begun to use two-decked quarter galleries generally similar in form to English, though they rarely made them open to the stern; but that in frigates and smaller ships a modified form of half-bottle remained in use much later.

Thus the *Boeken Roode*[7] of 1732 and the 64-gun ship of 1749[8] show galleries which are closely allied to English. The latter has her galleries both close; but the *Boeken Roode* has an open balcony running round outside the close part of the gallery on the quarter-deck level,

1. P. 134.   2. Plate 34.   3. Plate 49.   4. M.M. IV, 129.   5. Nance, Plate 39.   6. Plate 49.   7. P. 44, fig. (D).   8. P. 44, fig. (G).

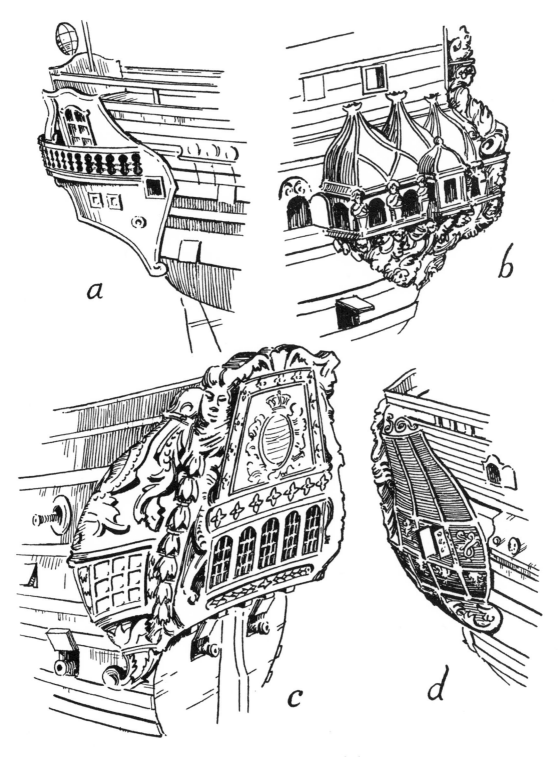

DUTCH QUARTER GALLERIES, 1696 TO 1747

(a) From an unnamed model in the Louvre.   (b) The "Kruisbark", or *William Rex* of 1696.
(c) The "Caravelle de Guerre" at Brussels.   (d) The *Mercurius*, E. Indiaman, 1747.

and opening aft between the quarter and fashion pieces, though there is no open stern gallery on that deck. The *'s Lands schip* of 1767[1] has a form which may perhaps be described as intermediate between the "half-bottle" and the English form; and the *Wageningen* of about 1780[2] has a very narrow high form clearly descended from the half-bottle. This last form is found in ships of the Baltic powers,[3] and even in Frenchmen, as late as the 19th century. Dutch line-of-battle ships in the last quarter of the 18th century had galleries entirely English in form.

Only two entirely abnormal Dutch forms occur. One, from the "Kruisbark", or *William Rex*, model of 1696, is the Dutch flat gallery with the triple turret finishing which was common in English ships about 1650-5.[4] A small bay abreast the middle turret, with a little dome of its own, corresponds to the more usual arched door in that position; and the normal seated quarter figure is not interfered with. The other is from an 18th century model in the Louvre described as a Dutch ship.[5] In this there is no close gallery, but merely a large badge with a window above and a gun port below, and an open gallery running round under a curved bracket from the quarter to the stern. The arrangement is decidedly French.

It has been seen that French ships of 1626 had quarter galleries in the Dutch fashion, but with little turrets at their two extremities. There is a gap in the evidence after this, and we do not know how this feature was developed in ships

built in France during the middle of the century. From the fact, however, that the *French Ruby*, captured in 1666, had open galleries both on the quarters and astern, and that the Colbert ship[6] of about the same date has galleries differing greatly from Dutch practice, it may be inferred that there had been transitional steps of which we have no trace. In the Colbert ship there appear to be three galleries. The lowest, on the upper-deck, is flat and close, like a Dutch gallery, but with mock balustrading under the lights; the second, on the quarter-deck, is flat but with small projection, leaving room for a straight open balustraded gallery outside it which opens through to the stern; and on top of the second, instead of a finishing, is a straight open gallery which ends at the quarter piece. This last feature has not been found in any other ship since the *Prince Royal* of 1610; but in her it ran all round the stern.

The *Paris*,[7] whose decorative features were designed by Puget about 1668, shows what appears to be a very early 17th century type of lower gallery, which, entered at the stern from the middle deck, has so much steeve that its fore end is level with the lower deck ports. There appears to be no close quarter gallery here, but only a couple of windows set flat in the side. Above this is a small upper-deck open gallery, not reaching aft to the quarter piece, with one large window also set flat in the side. The two galleries are connected by enormous carved spurs. These galleries are so unlike the form which shortly afterwards established itself that there is at first a temptation to dismiss them as

1. Plate 41.   2. Nance, Pl. 97.   3. *Ibid*. Pl. 102, 112.   4. P. 143, fig. (b).   5. *Ibid*. fig. (a).   6. Plate 40, No. 1.   7. Plate 33.

being entirely a freak of Puget's fancy; but they were not entirely so. M. de la Roncière[1] gives a contemporary illustration of the *Royal Louis* of 1668, with ornaments designed by Le Brun and carried out by Girardon, and this ship has, on three decks instead of two, open galleries similar in type to those of the *Paris*, and with even heavier carvings connecting them.

At the end of the 17th century French ships had their galleries, from the middle deck upwards, all entirely open, but with the side heavily ornamented and pierced for guns.[2] The galleries were connected with each other by pillars or spurs. In the 18th century the closing of the galleries began, but advanced slowly. Even in the middle of the 18th century, as seen from the *Royal Louis*,[3] while the middle deck gallery was close, that of the upper-deck was only partly closed, and above that of the quarter-deck there rose what was no more than an elaborate

badge with a window in it. Even the fore part of the lowest gallery seems to have been so close to the side that it was sometimes possible to cut a gun port in it.[4] In small ships there was no open gallery, and the projection was so small that it needs some attention to see that the structure is more than a badge.[5] The general outline of these quarter galleries is distinctly of the "half-bottle" order, and the resemblance is even more obvious in the transitional forms introduced shortly after 1750.

A feature common to all these early French ships was that the stern ran straight up from the counter, thereby exaggerating the projection of the gallery aft. The "Pic" model of 1755 shows the beginning of the change. She has a quarter gallery of the same fashion as the *Téméraire*,[4] but has the poop prolonged in a counter over the quarter-deck gallery which, as formerly, runs right round the stern from

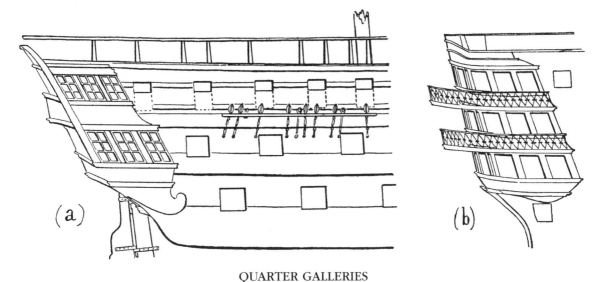

QUARTER GALLERIES
(a) *Duquesne*, 1803.   (b) *R. Frederick*, as designed 1841.

1. Hist. de la marine française, V, 380.   2. Plate 39.   3. Plate 51, No. 3.   4. Plate 41.   5. Plate 51.

quarter to quarter. There is the same badge arrangement on the quarters, the window of the badge being the aftermost of five square evenly spaced lights, placed where in an English ship there would be gun ports. When such ships became ours by fortune of war, we sealed up the lights and cut ports immediately below them, as is seen in the *Duquesne*, a prize of 1803. The *Protecteur*[1] of 1757 has moved a step further. Her gallery is very noticeably of the "half-bottle" type, but there is now a projecting close gallery to the quarter-deck, and a large quarter piece coming down as a spur from the counter of the poop to the open gallery. There is a small open space to the quarter between this spur and the gallery, much as in English ships of about 1730. The so-called *"Bien Aimé"* model at the Louvre, a first rate of about 1760, shows the same arrangement in a three-decker.[2] Similarly the Louvre model known as the *"Sans Pareil"* of 1760,[3] a 110-gun ship of slightly later date, shows the extreme point to which the "half-bottle" form could be carried. The quarter galleries are extended further aft and the stern built out below until it actually tumbles home from the middle deck upwards. The quarter galleries are all close and rounded to the stern, and there is a gun port in the lowest. The model of the *Artésien* of 1765[4] shows a type intermediate between the "half-bottle" and the English form, but still has an open gallery outside the closed part on the quarter-deck. The profile of the stern and the treatment of the quarter piece are as in the *Protecteur*, except that the close gallery of the upper-deck is carried so far aft under the quarter-deck open gallery that it ranges with the projection of the poop.

The form shown in the *Artésien* was that which was retained and developed, and the development followed the only possible course. French galleries became almost exactly the same as English, save that they kept the upper one open to the stern, as many English ships had done in the first half of the century. It was not until after 1790 that the upper gallery was made close to the quarter piece, as in English ships. These two forms are shown from *"Le Northumberland"* of 1780, and the *Spartiate* of 1796.[5] The difference from the English form is very slight, consisting chiefly in the greater length in a fore and aft direction of the upper gallery. This makes the whole structure look heavier than the English pattern, its fore edge being nearly in a straight line, and narrowing aloft only by a small step under the quarter-deck windows, instead of the marked step found in English ships. Soon after 1800 the French gallery was made even heavier, the fore edge becoming quite straight and parallel to the quarter piece.[6]

The frigate type of gallery shown from the *Oiseau*,[7] roughly a contemporary of the *Artésien*, is interesting as showing how un-English the English type of gallery might be made to look. This is due to the small rake of the stern, and especially to the French form of lower finishing. The flat upper finishing is occasionally found on an otherwise wholly French gallery from about 1740.

1. Plate 52, No. 2.   2. Nance, Plate 84.   3. *Ibid*. Plate 90.   4. *Ibid*. Plate 93.   5. Plate 42.   6. Plate 47, No. 4.   7. Plate 25, No. 1.

The quarter of a galley of Louis XIV[1] naturally shows very great differences from that of a ship. There is a quarter figure as a bracket to the poop, and another at the corner of the apostis, and there is an elaborate carved panel on the side of the carosse; but there is nothing corresponding to a quarter gallery. The elaborate painting of the hull down to the water-line was reserved for admiral galleys, and was never practiced in ships.

I have little about Spanish galleries. Down to 1639 they seem to have been left open, and to have been doubled in large ships. In the early 18th century forms corresponding to French or English were commonly used. A model in the Naval Museum at Madrid, described as of the early 18th century, is difficult. Its stern is given here, and is dated tentatively 1730;[2] a broadside view is given by Mr. Nance,[3] and raises a serious difficulty. The form of the quarter gallery is French, but with the upper-deck built out aft as far as the projection of the quarter-deck gallery, and with a spur from the tafferel to the gallery. The open gallery runs round the quarters under the spur, and the arrangement is one which the French did not reach until about 1760. It would appear that the Spaniards were combining a form of stern which occurs occasionally in early 18th century Dutch practice, with the normal French quarter gallery.

A Spanish frigate dated 1739,[4] the *Fenix* of 1749,[5] and the *Grana* frigate, captured in 1780,[6] show an entirely English form of quarter gallery. It will be noticed that in the illustration of the *Fenix* the aftermost light of the quarter-deck gallery is very faint. This is because in the Admiralty draught it has been inked in in green, to show an alteration to be made in fitting the ship as the *Gibraltar*. In the Spanish service the ship had no light there, her quarters being open through to the stern. Spanish ships in the second half of the century continued to use English galleries, but, like most other nations who did so, kept the quarters open long after they had been closed in English ships.

Such evidence as I have shows that in the 17th century the Baltic powers fitted their galleries in the Dutch fashion, commonly in the simple flat form, but occasionally with a turret rising out of it. This is shown particularly in the case of the Swedish ships of 1658,[7] which had their turrets right aft, but usually when a turret occurs it is placed, as in Dutch ships, some way from the fashion piece. Mr. Nance shows[8] a church ship from Bergen which is peculiar in having two quite independent galleries of Dutch form, with a high turret as a quarter piece closing the after ends of both, and a smaller turret at the fore end of the upper-deck gallery. This is interesting, as showing that in northern waters the Dutch form was subjected to developments which exercised no influence on the Great Powers. This ship is dated about 1610, a time when the Dutch had not adopted even a single closed gallery. It seems probable that it should be placed some 20 years later.

1. Plate 51, No. 1.   2. Plate 43, No. 1.   3. Sailing-ship models, Plate 85.   4. Nance, Plate 78.   5. Plate 48.   6. Plate 50, No. 1.
7. P. 134, fig. (k).   8. Sailing-ship models, Plate 14.

There is a history of French influence on Danish quarter galleries. This is seen in the modern model of the *Christianus V* of 1673, and more convincingly in the *Fyen* of 1746.[1] Each of these has her galleries distinctively French; but in the latter part of the 18th century, especially after the coming of Chapman, the Baltic states, like all others, adopted the English form of galleries. In doing this they, like other nations, kept the quarters open later than the English did, as for example in the *Adolf Frederick*[2] of 1767. From 1800 Danish ships introduced one notable difference from English practice. This was in connection with the Hohlenburg stern, which, when carried up to form a poop, as in the *Christian VII*,[3] was so narrow aloft that the quarter-deck gallery projected widely on each side in early 17th century fashion. But in other ships there was no poop, and then, as in the *Norge*[4] and *Princess Carolina* the quarter like the stern was treated frigate fashion, and given only a single quarter gallery,

close with very high windows. American frigates in the War of Independence had English pattern quarter galleries even when following French fashions,[5] because by that date the French had adopted the English form. In the war of 1812 there was no noticeable diversity of practice surviving anywhere.

From the accompanying illustration of the galleries of French round-sterned ships it will be seen that, though in principle the method of fitting them was the same as in England, yet there are differences of detail. In particular the quarter galleries are longer and heavier in the line-of-battle ship, fig. (a), than in English practice, the open gallery is roofed in, and is also open to the quarters in very much the 18th century manner. The frigate, fig. (b), on the other hand, has merely an open gallery on the quarter, and no close gallery or badge such as was given to English ships of the class,[6] as seen in the *Castor*.

FRENCH ROUND STERNS
(19TH CENTURY)

1. Nance, Plates 34, 83.   2. P. 105.   3. P. 108.   4. P. 107.   5. Plate 50.   6. P. 38.

QUARTER BADGE OF
A DUTCH SNOW

In England yachts can be trusted to afford good examples of quarter badges, but this is by no means always so with Dutch yachts, owing to the alternative method of building them with a glazed pavilion aft, as seen in Plate 44. Quarter badges from less ornamental small craft are not very easily come by, but a good example is offered here from a snow of 1768.

§ 2. ORNAMENT

The decoration of early galleries was limited to such as could be applied to their brackets, rails, and spurs, which appear to have been treated handsomely and picked out in colour.[1] When the galleries were closed the mullions between the lights, the frieze under

them, and the upper and lower finishings gave a more extended opportunity for ornament.

The mullions or brackets between the windows were treated in the 17th century as were those of the stern, which implies that they were commonly carved in terms or whole figures, or in less important ships in designs of flowers and foliage. But in early ships all the space available was not filled with windows. Thus the *Prince Royal* of 1610[2] had in the centre of her one close gallery an enormous panel of the Prince of Wales's feathers. The *Sovereign of the Seas*[3] similarly had a large device of the royal arms on each quarter, but in her case it was found possible to place it between the two tiers of lights. In later ships, both under the Commonwealth and in the early Restoration period, a large arch was sometimes substituted for this panel. The purpose of this is not too clear. Sometimes it seems to have been merely decorative, and flat to the surface of the gallery; but sometimes it was recessed, either to serve as a small open balcony, or as a niche in which to place a carved figure. When a figure was introduced, it seems safe to decide that it must have been symbolical of the ship's name, as the panels which the *Prince* and the *Sovereign* carried in that position had been. This arch was always axial to the central dome of the gallery, but its position altered vertically. In Commonwealth ships with two tiers of windows it had its crown below the upper tier, but after the Restoration it was placed higher. It does not seem to have been repeated after 1670.

1. P. 134, and Plate 1. 2. Plate 8. 3. Plate 9.

It will be noticed that, also from about 1650-70, gun ports were often cut in the galleries below the windows, a thing which sets us wondering how the guns which fired through them can have been mounted. The ports so cut were in English ships always treated decoratively, being given round wreath ports like those used for the upper stern chase guns.[1] In French ships the mounting of guns in these positions was possible until the middle of the 18th century, because, as has been seen, there was little in the nature of close galleries to prevent it.

In the *Prince Royal, Sovereign of the Seas*, and in other early ships, the surface of the gallery to be decorated was divided up into compartments, each of which carried its own ornament of a badge, trophy, or the like. There was little of this class of ornament after 1650, the heavy carving of the mullions being the chief feature; but occasionally there is in early Restoration ships a distinct trace of compartmenting. This is well shown by a Van de Velde drawing of the gallery of the *Charles* of 1667, which shows three of these compartments or panels, one over the other in the centre of the gallery, to the exclusion of a couple of windows. But from about 1670 it is approximately true to say that there remained no more gallery in a fore and aft direction than would carry the number of windows needed. Apart therefore from the brackets and finishings, there remained only the spaces under the windows to ornament. These from that time were either rails to open galleries, or were potentially railings,

so that their treatment was governed by that of the rails of the galleries of the stern. Balustrading began as early as about 1675, and became progressively more common in the 18th century. In the early 18th century, after the restrictive order of 1703, much attention was paid to these rails, and many of the designs used were very handsome.[2] Friezing, however, was still often used on the quarter galleries, as illustrated here from the *Augusta* of 1736.[3]

The ornamentation of the simple form of quarter gallery used by the Dutch in the 17th century was relatively small, consisting of small figures between the lights, a carved arch to the central door, when such was fitted, and sometimes a row of small independent figures or ornaments as an upper finishing. In French ships there was much ornament, both on the sides of the ship and on the open galleries; but a feature which was peculiar to them, and to ships which imitated their fashions, was the use of spurs or pillars between the galleries. Apparently when the artists and carvers had a free hand, Puget, Le Brun, Girardon and others, these spurs were, for the sake of ornament, often made preposterously heavy. A drawing of the *Royal Louis* of 1668[4] shows the quarters of the ship, as well as her stern, loaded with enormous whole figures and terms, whose only purpose is to support light open galleries. By comparison, even the great carved spurs of the *Paris* of the same date[5] are moderation itself. These were one of the chief features against which both the sea officers and the administration protested, and they

1. Plate 46, fig. (E).   2. Plates 28 to 31.   3. Plate 48.   4. La Roncière, V, 380.   5. Plate 33.

were drastically reduced. Even the *Soleil Royal*[1] has comparatively small brackets on her middle deck, and small terms on her upper-deck; and ships of slightly later date used light turned pillars or flat spurs with only a running ornament in low relief. The closing of the galleries in the middle of the 18th century did away with this feature.

§ 3. FINISHINGS

The "upper finishing" in English ships may be said to have been from the first a dome. Though not the first ship in which this occurs, the *Sovereign of the Seas*[2] may be made the starting point. In her the length of gallery to be covered placed a single dome out of court; and as there had already been instances of ships with a domed turret at each end of the gallery, and others of ships with a single turret in the middle of it, it no doubt seemed to be the natural thing to combine these methods. As there was no break in the gallery, which was flat throughout its length, the size and arrangement of the domes could be made to depend on the number of windows and compartments below. They were accordingly made nearly equal, the central one being but slightly larger than the others. Of the several drawings and paintings of this ship one, on four folding panels, shows small carved figures standing on top of the lateral domes. This may have been the first intention; but, as we know, the ship was completed with lanterns in these positions.

The *Prince* when rebuilt in 1641[3] had a much shorter gallery, to which a wide single dome was fitted, but till about 1655 the triple dome finishing appears to have been by far the most common.[4] Under the Commonwealth the central dome increased in size, and the lateral turrets dwindled proportionately, until it seemed not worth while to fit them. The last ships in which they are found, so small as almost to escape notice, are the *Prince* of 1663 and the *Charles* of 1667; but in general there remained merely a small ornament on the wing at each side of the central turret. The latest instance noted of this survival is of 1682.

The ships of Charles II seem without exception to have been fitted with a single dome as an upper finishing. Earlier examples of this appear to have been very heavy, projecting much from the ship's side, as in the *Old James*;[5] but in later ships they were made much lighter, being nearly flat to the side. The forming of an open gallery to the quarter-deck no doubt had its influence in bringing about this change. The dome was always ogee shaped, and crowned by an ornament, such as a plume, or bunch of foliage; but sometimes a figure was placed there, as in the *Charles* of 1667, which had what appears to be a statue of the king; or cherubs supporting a scutcheon, as in Mr. R. C. Anderson's three-decked model (perhaps the *St. Andrew* of 1670); or a large angel, as in the Van de Velde drawing which may be of the *Mountagu* of 1675. Anything, in fact, was admissible which could be placed on a narrow pedestal and was sufficiently decorative.

1. Plate 39.   2. Plate 9.   3. M.M. IV, 129.   4. Plate 46.   5. Plate 12.

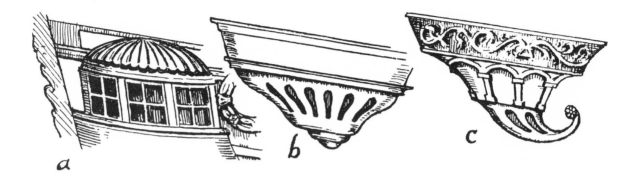

ENGLISH FINISHINGS, 18TH CENTURY

When, as first happened with the three-decked ships of the 1676 programme, a close gallery was formed on the quarter-deck, the old high dome could no longer hold its place. The first idea was to restrict it to the space remaining available above the quarter-deck lights. This made it very shallow and deprived it of its ornament, as seen in the *Coronation* of 1685. Apparently this arrangement was not liked, for three-decked ships at the end of the century reverted to the high dome. The *St. George*, 90, of 1701,[1] had the high dome instead of a quarter-deck gallery; the *"Britannia*, 1700",[2] kept the high dome, but put a window in it, thus making a badge of it; the *Royal Sovereign* of 1701[3] converted it into a regular gallery with three windows, thus reverting to the fashion of the *Coronation*.

In smaller ships from about 1675 the ogee dome began to give place to a concave turret finishing, which gave a wider pedestal at the top for ornamentation. This is seen in the Van de Velde drawing of the 60-gun ship which I have called the *Mountagu*, and

in an Admiralty draught of the *Charles Galley* of 1676. It is very well shown in the 80-gun ships of the 1690 Act, with the double crowns as an ornament.[4] But with a gallery on three decks in a three-decker, and on two in a two-decker, as became the rule early in the 18th century, there was little vertical space available for the finishing. It was a question of parting either with the dome itself or with the ornament which crowned it, and both methods were tried. Thus the Greenwich model which is thought to be the *Royal Anne* of 1704 has a Cupid riding a seahorse; but the "100-gun ship", which is a 90-gun ship of slightly later date, has a shallow fluted dome (fig. a, above). The *Princess*, 90, of 1711, had a similar dome, and the *Cumberland*, 80, of 1710, one even shallower with a plain knob on top; but two-decked ships of the same date show either the royal cypher, or a shell ornament within an arch. The dome, and later the slanting roof below the dummy gallery, were sometimes covered with scale work.[5] Both the dome and the shell arch became very uncommon after 1720, for before then a flat upper finishing, usually formed

1. Nance, Plate 59.   2. Plate 48.   3. M.M. IV, 69.   4. Nance, Plate 47.   5. P. 153.

ENGLISH FINISHINGS, UPPER, SIDE, AND LOWER, IN THE 18TH CENTURY

into a dummy gallery with a carved or balustraded rail, was almost always fitted.[1] This form is found in the *Royal George* of 1715 and in all subsequent first rates except the *Britannia* of 1719, which is shown in an Admiralty draught with an upper finishing formed of a narrow arch with a scroll before it. The latest dome I have found is in the model at the "Mercury" Museum known as the *Tartar* of 1734; and the latest arch noticed is in an Admiralty draught of the *Culloden* of 1744, which has an arch broken by a shell. This form is illustrated here from the *Augusta*, 60, of 1736.[2] The flat finishing was the regular 18th century fashion in ships great and small, and lasted as long as quarter galleries.[3] Yachts, as has been often said, are exceptions to all rules: thus the *Plymouth* yacht of 1754[4] had a large badge with a triple finishing, distinctly reminiscent of Restoration practice.

The finishing of the Dutch flat gallery of the 17th century has been mentioned. The "half-bottle" which succeeded this form was not ornamental, and had little space for an upper finishing, so that it was not until they adopted the English form of galleries that the Dutch made any notable use of upper finishings. This adoption began apparently about 1725, when the flat finishing was already by far the commonest form in England; but the Dutch preferred the older English fashion, and even accentuated it by placing a dome or group of carvings over the upper windows of the quarter gallery,[5] and it was not until about 1780 that they began regularly to use a plain finishing.

In France, as has been pointed out, there was no closed upper quarter gallery till the middle of the 18th century, so that strictly until then there was no upper finishing. But the ornamentation applied to the side in that position when seen from the broadside had much the appearance that a gallery with a finishing would have had. Its form did not appreciably vary from before 1690 till towards 1760. An arch of scroll work flat to the side enclosed important ornamentation in high relief. The *Soleil Royal*[6] shows the head of the "roi soleil" over a cornucopia, but in the 18th century[7] the decoration was less important. The "Pic" model of 1755, an early transitional form, without a close gallery on the quarter-deck, has a spread eagle as an upper finishing, not enclosed by the traditional scrolled arch. The transitional "half-bottle" form of gallery of the 1760's seems to have made room for a certain amount of carving on its top,[8] but the adoption of the English form of gallery, which followed very shortly, was thorough, and included the adoption of the English flat upper finishing.[9] In such a late transitional form as is shown by the *Oiseau* frigate, of about 1770, it is interesting to see the English gallery and upper finishing combined with the old French form of lower finishing.[10] Conversely, a flat finishing to an otherwise French gallery is found occasionally from about 1740.

Side finishings were something of a feature in the 18th century, especially in the early part of it, after ornament had been rigorously cut down. They never amounted to more than a small formal

1. P. 153.   2. Plate 48; and *cp*. Plate 4.   3. Plates 16 and 50.   4. P. 140, fig. (b).   5. P. 44, figs. (D) and (G).   6. Plate 39.
7. Plate 41.   8. Plate 52.   9. Plates 42 and 47.   10. Plate 25.

scroll, one being often placed before each tier of windows.[1] In English ships these scrolls were most commonly, but not always, plain; in foreign ships they were adopted with English galleries and outlasted the century. The Dutch in particular used them, preferring a slightly flory pattern to the plain scroll. A form which frequently occurs is the scroll, slightly ornamented, with its upper end carved into a snake's head. These little ornaments only catch the attention owing to the 18th century poverty in broadside ornament.

The lower finishing grew out of the brackets which supported the original flat gallery. There was this advantage in the brackets, that they permitted guns to be mounted very close under the floor of the gallery, as may be seen in the *Sovereign of the Seas*.[2] When the galleries were shortened into what has been called the "bottle" form, the brackets became few in number, and could no longer conveniently be placed in a straight row. The method then adopted was to case in the brackets, as seen in the *St. Michael* of 1669,[3] or to use something larger, often with wings, such as a spread eagle, or a pair of Cupids. As long as brackets were used uncovered a gun port could be cut through the finishing, even to the disturbance of the design. The *Prince* of 1670 shows a good example of this. Her lower finishing is a pair of Cupids with wings displayed; but in order to mount a gun between them the inner wing of each has been cut. The "*Britannia*, 1700", similarly has a port between a pair of brackets.[4] But by the end of the century it was the English

custom to build a shallow inverted cone under the galleries, and this might end either in a volute or a knob, or more rarely in a regular tail.[5] The *St. George* of 1701 has the knob form, which was perhaps the most common. Occasionally, as shown by the *Augusta*, of 1736,[4] the cone form might end below in an ornament instead of a knob, the Augusta having a fleur-de-lys; but in English ships this was rare. The volute type is seen in its usual form in the fourth rate of George I.[6] Occasionally it was made longer and ended in a fish's tail, as in the *Deptford* of 1729; but after the middle of the century the volute form in any shape was in a great minority.

Dutch lower finishings to the flat gallery were naturally rows of brackets, but from about 1660 these were often cased in, or a solid finishing built and the brackets applied outside it.[7] The "half-bottle" gallery ended round below, without much ornament; but when the English gallery was adopted the English forms of lower finishing came with it. The Dutch treated the volute form more freely than we did, and often made it into a long fish tail looped in the middle.[8]

The French lower finishing was in the main similar to the upper from 1690 to 1760. It was formed as an arch, and, though close to the side, was both deeper and heavier looking than the English cone form. Its flatness may be seen from the cutting of a lower deck port through it,[9] and it can certainly be said of it that its decoration was less formal than ours. In the latter part of the 18th century, in conjunction with

1. P. 153.   2. Plate 9.   3. Plate 27.   4. Plate 48.   5. Pp. 152, 153.   6. Plate 4.   7. Plate 34.   8. Plate 41; and P. 44, fig. (G). 9. Plate 39.

the English form of galleries, a volute
finishing was commonly used, which
differed noticeably from the English
volute.[1] This was not, however, newly
introduced, for it is found in some
French ships of the early part of the
century,[2] though then in an undeveloped
form. The cone finishing also was used,
but less commonly, until such things
came to their appointed end.

1. Plate 42.   2. Plate 51.

CHAPTER VIII

THE BROADSIDE

The features of the broadside of the ship have hitherto received far less attention than those of the head and stern. Though individually they are for the most part of minor importance, yet collectively their significance is great; so much so indeed that it is hardly an exaggeration to say that by them alone, leaving the head, stern, quarter galleries, and rig out of account, it would be possible in most cases to tell the nationality and date of a ship. They may be divided into two classes: those which were purely structural and utilitarian, and those which lent themselves to decorative treatment.

To the first category belong the Wales, the channels, the Anchor Linings, and perhaps the Rails and Bulwarks.

To the second belong the Gun Ports, the Entering Ports, the Lights to the cabins, the Hancing pieces, the Chesstrees and the early Pavesades with their successors the Waist Cloths and Armings. The Frieze will more properly be included in the description of how the hull was painted.[1]

§ 1. WALES

In early times, before the introduction of great guns, the side of a carvel built ship was treated much as was any other large timber structure which had to be made very strong, such for instance as a timber sea-wall or a groyne. As the thickness of plank necessary for the staunchness of the ship was not found to give her enough rigidity, it was sought to strengthen her by working a thick baulk, roughly square in section, fore and aft between every few strakes of plank.[2] These baulks, or wales, were at first evenly spaced, some three feet apart, and may be compared to the string-courses of architecture. If further strength was needed, in addition to that given by the internal framing of the hull (with which here we are not concerned), the practice was to clap on vertical external timbers crossing the wales and planking.[3] These were especially in demand for binding the superstructures or cage work to the hull proper. They were known as clench work, and were in effect external riders.

This clench work need not detain us, for it had no long vogue. It cannot have been much needed before the 15th century, when the upper works of ships began to grow lofty; and by Henry VIII's time its inconvenience or even danger, when lying board and board with an enemy, had become apparent, and it was entirely discarded in English ships except as a local strengthening in the wake of the chains. Spanish ships, however, as Brueghel and other artists show, kept it later, at least to the end of the 16th century.

The introduction of gun ports on the broadside affected the position of the wales, especially when, as happened from about 1540, gun ports began to be cut the whole length of the broadside. As the wales, especially the lower wales, curved up more sharply than the sheer of the ship, and as the decks more or less followed the sheer, it resulted that the line of ports intersected the wales.

1. Chap. X.   2. (Original) Frontispiece.   3. P. 177, fig. (a).

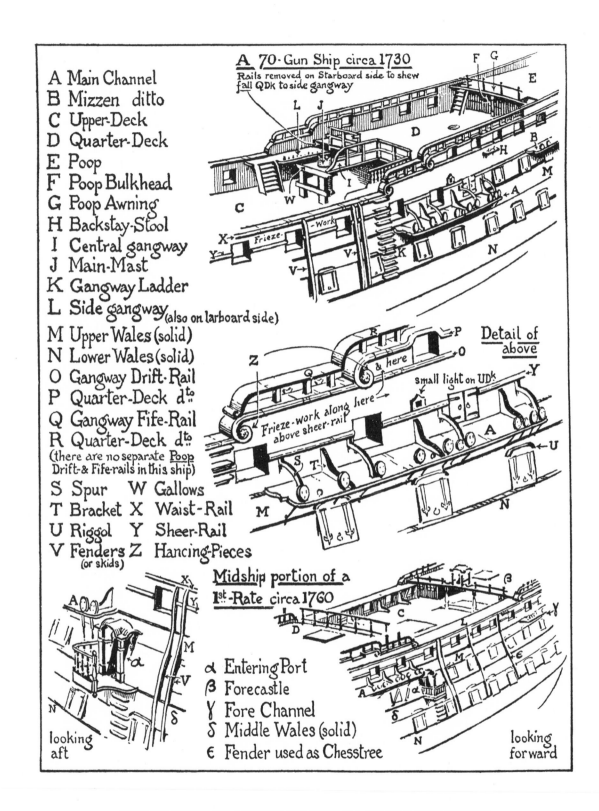

A **Main Channel**
B **Mizzen ditto**
C **Upper-Deck**
D **Quarter-Deck**
E **Poop**
F **Poop Bulkhead**
G **Poop Awning**
H **Backstay-Stool**
I **Central gangway**
J **Main-Mast**
K **Gangway Ladder**
L **Side gangway** (also on larboard side)
M **Upper Wales** (solid)
N **Lower Wales** (solid)
O **Gangway Drift-Rail**
P **Quarter-Deck d$\overset{to}{}$**
Q **Gangway Fife-Rail**
R **Quarter-Deck d$\overset{to}{}$**
(there are no separate Poop
Drift- & Fife-rails in this ship)
S **Spur**   W **Gallows**
T **Bracket**   X **Waist-Rail**
U **Riggol**   Y **Sheer-Rail**
V **Fenders** Z **Hancing-Pieces**
(or skids)

A 70-Gun Ship circa 1730
Rails removed on Starboard side to shew
fall QDk to side gangway

Detail of above

Frieze-work along here above sheer-rail

small light on UDk

Midship portion of a
1st-Rate circa 1760

α **Entering Port**
β **Forecastle**
γ **Fore Channel**
δ **Middle Wales** (solid)
ε **Fender used as Chesstree**

looking aft

looking forward

KEY DRAWING TO ILLUSTRATE DETAILS OF THE BROADSIDE

This involved cutting the wales, and thereby depriving them of a great part of the strength which was the reason for their existence. It took a long time to get over this difficulty, and there were different opinions about how it should be done.

One way was to make a step or hance in a wale in order to avoid a gunport;[1] another was to make a rise or fall in the deck.[2] In Elizabeth's reign these two methods were being practised concurrently: in that of James I the hancing of the wales stopped,[3] but the unequal spacing of them, which is first noticed in the drawing believed to represent the *Ark Royal*,[4] began to be regular, and the breaking of the line of ports by falls continued.

As is well known, one of the chief novelties about the *Sovereign of the Seas*[5] of 1637 was that she had three flush gun decks, that is to say, decks with no falls or rises in them. In order to keep her wales clear of the ports she developed the practice which had begun at least 20 years earlier,[6] and carried her wales in pairs, having one pair at the water line, a second pair between the lower and middle tiers of guns, and a single wale between the middle and upper tiers. She may thus be said to have initiated what became the standard practice in English ships for nearly a century. At first inevitably there was some variation. Under the Commonwealth, as for example in the *Naseby*,[7] the lower pair were a good deal wider apart than the upper; occasionally three were fitted instead of the lower pair. This is seen in the *London* of

1657;[8] in the three-decked model in the Mercury museum which probably represents an unrealised project, perhaps attributable to Anthony Deane;[9] and less infrequently in Dutch ships. Sometimes, until shortly after 1700, the lower wale of a pair is made somewhat thicker than the upper, but the difference is rarely enough to be very noticeable.

Even this improvement was not entirely successful, for the sheer of the ship, though gradually growing less, was still so great that the after ports cut the wales. This is a noticeable feature of the many pictures and models of ships of the Restoration period. Approximately from the Restoration the usage was to place the two wales of the lower pair close together, and from about 1670 the two of the upper pair equally close, and so they remained, one strake of planking apart, till the reign of George I.[10]

There is one small point to which it seems worth while to direct attention. In three-decked ships sometimes a pair of wales, sometimes only a single wale, was fitted under the upper-deck guns. It was tempting to consider that there might be some significance in this: that a pair in that position might be one of the marks of a first rate, and a single wale of a second rate. Had this proved to be so, it would have been of considerable use in the identification of models; but the theory when tested proved invalid. Both first and second rates, almost indifferently, had either a single wale or a pair in the upper position.

1. Plates 5, 6.   2. Plates 1, 5, 6.   3. Plate 1.   4. Plate 6.   5. Plate 9.   6. M.M. IX, 58, 59: the *Antelope*, 1619, and *Constant Reformation*, 1618.
7. M.M. II, 238.   8. M.M. IV, 27.   9. P. 35, fig. (a).   10. Plate 4.

After the early 16th century there was no renewal of the external clench work as such, but verticals played a considerable part in the ornamentation of the sides of the *Prince Royal*, of the *Sovereign of the Seas*, and probably in a less degree of other great ships of the early Stuarts of which we have no record.

There were, however, other vertical pieces, which were not fitted for ornament. These were the fenders in the waist, the purpose of which was to protect the ship's side from damage when hoisting heavy things on board, and especially to prevent the load from catching under the wales. Incidentally these fenders have another use, for they serve to mark an English ship. The Dutch did not use them, which is as much as to say that in the 17th century, when most nations except England took their maritime fashions from Holland, they were not to be seen in other northern ships. In English ships they began to be used about the time of the first Dutch war, the reason almost certainly being that it was then that the long boat was first hoisted in and stowed in the waist instead of being towed astern. Early in the 18th century, when Dutch influence was dying out in France, they begin to appear in French ships.

In England at first merely a pair were fitted,[1] widely spaced to take the chafe of the boat; but very shortly first three, then four became the rule. When there were three, these were placed thus: a pair two feet or less apart close before the entering steps, and one towards the fore end of the waist. Before the end of the century usage was more or less standardised, a pair near the steps, one well forward, usually with its upper end fitted as the chesstree,[2] and the fourth about half-way between the pair and the one. Thus they remained till there were no longer wales or rails on which things might catch. The purpose of the pair placed close together, which were sometimes called the skids, was to serve as a sort of railway for hoisting in barrels and cases; but occasionally, down to about 1675, the entering steps were placed between them, thus forming a ladder. In the *Britannia* of 1682 there was such a ladder, but reaching no higher than the entering port.

The "closing of the wales", that is the filling up of the space between the two of a pair so as to make one wide, solid band of thick timber, seems to have begun accidentally. Many of the later Stuart ships had to be "girdled" to give them greater stability. This meant increasing their beam at the water-line, a thing which might be done, and was done, in various ways. If not much addition of breadth was intended, the readiest and cheapest method was to fill up the space between the wales; and this was done in some cases. It was, however, never done to a new ship till the reign of George I, the earliest draught found showing a ship designed with solid wales being that of the *Newark*, 80, of 1717. The next available draught of this class of ship, that of the *Humber* of 1723, shows the same thing, which, as far as the evidence goes, seems to have been made at once an invariable rule in 80-gun ships. In

1. M.M. IV, 129. 2. P. 199, c.

both larger and smaller ships the change was made more slowly. Thus the *Royal William*, 100, of 1719, had the lower and middle wales built solid, while keeping the upper as a pair, the *Britannia*, 100, of the same date had them all open, and the *Prince George* and *Namur*, 2nd rates, of 1720, had them all solid. The change was approximately complete by 1730, after which date only occasional instances of an upper pair being left open occur, but none of a lower pair. Thus in 1745 the *Ramillies*, 90, was designed to have a pair of middle wales, but the lower and upper closed; though as completed in 1748 she had them all closed. The latest example of an open pair noticed in an English ship is in the *Pembroke*, 60, of 1752; but she was an experimental ship with several unusual features. In yachts, however, which followed rules of their own in several respects, a pair of wales was fitted till later. The Plymouth yacht, designed in 1754, had a pair; so had the *R. Carolina* as rebuilt in 1749.

The solid wales remained as broad projecting bands of timber till the end of the century, when the practice of tapering them off to reconcile with the planking of the side began, the under edge of the lower wales being the first to be so treated. This change, giving a smooth-sided ship, was complete by about 1820. It is possible that the introduction of the "Nelson fashion" of painting the hull, in strakes which followed the lines of the ports, may have conduced to the alteration.

FOREIGN PRACTICE

Abroad in the 17th century the treatment of the wales was similar to that in England. It has been noticed that three lower wales were not uncommon in Dutch ships though very rarely found in English; apart from this the only other difference seems to be that the Dutch kept the upper pair of wales spaced wide apart till somewhat later than we did. In England they all were being placed close together by about 1670; in Holland, and consequently in other northern countries, they were noticeably wider apart till some 10 years later. The French ships of the Colbert régime[1] at first followed the old Dutch fashion; but by the end of the century both Dutch and French practice had been assimilated to English.

It would seem that the Dutch adopted the solid wales at about the same time as the English.[2] In France, however, the old fashion died hard. To judge from the numerous sheer draughts of French prizes extant in the Admiralty records, pairs of wales, both upper and lower, were the rule in French ships until about 1750; the prizes of 1759 showed a solid lower wale but a pair above; and apparently from about 1765 all were made solid. It must be confessed however that this issue is somewhat complicated by the models of three three-deckers at the Louvre, all of which show the lower pair solid and the two upper pairs open. Admiral Pâris[3] calls them the *Bretagne* of 1780, the *Sans Pareil* of 1770, and the *Bien Aimé* of 1780. The explanation of the difficulty seems to be that the *Bretagne*, launched

1. Plate 14.   2. Plate 14, 49, *'t Wickelo*.   3. Musée de Marine, 68 *sq*.

in 1766, was necessarily designed a few years earlier, and therefore in her wales represents normal practice; and that the two other models are certainly wrongly described in name,[1] and represent ships also designed before 1765. No other nation imitated the French fashion in this matter of wales. Even the Spaniards, whose ships frequently show strong traces of French influence, preferred the English usage with regard to wales. Thus the *Princesa*, of 70 guns, built in 1730, had all her wales solid, though in the main she was rather a French looking ship; and such other evidence as is available seems to justify the statement that in this respect Spain closely followed English usage.

With regard to fenders, it would perhaps be true to say that only Swedish ships of Chapman's design, and perhaps some Spanish ships built by Englishmen, ever were fitted like English ships. The Dutch were very late in adopting them in men-of-war, which is curious, seeing that by 1700 or earlier their whaling ships[2] were using them freely to help in getting their boats out and in; the French seem never to have used the pair of skids near the gangway, unless, as a model of 1765 shows, with the steps between them; the Spaniards, Portuguese, and Swedes sometimes at least put the entering steps between the skids even after the middle of the 18th century.

As something of a curiosity, it may be mentioned that Chinese junks built 100 or so years ago, and therefore presumably also if built several hundred years ago, had half-round wales, very solid,

rising in a high sheer from below the water-line, and placed contiguously;[3] but whether this arrangement was general, or was confined to one or two of the many bewildering classes, it is for an Orientalist who is also a nautical antiquary to say.

§ 2. RAILS, PAVESADES AND BULWARKS

Representations of mediæval ships are for the most part on so small a scale that it is not easy to speak with certainty on points of detail; but it seems safe to say that from the time when fore and aftercastles were first used they were generally surrounded by a battlemented bulwark, for the convenience of the archers stationed on them. Sometimes, perhaps only in harbour, cloths emblazoned with coats of arms were hung over the sides of the aftercastle;[4] at sea the regular usage for long was to place painted wooden shields, or pavesses, along these superstructures, but apparently not usually in the waist, except in ships of the galley type.[5]

In ships armed for war the tradition of the shield bulwark of the Viking age survived down to a very late date. It would seem that the rise of heraldry gave a new impetus to this use of shields, for a display of the armorial bearings of the men of note who were on board was at once martial and ornamental. There is probably not enough evidence to admit of a decision as to when actual shields gave place to pavesses, which were large wooden shields fixed permanently to the sides

1. The *Bien Aimé* and *Sans Pareil* were two-deckers.   2. Scheepvaart Museum, "Platen Album", 34.   3. See *e.g.* M.M. IX, 90.
4. P. 177, fig. (b).   5. M.M. VI, 81.

and bulwarks of the ship. It is perhaps possible that during the Hundred Years' War the cognisances of all the men of distinction embarked were displayed; but we know that towards the close of the 15th century something approaching to a standard practice had been evolved.

From the evidence of the Rous Roll and of W. A. (who has been identified as Wohlgemuth) it is seen that ships not belonging to, or in the service of, the Crown contented themselves with a few pavesses to form a bulwark to what we would call the quarter-deck. These were contiguous along an open timber rail, and bore the arms of the nobleman or port to which the ship belonged, alternating probably with the national device. In English men-of-war by the beginning of the 16th century, the St. George's cross was commonly used, but sometimes the royal badges in conjunction with it. In French ships of war the national colours were less prominent, owing chiefly to the right conceded to the admiral of France of displaying his own colours and devices in the ships under his command, but partly also to the fact that France was not yet a homogeneous kingdom. In the war of 1512, for instance, Brittany was virtually independent, and her ships, though acting with the French fleet, wore the ermine of their province instead of the fleurs-de-lys of France. It must be admitted that there is considerable difficulty in ascertaining what French usage really was, not because evidence is wanting, but because there is a direct conflict between pictures and the written word. Jehan Bytharne, who in 1543 addressed

an essay on the conduct of a fleet to the admiral of France, is a valuable witness, in great measure because he is not original.[1] It has been shown that he copied from earlier writers on the same subject, and consequently that most of the practices which he recommended had been in vogue for some 50 years before he wrote. Now it is very noticeable that he advises the use of pavesses on the fore and after castles, while to the waist he assigns neither pavesses nor an arming cloth, such as was already in use for the tops. "Touts les pavez que fauldra au dessus de vos chateaux devant que derrière doibvent estre tout armoýe de vous armes et de vous devises ... Sur la grande hune du grandt matz debvez avoir tout à l'entour une mormonture de la largeur de la profondeur de ladite hune toute armoiée de voz armes." He does not mention the use of the royal arms; yet in fact the great majority of pictures agree in showing the royal arms far more prominent than those of the admiral, which, though they occur in banners, do not appear on the pavesses.

Although early in the 16th century ships with fore and after castles had no pavesses in the waist, the flush built ships introduced by Henry VIII carried them right fore and aft, after the manner of a galley. By 1540 too they had been introduced in the waist of great ships,[2] where they were placed wide enough apart for the intervals between them to serve as gun ports. Here they were fixed to an open timber rail, and formed the only protection. They were made of poplar, a wood which does not splinter, and were thick enough to be

1. N.R.S., Nav. Misc., I, 7.
2. P. 177, fig. (d). Perhaps copying Mediterranean fashion: *cp.* Pinturicchio's carrack in the "Return of Ulysses", *ap.* M.M. II, 376.

musket-proof. This use of them went on well into Elizabeth's reign, but seems to have died out before the end of it. It was certainly more useful than that shown by pictures of the end of the 15th and beginning of the 16th century as existing in French carracks. There the pavesses are commonly shown placed against the solid side of the ship, where they could serve no purpose save that of ornament. In one ship a double tier of them is represented; in another the after castle rises to the height of two decks above them. It is possible that these illogical fashions originated in the carelessness of an artist: they have not been noticed in English ships.

When pavesses had been finally laid aside other means were taken of hiding the men on deck from the enemy's fire. "Armings", which still earlier were called "Fights", were spread along the open rails wherever they existed. These armings were usually of kersey, and of the national colours. Thus in English ships they were red, or red with a white edging, the edging being added seemingly late in the 17th century and being continued till armings went out of use. The Dutch also used red armings, sometimes edged with white. In French ships the arming, which as the "pavois" retained the old name, was blue powdered with fleurs-de-lys, but here the process was reversed, and approximately a white edging may be taken as indicating the 17th century, and an absence of edging the 18th.[1] In the 18th century in all navies the practice was adopted of using the hammocks to form a barricade round the decks, and especially in the waist. The hammocks had to be protected from the weather by tarred or painted canvas, but the coloured "armings" continued to be spread over these covers; and this went on even after the issue of kersey for the purpose had been stopped. Even at Trafalgar the *Victory* had white cloths thrown loosely over her black hammock cloths. Old fashions die hard at sea; but this was probably almost the last surviving vestige of the shield bulwark of the Viking age, for within a very few years after this date the practice of berthing up, that is boarding up, the hammock stantions was generally adopted. Conservatism then shifted its ground, and continued to call these boarded-up racks "nettings", after the actual hammock nettings on which in the 18th century the cloths had been spread.

The pavesses and armings which have been described were the decorative finishing aloft, but between them and the uppermost of the wales there were several rails or ribbands. As an early 17th century writer[2] puts it, "The rails and ribbonds are next above the chain wales: as they rise higher on the ship, so they are made less for ease to the side: some of them are imbowed or wrought for more grace sake, which is the chiefest use of them." It is impossible to say that the fashion of rails had become standardised by 1630 as the evidence is too scanty, but under the Commonwealth usage settled down and was little changed thereafter.

Above the upper wale came the "great rail" running the whole length of the

---

1. Established respectively by the Ordonnances of 1670 and 1765, but believed to have been in use long before those dates.
2. An anonymous treatise on shipbuilding, *c.* 1625; Admy. Library, M.S. No. 44.

ship,[1] which, from its marking the sheer, came shortly to be called the sheer rail. In an official paper of the end of the 17th century it is mentioned that its chief use is to part off "the black work", that is the black topside, which was sometimes ornamented with a frieze, from the ship's side. When the upper wale is single, and the sheer rail lies close to it, as is often the case, it is easy to mistake these two for a pair of wales; but with a model, or with a large scale drawing, the mistake should not arise, for the sheer rail, like all the rails above it, was normally moulded, while a wale was always plain. In the *Sovereign of the Seas*[2] the sheer rail was below the upper-deck ports, and the frieze work was extended between it and the upper wale; but of these features the first ended about the Restoration, while the second, unless perhaps in the case of the *Prince Royal*, was probably unique. After the Restoration the sheer rail ran through the line of upper-deck ports and was cut all to pieces by them, so that it added nothing to the strength of the ship.

Above the sheer rail came the waist rail, which was morticed over the heads of the top-timbers in the waist, and was covered by the "planksheer", just as a boat's gunwale is covered by a capping. The seamen corrupted planksheer into plancher, plainser, and a dozen other forms. It commonly happens that seamen and shipwrights have different names for the same fitting; thus the waist rail and planksheer combined were known at sea as the gunwale, a name reminiscent perhaps of the early 15th century.

The treatment of the waist rail varied widely. The early tendency was to make it run right fore and aft, thus helping in the scheme of ornamentation by compartments. It is so shown in the *Sovereign of the Seas*; but by the Restoration it was often stopped short at some distance from the stern. Thus in the *Naseby* of 1655 it ends at the poop hancing piece, and in the *Prince* of 1670 at the quarter-deck hance. The arrangement seen in the *Prince* was the rule, so far as there was a rule, for the later Stuart navy; but shortly before 1700 there was a reversion to the old mode, and the waist rail was often carried the whole length of the ship, and it so continued till the end. The *Belleisle* of 1815, for instance, had only one rail on her side, and that one was the waist rail running from cathead to quarter gallery. It must be understood that there were always exceptions, especially in small ships. Sometimes this rail was not continued beyond the waist; occasionally it ran forward but not aft; but these variants seem to be of no significance. They might help to identify an individual model with a draught, but they do not help to date an unknown ship. There is one variant, however, which does help. During the period of the shipbuilding establishments the waist rail often hanced up under the quarter-deck hance, and was thence continued aft on the higher level.[3] The earliest examples noted of this are the *Ossory*, 90, of 1706, in which the waist rail hanced up twice, at the quarter-deck and poop hances; and the *Cumberland*, 80, of 1710, in which it rose at the hances of the gangway and quarter-deck. But this double rise is uncommon: from 1706

1. P. 158.　　2. Plate 9.　　3. P. 174, fig. (c) and (e).

to about 1740 several instances occur, all of them showing only a single rise under the quarter-deck hance. As a somewhat extreme instance to show the lack of standardisation, it may be mentioned that in the *Resolution*, 70, of 1708, the waist rail ended at the quarter-deck hance; in the *Ripon*, 60, of 1712, and the *Gloucester*, 50, of 1711, it was not extended beyond the waist: its treatment in the contemporary three-deckers has already been mentioned.

To speak next of the rails that rose above the decks. About 1540 there seems to have been, in all parts of the ship, a low bulwark about 2ft. high with guns firing over it, and above this the open rail which was decorated with pavesses. In the 18th century these rails would have been called the drift and fife rails, but we do not know their Tudor names. It may be noticed, however, that the uppermost rail of all, the fife rail, took its name from its position, for "fife", as early usage shows, is a corruption of "fifth". How the rails had to be counted to make it the fifth remains for future discovery. In sea speech one of the meanings of "drift" is "distance between": thus the drift rail of the poop is the rail which extends the distance between the quarter piece, where the poop begins, and the hance which marks its fore end; and so of the other drifts. The shipwrights of the 17th century spoke of the 1st, 2nd and 3rd drifts, counting from aft, but it will be more convenient to refer to them as the drifts of the poop, quarter-deck, and gangway. The corresponding rails of the forecastle were apparently not always

called drifts, probably because till after 1700 they were commonly fitted differently from the after rails.

The *Sovereign of the Seas*[1] will serve as an illustration of Stuart practice. Her three drifts aft were to the poop, quarter-deck, and half-deck which reached to the main mast. Later ships which had only quarter-deck and poop kept the third drift, presumably in order to avoid having too deep a hance at the break of the quarter-deck; and then by degrees they added little side gangways leading forward from the quarter-deck to the ladders which went down into the waist. At first these gangways were very short, as in the *Prince* of 1670, and it was not till after 1700 that they were carried forward to the entering place. The progressive lengthening of the quarter-deck is a noticeable feature. It went on from the middle of the 17th to the middle of the 18th century, by which time the quarter-deck had reached almost to the main mast, and had in fact grown into a half-deck. Later in the 18th century it was carried still further forward, to the main topsail sheet bitts; but these changes did not affect the drifts, which, as long as they were used, continued to reflect the usage of the late Stuart period.

The drifts varied somewhat in length from time to time. In the *Sovereign of the Seas* they were all three of nearly the same length; a table of dimensions of about 1675[2] gives their lengths as roughly 9, 6, 4 in three-decked, and 9, 4, 4 in two-decked ships, and these proportions remained fairly constant

1. Plate 9.   2. Admy. Library, M.S. No. 44.

till after 1700. There was, however, this important exception, that from about 1690 the poop drift was entirely omitted in ships of 50 guns and below, because their poops had been shortened till they became negligible. This lowering of the sheer was advantageous, and from very soon after 1700 it was generally adopted in two-decked ships, and even in three-decked third rates, which thenceforward rarely, if ever, had a separate poop drift. The quarter-deck drift in these ships was continued aft to the tafferel.[1] The same change was eventually made in first and second rates, but with some hesitation. The *St. George*, 90, of 1734, was designed with a poop drift, but completed without it; the *Ramillies*, 90, of 1748, was in the older fashion; but the *Blenheim*, of 1761, and later ships had no poop drift. The change took place at about the same time in first rates: Balchen's *Victory* of 1737 had a very long poop drift; Kempenfelt's *Royal George*, designed soon after the loss of the *Victory*, had hers much shortened; so had the *Britannia*, designed in 1757; but Nelson's *Victory*, designed in 1759 and launched in 1765, in a first draught, and in the model at Portsmouth, shows drift and fife rails to the poop, but in the corrected draught shows only a fife rail.

From about 1730, or perhaps a little earlier, to 1800, the third or gangway drift was only about 10 or 12 feet long, so that the two drifts which remained when the poop had none were in the ratio of seven or eight to one. Probably a good deal of advantage is to be gained by careful plotting of these changes, but it is impossible here to give more

than the above general indication of the course they took.

Apart from their lengths, useful indications are to be had from the way in which these rails were fitted. From Tudor times[2] the drift rail was a little above the deck to which it belonged, and above it rose stantions to which a bulwark was nailed. But this bulwark did not come right down to the drift rail: it ended about a foot above it, leaving the stantions exposed. In early ships, such as the *Sovereign of the Seas*, and some Commonwealth ships, the stantions were carried up a few inches above the bulwark, presumably to serve as pins, and occasionally an open fife rail was fitted above the bulwark. Such an open rail is shown by Van de Velde on the forecastle, on the half-deck and in the waist, in his drawing of the *Sovereign*,[3] but not on the quarter-deck or poop. The *Prince* of 1670 has the bulwark as described between the gangway and quarter-deck hances, but not elsewhere.[4] In the waist she has nothing above the waist rail, which is extended forward to form the drift rail of the forecastle. Above this drift the forecastle has another heavy rail, raised on short stantions which are not planked in; and she shows no timber heads above this upper rail.

Several Stuart models illustrate variants of the above arrangement, but, as practically all of these models are as yet unidentified, it seems impossible to say more at present than this: that the bulwark with a gap below it was not used after about 1675, but instead was built up solid to the drift rail raised to

1. Plate 4; and P. 158.   2. Plates 1, 6.   3. Plate 9.   4. P. 174, fig. (a).

some three or four feet above the deck, and was surmounted by an open fife rail which was now placed as a capping on top of the stantions. The heavy upper rail on the forecastle was general till about 1715, though a fife rail instead of it is in a few instances met with before that date, as for example in the *Marlborough* of 1708.[1]

A small point which may have some significance is the presence or absence of timber heads above the forecastle rail. They are often absent when we would expect to find them, and at present it does not seem safe to say more than that in early cases where they occur only some three or four a-side are fitted,[2] and always on the fore part of the rail; from perhaps 1670 when present they run the whole length of the rail on both sides;[3] but that apparently they were more often omitted than not until after the heavy rail had been replaced by a fife rail. With the general adoption of the fife rail they became universal, and remained so till the end of the 18th century.

A feature which was very common and noticeable in English ships all through the 17th century was the continuation of the upper rails one drift aft. Thus the quarter-deck drift was continued under the poop drift to the stern, the gangway drift under the quarter-deck drift to the poop hance, and similarly the waist rail under the drifts of the gangway and forecastle. The result was that the side, except in the waist, ended aloft in triple rails, which, moulded themselves and reconciling with carved hancing pieces, were painted gold or perhaps sometimes yellow on the background of the black topside. The wreath ports also contributed to this decorative scheme, which left no need for carved or painted frieze work. This arrangement seems to have been less common after the restrictive order of 1703.[4]

In the 18th century the treatment of the rails was almost standardised, and an English-built ship, whether built in England or by English builders abroad, could be recognised by her rails. There

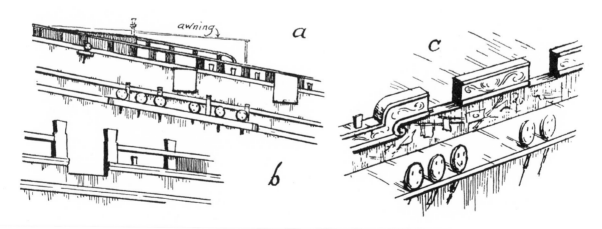

DETAILS OF RAILS (FROM MODELS)
(a) *Cambridge*, 1755.   (b) *R. George*, 1756.   (c) *Q. Charlotte*, 1790.

1. From the model formerly in the London Museum.   2. *E.g.* in the *R. Charles* in 1667, built in 1655 as the *Naseby*.   3. Plates 11, 12.
4. P. 174.

was always some slight diversity of practice, but in general two features were present: the rails, except to the quarter-deck, were extremely low, so that they afforded no protection whatever and served merely for ornament; and the fashion of continuing all the drifts aft to the stern died out, thus leaving the "black work" above the sheer rail free for embellishment by painted frieze work.

The lowness of the rails in English ships deserves some comment, for it was a peculiarity of English fashion. It has already been mentioned[1] that early in the 18th century the poop drift began to go out of use, thus lowering the sheer. It lasted longest in first rates; and it is a fair conjecture that the disastrous loss of the 1737 *Victory* in 1744 – a ship with a very high side and high rails, wrecked, it is believed, from sheer leewardliness – had much to do with the subsequent extreme cutting down of the rails. This reached such a pitch that it is commonly found in line-of-battle ships from about 1740 that at the break of the poop even

the fife rail was actually below the level of the deck. When this was the case either an extra fife rail was worked on top of that which had been, so to speak, submerged, or a mere filling piece was added without any pretence at ornament; or both the fife rail and the filling piece were added (P. 168, fig. a).

What the ships gained in weatherliness by this lowering of the sheer they lost in defensive qualities, and the Navy Board papers of the early part of the century are full of projects for protecting the men on deck from the enemy's shot. This was done partly by the use of "armings", which screened but did not protect them; partly by the building of "awnings", or extensions of the poop and quarter-deck, which were much in favour because they also afforded shelter from the weather; and partly by fitting "barricades" round the exposed decks. These barricades in turn were objectionable. As in the previous century, they were made of junk, and, though theoretically temporary structures, tended

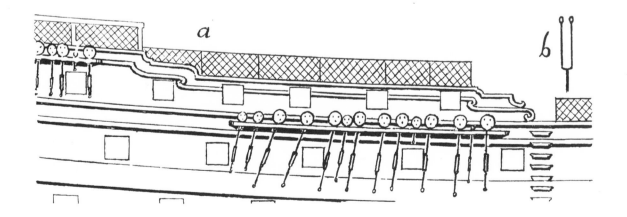

RAILS AND NETTINGS OF THE "ADOLF FREDERICK" (SWEDISH), 1767

1. P. 167.

to become permanent. Their height and weight wronged the ship more than a timber bulwark would have done, and it is not remarkable to find the Navy Board, soon after 1740, experimenting with cork shavings and hair as a substitute for junk. These experiments failed, for the new barricades would not stop a musket bullet; and then, seemingly almost by accident, the idea occurred of forming the barricades of the hammocks.

It is not known how early the hammocks were stowed in nettings on deck, but a paper of 1746[1] shows that they were already so disposed, though without provision for keeping them dry. The inference is that hammock nettings were then of recent introduction. It was at this time that tarpaulin covers were first authorised, thus solving the barricade question. For 50 years this hammock barricade continued to give almost the only shelter available on deck.[2]

A small but noticeable change which began to be common about 1780 was the planking up of the space hitherto left between the drift and fife rails. The effective height of the protection was thus raised by about a foot, and an adequate bulwark was formed to the after part of the quarter-deck; but as the rails sheered down from aft forward, the fore part of the quarter-deck, and still more so that part of it which was abreast of the gangway drift, was still dependent in great measure on the barricade of hammocks for its protection.

In the frigates of the Seven Years' War a high open quarter-deck rail was worked above the fife rail. The ports were formed in this by stantions, as later in the poop rail of line-of-battle ships; and the barricade was presumably formed of hammocks. This rail for frigates continued in use till the early years of the French Revolutionary war, and then gave place to solid bulwarks,

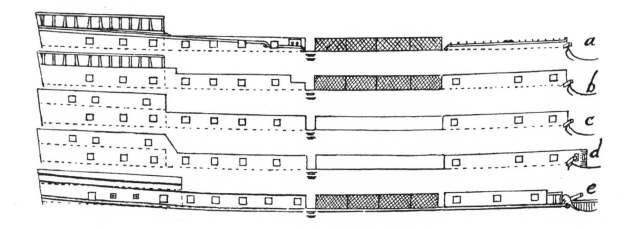

SQUARE HANCES
English: (a) 1797.   (b) 1800.   (c) 1810.   (d) 1820.   French: (e) *c.* 1800.

1. Navy Bd. to Admy. 26 Sep., 1746.   2. P. 169, fig. (a) shows the nettings from poop to waist. Fig. (b) is a netting crank.

which, introduced first in the frigates, were soon extended to ships of the line. These bulwarks ran parallel to the deck, their height being nearly 5ft., that is, high enough for the rail to close the upper edge of the ports, some of which hitherto had risen above the rail. This was first done on the quarter-deck, the most important station in action, then on the forecastle, and finally on the poop,[1] which from the introduction of carronades in 1780 had had an open timber rail some 4ft. 6 in. high. By 1800 this change was complete and was confirmed by a standing order. All new ships were so fitted, and all old ships as they came in hand for repair. The only exception was that ships with no poop carronades went without the poop bulwark till 1807, after which date poop carronades, and consequently the bulwark, became universal in ships of the line.[2]

This raising of the bulwarks, coupled with the tendency to flatten the sheer, greatly altered the appearance of the ships, and apparently old seamen regretted the change. The ship now looked more or less flat from end to end, with a high sharp rise for the poop; and the method of stowing the hammocks, so that the height of the nettings on quarter-deck, forecastle, and in the waist, was approximately the same, accentuated the absence of sheer. The old drift and fife rails were no longer of use, and consequently were abandoned in all new ships; but naval conservatism had its say, and for a few years the old rails were nailed on as mouldings on the outside of the bulwarks in old ships which had been altered to the new mode.[3] Thus

it is practically certain that at Trafalgar there were ships with the plain square unornamented bulwarks;[4] others, probably including the *Victory*, with the same bulwarks having the old rails nailed on to them and painted yellow;[3] and some ships, not recently in dockyard hands, with the old drift and fife rails, and the range of timber heads along the sides of the forecastle.

FOREIGN PRACTICE

From an early date the tendency was strong in Dutch ships to carry all rails right aft, and from the Dutch this fashion spread to the French and to other nations. Until more examples of foreign ships have been plotted it will not be possible to speak with certainty, but by 1730 the Dutch were building ships in which the drifts were not continued. This change of fashion, however, was probably never universal, and certainly was not permanent, for at the end of the century we again find the drifts all continued in Dutch ships,[5] as they are commonly seen also in the numerous bone models of French ships made by prisoners of war in England during the Napoleonic wars. Another minor feature which is found in both French and Dutch ships, and indeed commonly in all foreign ships save those which notoriously followed English fashions, was that as the quarter-deck was lengthened so was its drift, which was placed abreast the actual break of the deck, instead of remaining, as it did in English ships, in the position it had occupied early in the 18th century,

1. P. 170, figs. (a), (b), (c).   2. *Ibid*. figs. (c), (d).   3. *Ibid*. fig. (a).   4. *Ibid*. fig. (b).   5. *E.g.* Nance, Plate 105, the *Chattam*.

when the quarter-deck broke many feet abaft the mainmast. In other words, this means that in Dutch ships of the second half of the century the quarter-deck and gangway hances were very close together,[1] instead of being 12ft. or more apart; and in French ships sometimes there was a double hance[2] as in Dutch ships, or, more commonly, only the one break at the gangway.[3]

The French also were before us in raising the forecastle and poop bulwarks. In the middle of the century we still find an open rail and timber heads on the forecastle, but above a relatively high drift, and sometimes with a rail on top of the timber heads for part of the length of the forecastle, thus closing the upper side of the ports; but a solid bulwark to the poop seems to have become the rule during the American War, and to the forecastle from very soon after it. Another obvious feature is that from about 1740 French ships were built with less sheer than English; and as their high bulwarks ran at first nearly, and from about 1770, quite parallel to the decks, the absence of sheer and the hard breaks in the rails become useful for the purpose of identification.

No doubt these high bulwarks were there for the protection of the crew; and in this connection it is of interest to notice that Admiral Pâris thought[4] that in French ships the hammocks were not stowed in nettings till towards the end of Louis XVI's reign. It may well be that he places the date too late, for the point is a difficult one to determine; but we are probably justified in accepting the explanation that the high bulwarks were introduced as a substitute for the hammock barricade of English ships. It is interesting, therefore, to notice that by 1800 England had adopted the French fashion, and that France and other nations had copied the English method of stowing hammocks, so that the combination of the two methods was general. The French fashion of about 1800 is illustrated.[5]

§ 3. HANCING PIECES

A "hance" is a shoulder, or haunch, and in naval architecture means the step made by the drop of the rail at the top of the ship's side to a lowel level. Thus we have a hance where the poop rail ends, another for the quarter-deck, and others at the ends of the waist. As in early ships[6] these breaks were square and unsightly, the idea of disguising them by the application of ornament was introduced. In late Tudor ships this took the form of a plain bracket piece on top of the rail. In the early 17th century the fashion for compartmenting[7] seems to have suggested the addition of long drop hancing pieces, running several feet down the ship's side,[8] which are found sometimes alone, sometimes in conjunction with dogs or dolphins[9] on top of the rail. It will be seen that the famous *Sovereign of the Seas*[10] combined these modes in an interesting manner. At the ends of the waist she had bracket pieces with life-size human figures seated on them; at the other hances she had small brackets on the rail and drop pieces externally, that of the poop being continued by

1. *E.g.* Nance, Plate 105, the *Chattam*.　2. P. 176, figs. (b), (c), (e).　3. Nance, Plate 90; and p. 176, figs. (k) & (l).
4. "Musée de Marine", p. 70.　5. P. 170, fig. (e).　6. Plates 1, 5, 6.　7. P. 14.　8. P. 173, fig. (a).　9. P. 175, fig. (a).　10. Plate 9.

one of the verticals belonging to the compartmented scheme of decoration. The same system prevailed under the Commonwealth, though on not so elaborate a scale. The *Naseby* (fig. b), which may perhaps be accepted as the most elaborate ship of that period, had miniature seated figures, about 2ft. high, at the ends of the waist and at the poop hance, and had in addition standing figures, some 5ft. long, externally as drop pieces at all her hances.

These square drop pieces continue to occur in post-Restoration ships, but very much shortened, being generally only made long enough to act as terms to the rails which ended at each hance. They are perhaps of some interest, for it is possible to see in them the last trace of the verticals which the early Stuart ships borrowed from Tudor design; and they continued to be used, as an alternative method, till the reign of Anne, by which date they had become simple mouldings.

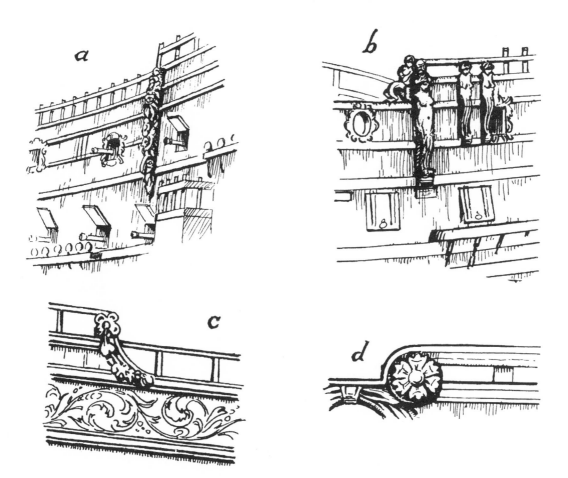

ENGLISH HANCING PIECES
(a) The *Constant Reformation*, 1618.   (b) The *Naseby*, 1655.   (c) The *Peregrine* galley, 1700.
(d) A 50-gun ship of 1703.

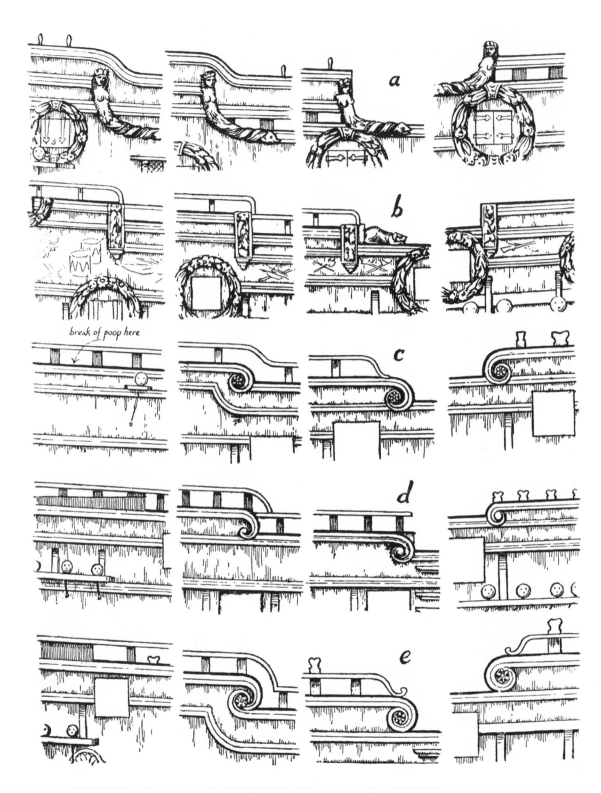

break of poop here

ENGLISH HANCING PIECES AND RAILS
(1670 TO 1730)

In Charles II's reign bracket hancing pieces continued to be combined with the drop pieces, usually taking the form of dogs, not uncommonly in ungraceful attitudes (fig. a). In William III's reign these dogs are found under the fife rails, as in the model of the *Boyne* of 1692 at Greenwich. It will be noticed that, when whole figures are used for drop hancing pieces, the hips and legs are often made disproportionately small.[1]

Instead of the drop piece a quadrant piece[2] was frequently used. It certainly occurs in northern ships before 1650 (*e.g.,* in the *Norske Löve*), and may have been used in English ships, though no certain instance of it earlier than 1660 has been noticed. It acted as a term to both fife and drift rail, its head frequently being carved into a bust, and its tail reconciled with the continuation aft of the drift next before it. It was thus the form most convenient to that fashion of rails in which each drift rail was continued aft under that next abaft it; and as that was the commonest fashion of rails from about 1670 to

about 1700, so too was the quadrant the commonest form of hancing piece.

Other fashions began to come in shortly before 1700, first the rosette, then the volute. The rosette by itself had no long vogue. It is found in 1703,[3] and till about 1730 a small rosette is often placed as a centre to a volute;[4] but the restrictive order of 1703 banished all but the most meagre ornamentation of the side, and thenceforward quadrant pieces, carved drop pieces, and dogs for brackets are seen no more. The volute almost immediately became universal, and so continued throughout the 18th century. There is little to be said about it, for it admitted but slight variation. It might be made single, where a rail ended, or double, when it formed a junction between two rails on different levels. It might be laid on top of the drift next to it, or the next rail might butt against it, these variants being decided by the height of the rail to which it was the term. Unlike the older finishings, it concerned one rail only, the drift rail. The corresponding fife rail was

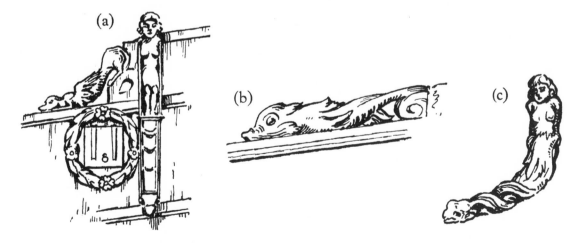

ENGLISH HANCING PIECES (17TH CENTURY)

1. *Cp.* p. 192.   2. P. 174, fig. (a); and p. 175, fig. (c).   3. P. 173, fig. (d).   4. P. 174, figs. (c) and (e).

DUTCH HANCING PIECES

otherwise disposed of, either hancing down in a quadrant when it was to be continued, or having its end curved up for a term.[1] Slight variants occur, but not often. With the raising of the bulwarks in 1800 hancing pieces of every kind were discontinued, the square breaks being entirely undisguised. It may be noticed as a curious throw back that the ironclad *Zealous*, of 1864, had life-sized female busts as poop hancing pieces.[2]

FOREIGN PRACTICE

In general no other nation used hancing pieces to anything like the extent that the English did. The Dutch in the 17th century not infrequently used dogs or the like as bracket pieces, but external pieces of any kind were little used. When there was no dog the hance was frequently quadrant shaped, but small and inconspicuous.[3] In the 17th century Dutch fashion seems to have pervaded Northern Europe, to be replaced in the 18th by the

English fashion of volutes, which towards the end of the century had become almost universal except in France. There were naturally minor differences: the Dutch, for instance, sometimes ended a rail in a convex quadrant, without forming a volute,[4] and occasionally they added some floral embellishment to a volute such as

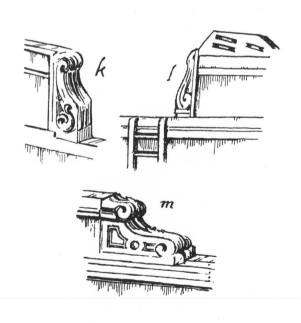

FRENCH HANCING PIECES

1. P. 174, figs. (c), (d), (e).　　2. I am indebted to Mr. Philip Castle for this information.　　3. Fig. (j).　　4. Fig. (c) is *c*. 1750; fig. (d) is 1804.

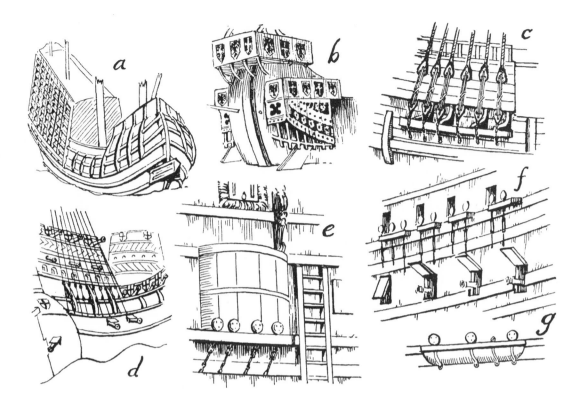

MISCELLANEOUS BROADSIDE FEATURES

(a) Clench work, *c.* 1560. (After Breughel.) (b) Pavesses and Hangings, 15th century. (After
Ambrogio.)   c) Channel with knees, *c.* 1520. (After Holbein.)   (d) Channel with clench-work,
c. 1540. (After Cott. Aug. I., ii., 57b.)   (e) Entering ladder and house in chains: the *Naseby*, 1655.
(f) Channel: the *Eendracht*, *c.* 1665. (After Van de Velde.)
(g) Chock under channel: the *Swift*, sloop, 1721. (Admy. draught.)

English ships never had.[1] The Spaniards
followed the English fashion closely.
Chapman introduced the same fashion
into Sweden and handled it with an added
grace.[2] Only the French were nearly
immune from the volute. When they used
any hancing piece at all, it was almost
invariably a bracket piece on top of the
rail, a beast or a beast's head in the 17th
century, but in the 18th a plain bracket
lightly carved on its out-board side.[3] The
very plain hances with Greek key (facing
page) are from a Mediterranean polacca
of the early 19th century.[4]

§ 4. CHANNELS

Channels are hardly ornamental in
themselves, but they force themselves on
the attention. The word itself is a corruption of "chain wale", the wale to which
were fastened the chains which held the
lower ends of the shrouds. At first clearly
the shrouds were brought down to one of
the wales already existing (fig. d), and it
may be assumed that, when ships began
to be built with a great tumblehome, the
spread thus gained was decided to be inadequate, and in consequence a projecting
shelf was added to the wale. This would

1. P. 176, figs. (a), (b) are 1768; figs. (e), (h), (i), are *c.* 1800.   2. P. 169.   3. P. 176, figs. (k), (l), (m).
4. Dutch by ownership, but probably not so by origin.

seem to have begun in the 15th century,[1] for the mainmast only, the foremast still being relatively insignificant. Even in the middle of the 16th century the main and fore channels were still at different levels, the main being low on the hull proper, while the fore shrouds, like those of the mizzen mast, ended on the superstructure; but it is by no means certain that a projecting shelf was, even in Elizabeth's reign, always or even usually fitted. As late as 1540 there was sometimes no shelf, and clench pieces were fitted between the chains to strengthen the side locally.[2] But whatever the usage, in this reign the foremast came to be on a par with the main, and its shrouds, however attached, were brought down to the same level.

The "chain wale", certainly from 1590 and probably a good deal earlier, was the wale above the lower deck guns, as it continued to be till after 1700. When, in the 17th century,[3] the wales came to be placed in pairs, the "Channel wales", as they had now come to be called, were the middle pair in three-decked ships, and the upper pair in two-deckers. The channel was attached to the upper of the pair, and had for its support chains below and curved spurs or knees above. A drawing by Holbein, *i.e.*, of *c.* 1520, in the Städel Institute, Frankfort, shows a ship with knees above her channels.[4] It may perhaps be inferred that the spurs, which seem to have been commonly fitted in large ships in the 17th century, became necessary as the width of the channel increased. The chains were carried only to the lower wale of the same pair, which gave them a sharp angle with the shrouds. This arrangement lasted till 1706, when,

after experimenting with two ships, the Navy Board decided to raise the channels of three-deckers to the wales above the middle deck guns. In some small craft, instead of brackets of any kind, a solid chock was fitted under the whole length of the channel. The drawing[5] shows how this was done in the *Swift* sloop of 1721.

This change brought another; for, there being often only a single upper wale in three-decked ships, a new way of attaching the chains had to be devised. They were carried down to the wale next below, *i.e.*, to the upper middle wale, a change which by reducing the angle which they made with the channel must have increased their strength greatly. Shortly afterwards the strain was still further distributed, the end of the chain being attached to the ship's side at two points instead of one. This gain in strength lessened the need for the spurs above the channel, which immediately began to go out of use. From about 1705 to 1735 they are still met with, but in the latter part of this period never alone, half or all of them being replaced by small knees or brackets.[6] Then the brackets went on alone for a short time, and finally disappeared in their turn. The experience of the three-deckers with the improved attachment of the chains being satisfactory, the new mode of fitting them was immediately copied by two-decked and smaller ships, which however did not shift their channels up a deck. Thus all ships from 1704 for 40 years had their channels under the upper-deck guns. In English ships of force the gun ports were never allowed to cut the channels, but in small craft apparently this sometimes happened.

1. M.M. II, 283.   2. P. 177, fig. (d).   3. P. 159.   4. P. 177 fig. (c).   5. *Ibid.* fig. (g).   6. P. 158.

Probably, however, this was rare, for only one instance of it, that of the *Cruizer*, sloop, of 1732, has been noticed. In her both the fore and main channels were neatly bisected by a gun port.

The next change was to raise the channels above the upper-deck guns, and this was done in all ships in or about 1745. Once up, they remained up in two-deckers and the smaller ships, but curiously enough in the three-deckers they were lowered again a dozen years later. Thus Kempenfelt's *Royal George*, launched in 1756, had them above the upper-deck guns; but Nelson's *Victory*, begun in 1759 and launched in 1765, had them between the middle and upper tiers.[1] About thirty years later they were again raised, this time for a full due. The two-decked or "spar-decked" frigates of the early 19th century did not count as two-deckers, and, at least at first, kept their channels below the upper tier of guns.

What has been said refers only to the main and fore channels: those of the mizzen, relatively insignificant, were almost invariably placed a deck higher; but after the final raising of the main channels, the mizzen sometimes were not raised, but were left on the same level as the others. Backstay stools can only be said to have been placed where convenient in order to be clear of the ports; but latterly, when the channels came up above the upper-deck guns, there were fewer ports to avoid, and it was often found simplest to place the deadeyes of the backstays on the after end of the

channel. A stool when used was generally placed higher than the channel.

Perhaps it is desirable to mention the little house in the main chains, which though not very often shown in pictures, and never in models, was a regular feature of ships of the 17th century.[2] About 1705 – the exact date has not been determined – it was entirely superseded by the round houses of the head.

FOREIGN PRACTICE

In the 17th century the Dutch seem to have suffered some inconvenience from their keeping the wales of each pair wider apart than we did. One result of this was that if the lower of the pair of channel wales was placed high enough to clear the lower deck guns, the upper of the pair as it sheered up, especially aft, was cut by the upper-deck ports. If, therefore, the channels were to be placed on this wale they would have to be in bits between the ports; and this was commonly the case in Dutch ships down to about 1680.[3] Then they got out of the difficulty by raising the channels to above the guns; and when after 1685 they experimented for awhile in building three-deckers, they placed the channels above the middle tier. The French seem to have been the first to place the channels above the upper-deck guns. They are so shown in 1626 (M.M. III, 376), in a two-decker, and also about 1665.[4] After the Seven Years' War they raised them also in three-decked ships.

1. *Cp.* p. 158, "1st rate *c.* 1760", with the *Victory*, Plate 53.   2. P. 177, fig. (e).   3. *Ibid.* fig. (f).   4. Plate 14.

Thus England was the last to raise the channels. A notable peculiarity is that in the latter part of the 18th century the Dutch, keeping all three channels on the same level, sometimes joined up the main and mizzen channels into one long shelf, which ran nearly half the length of the ship. In a model this feature is conspicuous:[1] in a picture probably it would rarely show. One is tempted to see in this shelf a lineal descendant of that which seems sometimes to have been fitted about 200 years before;[2] and it is at least permissible to assume that, as formerly, it was used for stowage of some kind, whether of steep tubs and harness casks or of spare spars. The same feature is found in the French 100-gun ship *Hercule* of 1837.[3]

The curious little turret on the side of the upper-deck, close abaft the head, in the "Navire Royale" of Hondius (M.M. IV., 33), and in another French ship built in Holland, also in 1626 (M.M. III., 376), has been found in no other ship. It seems to have been peculiar to the French, and there is little doubt that it was the ancestor of the later round house in the head, which is found in French ships about 1690. Just as in English ships, the house was moved forward from the fore end of the quarter gallery to the main chains, so it is possible that in French ships it may, at about the same time, have been moved aft from its position of 1626 into the fore chains. But this has not been proved.

Apparently the Dutch kept the very short chains, of 17th century fashion, to a later date than other nations. A model of a 40-gun two-decker (unnamed, but assigned to 1756) in the Scheepvaart Museum shows them so fitted. Also models show knees securing the channels of French ships at least as late as 1785: these are of the *Protecteur*, and an unnamed 40-gun frigate with four gun-ports and 20 oar-ports a side on the lower deck, both in the Louvre. Backstay stools rarely appear in Dutch ships.

§ 5. GUN PORTS

A port literally means a door; and from this name alone, were not the fact otherwise established, it would be possible to decide that the entering port was the first port to be so described. From this all other considerable openings in the ship's sides derived their name, so that we have gun-ports, oar-ports, ballast-ports, the helm or rudder-port, and in merchantmen "raft-ports", which later were called timber-ports. The only purpose in mentioning the raft-port is to call attention to its presence in the famous carrack drawing by W.A., which seems to show that it existed before the gun-port.

The 15th century ship of war mounted very few heavy guns, and such as she had fired over the gunwale in the waist.[4] The rest of her armament consisted of small pieces, mounted in the superstructures, that is, above the hull proper. The scheme of decoration which came down from the dark period of the Middle Ages[5] provided openings in the sides of the superstructure by

1. *E.g.* in the *Washington* model in the "Mercury" Museum.   2. M.M. III, 321.   3. Pâris, "Musée de Marine", Plate 47.
4. (Original) Frontispiece.   5. P. 11; and Plate 5.

a free use of arcaded work. The many arches so formed served as windows to the cabin space, as loopholes for archers, and, when guns came to be mounted, as holes for the guns to fire through. Thus as long as the small guns that could be carried high up in the superstructures formed the greater part of the armament, as they did till about 1500, there was no need to cut holes for the guns in the sides of the ship: those which already existed answered the purpose.

Whether or not we believe that an ingenious shipwright of Brest invented gun-ports, cut through the solid side of the ship, in 1500 – remembering that whoever did so quite probably drew his inspiration from pre-existing raft-ports or scuttles – it is at least certain that gun-ports began to appear about that date. At first they seem to have been round, presumably because a gun was cylin-drical; but very shortly they were made square because, as we may suppose, it was not easy to contrive a close-fitting lid to a round hole. The attempt, however, seems to have been made occasionally, and for over a century a few instances of round-lidded ports are met with.[1]

We are not here concerned with the development of the gun armament, and may pass it by with a bare mention that by 1540 there was a complete lower deck of guns, mounted in square-lidded ports, while for the guns above that deck the old method sufficed. As the century went on there was considerable simplification in the armament, till towards the end of Elizabeth's reign ships had in all essentials assumed the features which lasted to the end of the wooden ship era. But unless importance is attached to a doubtful mention of 1598, they had not yet begun to treat

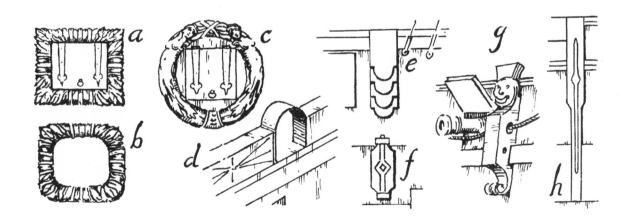

MISCELLANEOUS BROADSIDE DETAILS
(a) (b) (c) English wreath ports, 17th century.
(d) Entering port of French 120-gun ship. (Prisoner-of-war model.)   (e) to (h) Chesstrees, viz.:
(e) Dutch, 1796.   (f) French, 1780.   (g) Danish, *c.* 1630.   (h) Swedish, 1767.

1. Pp. 182, 187.

their ports decoratively.[1] The gun-port was plain and square, with its lid, as afterwards, usually hinged on the upper edge; but this was not an invariable rule, for occasionally, especially in Spanish ships, the port-lid was hinged like a door at its fore edge; as also in Dutch cromsters of *c.* 1600.[2]

This was man-of-war fashion. We have Raleigh's testimony that Easterling hulks "were wont to paint great red portholes in their broad sides, where they carried no ordnance at all", from which we may infer that round ports, probably carried high above the water, were still common enough in merchant ships.[3] There is indeed other evidence of it besides Raleigh's.

The great growth of ship ornamentation which began in 1598 soon extended itself to the ports, and from James I's reign those of the upper-deck and above began to be surrounded with carvings. The earliest instances available are the *Phœnix* of 1612,[4] which has in her forecastle circular chase ports surrounded by intertwined snakes; and the *Constant Reformation* of 1618,[5] which shows two arched wreath ports a side on the half deck, all the rest being plain. The *Prince Royal* of 1610 had "great lion heads for the round ports" of the upper-deck, but no representation of these is to be had. It may be assumed that they were similar to the mask quarter ports of the *Prince* of 1670,[6] one of which is illustrated.

But lions' masks for ports were not common; the decoration was usually in the form of a wreath of foliage with or without flowers and fruit,[7] but more rarely was composed of two figures.[8] When on an open deck these ports usually had no lids and could without inconvenience be cut round, but when in the cabin spaces they had a square lid fitted inside the wreath. Such ports as were above the channels commonly had their lids fitted as a pair of folding doors,[9] because there was not room inside the shrouds to haul up a lid fitted in the usual way. Double casement lids are also found to the wreath ports in the waist of the *Prince* of 1670, and of the *Britannia* of 1682. They occur also, perhaps experimentally, under the channels of a frigate of about 1760.[10]

It would be too much to say that wreath ports were a peculiarity of English men-of-war, because they occur occasionally in ships of most, or probably of all other nations; but quite certainly they never became elsewhere the invariable rule as they did in England. It may be that the *Prince Royal* was the first ship to show this kind of decoration in any form; but it would seem that the fashion established itself, for a painting by Willaerts, dating from 1619,[11] shows a complete tier of wreath ports on the upper-deck of a large English ship. The *Sovereign of the Seas*,[12] however, had wreaths only to her half-deck, quarter-deck, and forecastle ports. Her upper-deck ports were ornamented by vertical carvings, which were carried up to the gunwale: indeed the position of these verticals, which form a conspicuous feature in the compartmented scheme of decoration adopted

1. Oppenheim, "Administration of R.N.", 131.   2. M.M. V, 48.   3. *Cp.* M.M. II, 65 *sq.*, esp. p. 74 (13).   4. Plate 1.   5. M.M. IX, 58.
6. P. 184, fig. (e).   7. P. 175, fig. (a); p. 174, figs. (a), (b); p. 192.   8. P. 181, fig. (c).   9. P. 158; P. 184, fig. (a); and Plate 4.
10. M.M. VII, 49.   11. M.M. III, 321.   12. Plate 9.

for the *Sovereign*, was determined by the position of the ports.

A drawing believed to represent the *Prince Royal* as rebuilt in 1641 shows the ports unornamented,[1] but the great ships built under the Commonwealth all show some wreath ports. The *Naseby* of 1655, for example, had square wreaths to her upper-deck ports except in the open waist, where they were round; her quarter-deck ports also had round wreaths, and the aftermost of them was abaft the upper finishing of the quarter gallery.

Several of Van de Velde's drawings,[2] and the draughts of ships of all rates in Anthony Deane's "Doctrine of Naval Architecture", show that the early Restoration ships, or at any rate some of them, followed the Commonwealth fashion in this matter of square wreaths;[3] but the circular wreath prevailed, and within a few years had become almost universal. When we think of the typical late Stuart or William III ship we picture her, quite rightly, with round wreath ports everywhere from the upper-deck upwards; but a few instances of square wreathed ports are still to be found. A quarter-deck port abaft the upper finishing is seen in the *Prince* model of 1670, after which date, by the growth of the gallery, there ceased to be room there for it.[4] It will be noticed also that the circular gun-ports in both the quarter galleries and the stern, which are very conspicuous in Commonwealth, and less so in early Restoration ships,[5] soon ceased to be used. Towards the end of the period all stern chase ports, of which as many as 14 are found in a

three-decked ship, and also the chase ports in the beakhead-bulkhead, were cut square, their port lids usually being elaborately carved[6] to harmonise with their surroundings.

An order issued by the Navy Board in March, 1687, forbidding the fitting of wreath ports in ships of 50 guns and under seems to have had no effect. There were in fact no small new ships, if we except a bomb vessel or two, built during the rest of James II's short reign; and after the Revolution the order was certainly a dead letter. Wreath ports to all guns on the upper-deck and above it continued to be the invariable rule till 1703. The restrictive order of that year succeeded in banishing them entirely from the upper-deck; but on the quarter-deck and forecastle they lingered for a few more years, and then for yet another few years circular mouldings surrounded the quarter-deck ports. It is doubtful if any ship launched after the accession of George I had even the round mouldings.

There are two minor exceptions to this rule. Royal yachts continued throughout the century to have wreaths to their ports, and these wreaths occasionally, as in the *Catherine* of 1720, were intermediate between round and square.[7] Also frigates, which had a pair of round or oval chase ports in their tafferel, sometimes during the American War and down to 1796 had light wreaths of carved foliage round these ports. In ships built in India this seems to have occurred at least as late as 1809.[8]

1. M.M. IV, 129.   2. *E.g.* Plate 11.   3. P. 181, fig. (a).   4. The *Prince* of 1670 had a light as well as a port in this position.
5. Plates 11, 27.   6. P. 184, fig. (h).   7. P. 181, fig, (b).   8. Plate 37.

From at least the date of the *Sovereign of the Seas* it had been common to decorate the inside of port lids with painted masks of lions:[1] indeed one draught suggests that the *Sovereign* may also have had carved lions' masks on the outside of her port lids. The fashion continued for the inside of the ports at any rate till George II's reign, before which time, if the evidence of models may be accepted, the masks were sometimes replaced by human faces. These were occasionally full face and after the Chinese manner,[2] occasionally of Greek type, either full face or in profile.

Very little reference is necessary here to half ports, which were neither conspicuous nor ornamental; but it is worth noticing that because, as is commonly the case, upper-deck ports in the 18th century are lidless, it does not follow that they could not be closed. It was a complaint of the Navy Board that when port lids to upper-deck guns were provided, the captains frequently unhung them and left them ashore, preferring to use half ports. The difference of opinion seems to have been due to the gradual abolition of lights cut through the side;[3] and the solution of the difficulty to have been found in the fitting of glazed sashes to the ports in the cabin space under the quarter-deck, while retaining the lids of the ports.[1]

It is noticed elsewhere[4] that the introduction of carronades caused a rail with

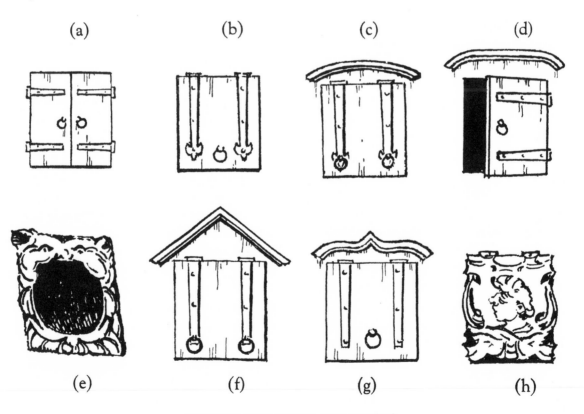

ENGLISH GUN-PORTS AND RIGOLS

1. P. 195, fig. (b).   2. P. 18, figs. (a), (b), (c).   3. P. 196.   4. P. 170.

ports to be built on the poop, and that after a period of experimenting a definite order was issued in 1800 that the quarter-deck and forecastle were to be barricaded for carronades. This affects the ports in two ways. First, because with the old low drift and fife rails the forecastle ports and the foremost ports on the quarter-deck were open on top;[1] or, in the case of the quarter-deck ports, had their tops closed by arching the fife rail over them, as was commonly done in French ships. Secondly, because a carronade port was much bigger than that for a 6, 9 or even 12 pr. long gun. It will be found that during the carronade period the quarter-deck and forecastle ports are frequently of two sizes, large ports for carronades, small ports for long guns in wake of the rigging.

It is perhaps worth mentioning, as a thing very noticeable both in models and pictures, that while English frigates carried two or three guns a side on the lower deck from 1676 to the establishment of 1741, this fashion was continued in France till a much later date, and at the time of the War of Independence was adopted by the Americans, presumably from their allies. Thus the *Bonhomme Richard*, French-built East Indiaman, and the *Alfred* and *Columbus*, American-built ships, were armed in this way. Indeed, the French still had ships mounting guns thus during the early part of the Revolutionary War.

One or two small changes were made in the fitting of ports towards the close of the century. Thus in 1778 it was ordered that a scuttle should be cut in every other gun-deck port, and in 1789 that it should be cut in every port. These scuttles, for lighting and airing the lower deck, were like oar-ports and hinged laterally.[2] In 1809 in addition "illuminators", which was the official term for glass bull's-eyes, were fitted in the same ports: they were not needed for the middle deck and above, on which half ports were regularly used in moderate weather. Finally in 1796 there was an order that the lids of stern chase ports, when heavy or inconvenient, might be hinged in two pieces, an upper and a lower.[3] The *Victory* was one of the ships so fitted, and has her chase ports thus to-day.

Small points which have not been noticed are that the strap hinges of the ports in the 17th century were gener-ally made flory at the ends, whereas in the 18th they were square; also that after about 1700 two rings for port ropes were put on the outsides of the ports of the heavier guns, instead of only one as formerly.[4]

FOREIGN PRACTICE

To compare Dutch ships with English is not always entirely satisfactory; for many of the best models of Dutch ships represent East Indiamen, whereas of English East Indiamen recognised models are exceedingly rare. The case with regard to pictures is the same, though to a less extent, for there are some good English oil paintings of East Indiamen from the latter part of the 17th century onward. In the main it may be said that the Indiaman was very like the man-of-war, in England even more so than in the Netherlands.

1. P. 168, figs. (b) and (c).   2. P. 186 fig. (f).   3. As in the *Adolf Frederick*, p. 105; not closing round the gun as in p. 186, fig. (e).
4. P. 184, figs. (b), (c), (f), (g).

So it happens that when it is noticed that Houtman's ship has her upper-deck ports in the waist all fitted with double casement lids, or that the *Prins Willem* model of 1651 and the *Ary* of 1725 have upper-deck wreath ports,[1] it is impossible to decide from such examples what was regular Dutch usage. But it is probably not far wrong to say that in the States' ships the upper-deck ports were square, lidded, and plain in the 17th century, and that early in the 18th century the fashion came in of finishing them with a square moulding,[2] which was retained till late in the century, perhaps till about 1780. Two examples are also given, from models of about 1800, of Dutch ports fitted as lights.[3]

Another minor feature of 17th century Dutch Indiamen was the fitting of a board loop-holed for musketry in the waist.[4] This seems to have been fairly general, and perhaps if we had models of English Indiamen of the middle 17th century, we might find it in them too. These loop-holes also occur in a Dutch 40-gun two-decker of 1756, as shown by a model in the Scheepvaart Museum. In the interesting Mediterranean ships illustrated in "Ancient English Shipwrightry" something of the same kind is seen. Between the upper and lower deck guns there is a third tier of ports, which are round and very small. From the size of the ship and of the ports these cannot represent a middle deck of guns; but

DETAILS OF DUTCH GUN-PORTS AND LIGHTS

1. The *Ary*'s being square: *cp.* p. 186, fig (d), from a 17th cent. merchant ship.   2. P. 186, fig. (a).   3. *Ibid.* figs. (b), (c).   4. P. 199, fig. (a).

as it is easily calculable that the loop-holes are not more than 5ft. above the lower deck, the inference seems clear that they were for the use of small arm men, probably arquebusiers. A similar arrangement has not been noticed in extra-Mediterranean ships, whether of the late 16th century or later.

The examples collected by Mr. Nance[1] show that in the 17th century wreath ports were to be found on the open decks, *i.e.*, the quarter-deck, forecastle, and even in the waist, of the ships of most Northern nations, but never right along the upper-deck, or elsewhere where the ports had a deck above them and consequently needed lids. An interesting Danish ship of the early 18th century combines casement[2] ports in the waist with double casement lids in the wake of the rigging and circular ports on the quarter-deck. To English seamen this, apparently studied, lack of uniformity must have seemed incongruous. Corresponding to the lion faces in English ships, other nations also painted national emblems on the inside of their port lids.

In French ships ports with round lids opening sideways are found once, in 1626. At the end of the 17th century the upper ports were either surrounded by mouldings or made plain, but arched;[3] and traces of this fashion survived till late in the 18th

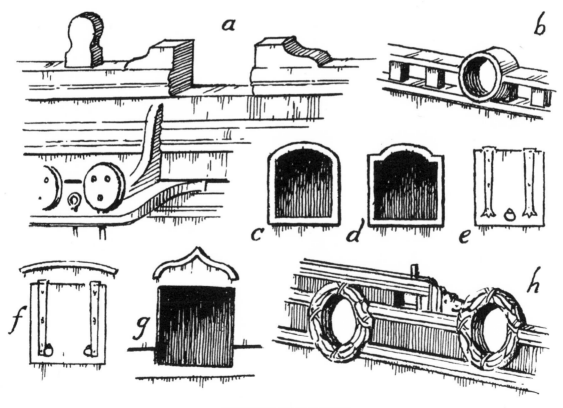

FRENCH GUN-PORTS

1. "Sailing-ship Models" plates 36, 41, 47, 79.   2. P. 184, fig. (a).
3. P. 187, fig (d) is from the *Soleil Royal*, 1690; fig. (c) from the *Royal Louis*, 1758. *Cp.* p. 42.

century in the occasional arching of the rail over a quarter-deck or forecastle port. It does not seem to have been imitated elsewhere, unless we accept as authentic in all particulars the modern model of the *Christianus V* of 1673,[1] which in almost every respect shows a remarkably French-looking ship. The so-called "*Royal Louis, 1692*", model at the Louvre, which seems to represent the ship launched in 1758, has wreath ports on her poop and forecastle;[2] the *Paris*, ornamented by Puget, has a few wreaths;[3] while the *Soleil Royal*, Tourville's ship, had plain rings[4] let into the poop and forecastle rails. The lower deck ports of the same ship show flory hinges very slightly different from the English pattern.[5] The "Pic" model of 1755, and that of a heavy frigate of 1785, both at the Louvre, show guns firing over a rail with a cleat on each side to form a port.[6]

The chief peculiarity of Spanish ships of the early 18th century was the smallness of their ports; but occasionally a trace of Dutch influence appears in a square moulding round those of the upper-deck. Occasionally a port may be found ornamented when it served for a light: this is shown, for instance, in the draught of the frigate *Grana*, taken off in 1781, which has over her aftermost gun-deck port a carved canopy or rigol supported by carved brackets.[7]

As is well known, French ships, till quite the end of the 18th century, put no guns in the great cabin, which means that the two or three aftermost quarter-deck ports were omitted, and lights placed there instead; but as these lights were both smaller than ports, and a couple of feet higher from the deck, they cannot be mistaken for gun ports.[8]

§ 6. ENTERING PORTS

Entering ports, as distinct from entering places, appear to have been essentially a feature of English ships. As long as the side was only a deck or two high, men were content to climb up it at its lowest point and enter the ship over the gunwale of the waist; but when the side rose to three decks the climb, especially in a ship at sea, was a stiff one, and an entering port, a regular door, was generally provided on the middle deck. The Hampton Court picture of the embarkation of Henry VIII shows the king himself climbing a ladder from a boat alongside to the waist, no great height in those days; but two or three centuries later to enter a three-decker over the nettings was something of a feat. St. Vincent recommended it for exercise: "Calder," we remember him saying to his first captain, "the lieutenants of the fleet are running infernally to belly. Seal up the entering port, and make them come in over the hammocks."

Apparently no Tudor ships, not even the *Ark Royal*, were thus provided, and the earliest entering port noticed is that of the *Prince Royal*. As in the *Sovereign of the Seas*[9] it was on the middle deck at the fore end of the main channel, but the several pictures of the *Prince*

---

1. Nance, Plate 34.   2. P. 187, fig. (h).   3. Plate 33.   4. P. 187, fig. (b).   5. *Ibid.* fig. (e).   6. *Ibid.* fig. (a).   7. Plate 50.
8. P. 145, fig. (a), which shows the lights altered to ports.   9. Plate 9.

leave so many details obscure that it is not certain whether in her it did not take the place of a gun port. In the *Sovereign*, as was the regular practice for 100 years, it was between two gun ports. The early Stuart practice, as may be seen from the *Constant Reformation* and *Antelope*,[1] was to put an entering port on the middle deck of all three-deckers, however small, even though, like the *Antelope*, they were not in the later sense three-deckers, but had only a spar deck in the waist. These ports had elaborate carvings, but no wide projecting canopy over them as was introduced later. There were cleat steps up the side for ordinary mortals, but an accommodation ladder of modern pattern was rigged on occasion.[2] The stowage of such a ladder in a relatively small ship must have been a nuisance, but it was not till 1756 that accommodation ladders were abolished by order.[3] The cleat steps ran past the entering port to the gangway, so that entrants according to their degree, and the discipline of the ship, might use the one or the other. Sometimes in the 18th century a step here and there, roughly every sixth one, was made longer than the others; presumably both so that men might stand aside to allow others to pass, and also for the use of the side boys. In one Dutch ship of the early 19th century a step near the top has on each side of it a little cleat step quite separate from it.[4]

One little riddle connected with entering ports is as to whether they were fitted on one side of the ship or on both. If we assume, as perhaps etymologically

we are entitled to do, that the original entering place was on the port side, we would expect to find that ships having only one entering port had it on the port side. Thus, because the pictures of all the ships already named show only the port side, we have no certain means of knowing whether they had not also a port on the starboard side; but an artist's preference for the port side seems to suggest that this decorative feature was absent from the other.

The experience of later ships bears out this supposition, for down to about 1670 whenever an entering port is shown it is on the port side; and when the starboard side is shown there is none.[5] Early Restoration three-decked models confirm this. The earliest model showing an entering port on each side, which can be dated with any degree of certainty, is that in the Royal United Service Institution, which probably represents the *Royal James* of 1671, while Van de Velde's draught of the *Royal Charles* of 1673 shows none to starboard. After this date it seems likely that all first-rates had two entering ports; but the second-rates of the 1676 programme appear to have had either one or two indifferently. From the fact that some at least of the 80-gun ships of the 1690 programme,[6] which had not yet developed into three-deckers, had two entering ports, it may probably be inferred that the rule in that reign was to fit two or none. There is even one remarkable model at Greenwich (which is described as the "*Victory*, 17th century", but probably represents the *Royal Anne* of 1704) which has four entering ports, two a side.[7] These consist of a pair on

1. M.M. IX, 58, 59. 2. Plate 9. 3. Admy. Navy Bd. 2507, No. 440. 4. Fig. on p. 194.
5. M.M. II, 238; IV, 27, 129; and *cp.* N.R.S. "First Dutch War", I, 11. 6. Nance, Plate 46. Seemingly a later ship of the class: the *Boyne* has none.
7. P. 190, fig. (d).

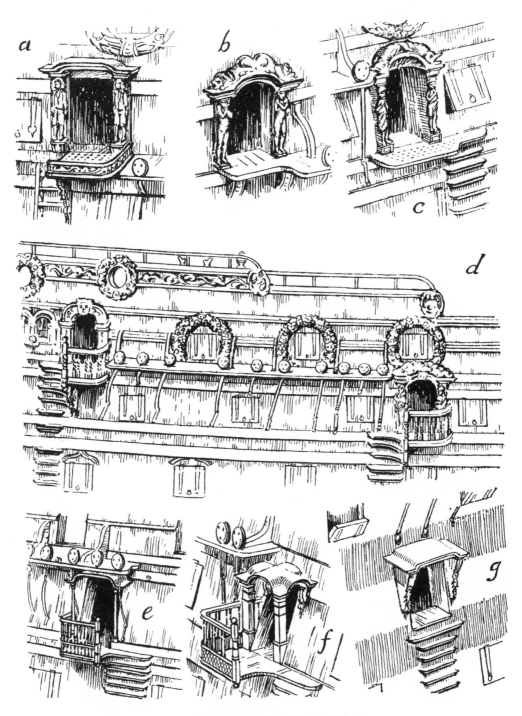

ENGLISH ENTERING PORTS

(a) The *Prince*, 1670.   (b) Mr. R. C. Anderson's model (? the *St. Andrew*, 1670).
(c) Based on the "100-gun ship" model (*Greenwich*).   (d) The "*Victory*, 17th century",
probably the *R. Anne*, 1704. (*Greenwich*).   (e) The *Victory*, 1737.   (f) The *Victory*, 1765.
(g) The *Queen*, 1839.

the middle deck in the normal position, between the 6th and 7th gun ports from aft, and of another pair on the upper-deck made out of what should be the 4th gun ports from aft. This, it should be said, is the first certain instance of the use of a gun port for an entering port, though there is an unidentified draught of the middle of the 17th century, believed to represent a project which was not carried out, and showing the middle deck gun port next before the main channel converted to an entering port and fitted with double doors. The next earliest example noticed of the use of a gun port is of 1717; the latest of an entering port between two gun ports is 1725. This applies to all three-deckers, 100, 90 and 80-gun ships alike.

One peculiarity of the official sheer draughts of English ships is that they invariably show the starboard side; thus when they show an entering port at all, they imply the presence of one also to port. Now from ships laid down in 1706 onwards they show, with a few exceptions which probably can be explained, an entering port in all three-deckers, including the first of the rebuilt 80-gun ships, to starboard.

Just as during the Napoleonic wars we occasionally hear of a ship increasing her force by putting a gun, unofficially perhaps, in each entry port, so in the middle of the century we find the same thing done officially. At the end of the Seven Years' War it was decided to increase somewhat the armament of the second rates, and the draughts show that, in ships launched between 1766 and

1777, this was done by fitting a gun port instead of an entering port. There seems to be no doubt as to the omission, for there were in those ships as many middle deck guns as there were ports. In a few draughts, however, of other classes, *e.g.*, the *Britannia*, 100, of 1757, no entering port is shown, though a comparison of the number of ports with the number of guns shows that there was a port to spare for the purpose. Presumably in these cases the entering ports were fitted; but it is at least curious to find that, in a model made from such a draught, the entry port may be equally omitted. This is shown for instance, in the model at the Royal United Service Institution illustrating the project, not carried out, for rebuilding the *Victory* in 1802 as a 110-gun ship. It would be idle to suppose that there was any real intention then of sending her to sea without entering ports. There is nothing to add of later practice, which accepted the two entry ports as regular and inevitable.

As for the ornamental design of these entry ports not very much can be said, for pictures almost without exception are too small to show detail, the sheer draughts only show them in one or two instances, and there are relatively few models to help, owing to this feature having been almost confined to three-deckers. To a considerable extent the design followed that of the belfry. In the 17th century there was always an arch over the port, and this was usually but not invariably carved. For example, the *Prince* of 1670 has a plain arch supported on caryatids,[1] while another model of about the same date[2] has two

1. P. 190, fig. (a).   2. *Ibid*. fig. (b).

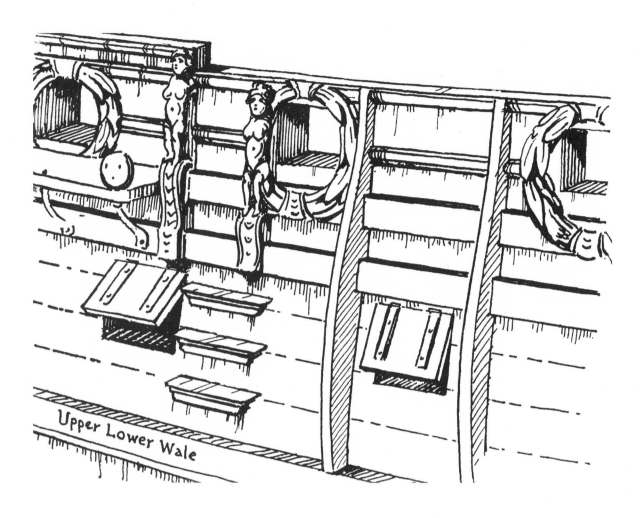

Upper Lower Wale

ENTERING PLACE OF THE *MORDAUNT*, 1682

lions lying on the arch. The restricting order of 1703 did away with the lions and other beasts with which the arch had been overloaded.[1] The graceful flat arched canopies of the 18th century were supported on their outboard side by turned or square pillars, the heels of which, owing to the great tumblehome of the middle deck, rested on the side of the ship. These canopies early in the century were most commonly formed of a flat single arch,[2] under which and above the port a shell design was sometimes worked; but from about 1740 the canopy of crossing arches became the usual form.[3] A gable instead of an arch is found in one of the three-decked 80-gun ships, the *Somerset* of 1731; but this form seems to have been rare. About the end of the century, when the tumblehome of the side had been much reduced, this wide canopy and its pillars were replaced by a narrower single arch carried on carved brackets, a form which continued in use in the 19th century. The example of it illustrated is taken from the model of the *Queen* of 1839.[4]

1. P. 190, fig. (c).   2. *Ibid*. fig. (e).   3. *Ibid*. fig. (f).   4. *Ibid*. fig. (g).

The earliest entry ports had no platform or landing in front of them, and the steps ran up under them; but in the Restoration period it became the rule either to fit a landing or to use the fore end of the main channel as such, and this necessitated the placing of the steps at the side of the port. After 1704, when the channels went up above the middle deck guns, an entering port platform continued to be fitted till about 1760, from which time the steps under the port again became the rule.[1] These platforms were balustraded, often very handsomely. Commonly the steps were on the fore side of the port from the Restoration onwards, but in a few cases entrance was from the after side of the platform. This is shown in the *Sovereign of the Seas*; in a model belonging to the Earl of Sandwich and representing possibly the *Royal James* of 1675; and also in the so-called "*Victory*" model at Greenwich, which is believed to be the *Royal Anne* of 1704.[2]

The entering place on the upper-deck had normally no ornament, unless the gangway hancing piece may be placed to its credit. Once in a way, however, when there was a drop hancing piece at the fore end of the gangway, *i.e.*, at the after side of the entering place, a second similar piece was fitted so that the entering place lay between the two. This feature is illustrated from the model of the *Mordaunt* of 1682[3] in the "Mercury" Museum at Hamble. It appears also in the model of one of the 90-gun ships of the 1676 programme, now in the possession of the New York Yacht Club.[4]

Oar ports were never treated decoratively. They were about a foot square, strengthened with a horseshoe band, the ends of which formed the hinges on the fore side of the port.[5] There is a continuous history of auxiliary oars in men-of-war from the balingers of the Middle Ages, through the row-barges of Henry VIII, the pinnaces of Elizabeth and James I, the Whelps, and latterly through galleys and frigates right down into the 19th century. In smaller ships, which hoped to get some degree of speed with their oars, the ports were commonly placed either on a deck below the guns, or one on each side of a gun-port; in larger ships there was one between each pair of gun-ports, but latterly only six or eight a side were fitted.

FOREIGN PRACTICE

The Dutch never used entering ports, presumably because they only once attempted the building of three-decked ships, and that for so few years that the innovation had not time to make its way. It is more curious that the French, who from the 17th century onwards built many three-deckers, also almost invariably did without them. A drawing by Goussier after Belin, in the French Encyclopædia of 1769, shows an entry port on the starboard side of the middle deck in a ship of about 1700 or soon after. Belin's date was 1703 to 1722; but it may be doubted whether the drawing represents an actual ship. With this one possible exception, until the middle of the 19th century, the French entering

1. Plate 53, from the Portsmouth model: p. 190, fig. (f) from the Greenwich model, which appears to be the earlier.   2. P. 190, fig. (d).
3. P. 192.   4. M.M. VII, 240.   5. As in p. 196, fig. (c).

place was always at the gangway, and though commonly no ornament was fitted there, at least one "prisoner of war" model[1] shows an arched doorway rising above the bulwark and netting on both sides of the ship. The *Hercule*, 100-gun ship of 1837, had her main channel carried forward to form a platform at the entering place.[2] The *Valmy* of 1847 had middle deck entering ports with folding doors; thus, although no other examples of this have been noted, it seems likely that other French three-deckers of the mid-19th century may have had the like.

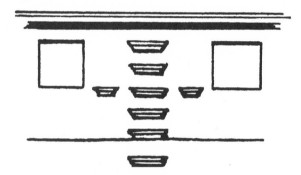

DUTCH ENTERING STEPS
(From a model of the early 19th century)

In the English Navy after Charles II's reign oar-ports were not fitted to ships of more than 40 guns; but both French and Spanish 50-gun ships had them in the early part of the 18th century. This was natural, for they were of considerable use in chasing the Barbary corsairs. In foreign frigates and smaller ships oars followed much the same course as in the English navy; but some heavy French frigates, as shown by a model in the Louvre, kept as many as 20 oar

ports a side on the lower deck even after 1785, when corresponding English ships had but six or eight, and those placed between the guns. The specially designed classes of oared men-of-war peculiar to the Baltic do not come within the scope of this book.

It has been noticed[3] that in the 18th century most foreign navies continued to fit their entering steps between a pair of skids, as a regular ladder, a practice which in England was dropped during the Restoration period. A late French example of this is the *Protecteur* of 1757: a remarkable Dutch example is seen in the Scheepvaart Museum's model of a 40-gun ship assigned to 1756. This model shows the bulwark in the waist, which has no gangways, cut into an entering place, and shows also the ladder fitted with hand rails instead of man-ropes.

§ 7. LIGHTS

From at least the early part of the 17th century the practice began of cutting lights or windows through the ship's side in the cabin spaces, and this went on for about 150 years. At first few, these lights increased in size and number as time went on, though for a short space the development of the quarter galleries checked the tendency. Thus the *Sovereign of the Seas*[4] with her two tiers of quarter gallery windows contrived to do with only one added light a side, this being under the quarter-deck. But the *Naseby*, for instance, of 1655, besides

1. P. 181, fig. (d).　2. Pâris, "Musée de Marine", Pl. 47.　3. P. 160.　4. Plate 9.

several other lights, had a range of six a side under the half deck (fig. a); and though this profusion seems to have been unusual, lights to the several cabins are regularly found throughout the Restoration period. It may be that there was already trouble from captains cutting unauthorised scuttles through their ships' sides, a practice against which an order was issued in 1692, while in 1701 an establishment was made of the glass allowed for the several rates, with a detailed specification of the lights and windows for which it was to be used. The high-water mark seems to have been reached in George I's reign, in the *Britannia* of 1719, which had

two lights a side on each of the lower and middle decks, seven a side on the upper-deck, and three on the quarter-deck, besides the usual two a side to the warrant officers' cabins under the forecastle. From this point they declined in numbers, till in ships launched after 1760 they are no longer found. The reason for this was that the practice had been adopted of fitting sashes to the gun-ports in the cabin spaces instead.

These lights were almost invariably decorated. In the 17th century they were commonly given wreaths, similar to the square wreaths of gun-ports (figs. a, c, d); but sometimes the decoration took

ENGLISH LIGHTS
(a) *Naseby*, 1655.   (b) *R. George*, 1756.   (c) (d) ? *S. Andrew*, 1670.
(Mr. R. C. Anderson's model).

the form of an arch broken by a small ornament. This fashion was continued in the 18th century to a small extent (fig. e), but commonly in the Georgian period the arch, whether whole or broken, was plain, and filled by the royal cypher or a shell design (figs. a, d, f, g, h). Often instead of an arch a flat canopy carried by brackets was fitted, while the small lights under the forecastle had merely a moulded frame (fig. b). Small lights in the mid-eighteenth century were often quite plain, and were sometimes closed by a hinged lid like an oar-port (fig. c).

FOREIGN PRACTICE

In all foreign ships lights were much more sparingly used than in English ships. While they kept to the lean-to form of quarter gallery on one deck only, the Dutch occasionally put a quarter-deck light above it; and the French about 1670-80, when they used an open gallery on the quarter-deck with a light in the finishing above it, at least occasionally added other lights on the same level;[1] and in both cases these lights had carvings round them. But such instances are

ENGLISH LIGHTS, EARLY 18TH CENTURY
(a) Model of *c.* 1715, called the *Royal George* (*Greenwich*).   (b) Ditto: from a forecastle cabin.
(c) Light with an oar-port lid: "*Ruby*" model (*Mercury Museum*).   (d) The "*Victory*, 17th century"
model; *i.e.*, probably the *Royal Anne*, 1704 (*Greenwich*).   (e) The earlier "*Royal William*, 1719"
model (*Greenwich*).   (f) As (a).   (g) A 4th rate of George I (*S. Kensington*).   (h) As (e).

1. Plate 39.

the exception in men-of-war, even in the 17th century; and in the 18th, while the Dutch used no lights at all save those in the quarter galleries and such as they fitted in the aftermost ports, the French adopted the practice of omitting the aftermost quarter-deck ports, the number varying from two or three to as many as five, and placed plain square lights in their stead, but so small and so high from the deck that they could not serve as gun-ports. In a few cases, however, as instances of 1755-65 show,[1] they fitted lights as large as ports. An instance has been cited[2] of a Spanish frigate, captured by the English in 1780, which had her aftermost gun deck port converted into a light, and elaborately carved.

Once in a way a light was fitted just before the quarter gallery in Dutch East Indiamen, light carvings being added in the 17th century,[3] but in the 18th the form being arched with a casement deadlight.

In the 19th century the lower deck of a frigate, for the sake of light and air, was given a row of scuttles fitted like oar-ports, but each with a bull's-eye in it. From their position close up to the gun-deck beams these scuttles cannot be mistaken for oar-ports. A good example of this is to be seen in the Louvre model of the *Alceste* of 1846.

§ 8. RIGOLS

This name, otherwise almost obsolete in English, means in naval speech a gutter fitted over a port or scuttle to prevent the rain from running into the ship when the port is open. The first certain mention of them is in a shipbuilding contract of 1691,[4] in which they are so mentioned as to show that they were then in common use. From first to last there were four forms of rigols in wooden ships. At first the ogee pattern; then the arch, which was either a true arc, or was flattened; and finally the gable shape.[5] The ogee and arch forms are found almost concurrently, examples of both sometimes being present in the same ship. The gable pattern has not been noticed before 1750, but it survived the others, and in 1815 was established by Navy Board order to their exclusion. Evidence on this small feature is scanty, for rigols are never shown in

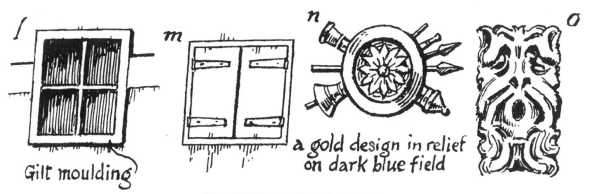

BROADSIDE DETAILS: FRENCH

1. P. 197, figs. (l), (m); and Plate 41.   2. Plate 50.   3. P. 186, fig (g).   4. Add. MS. 22153. f. 202.   5. P. 184, figs. (g), (c), (d), (f).

sheer draughts, they are too small to appear in any but the largest pictures, and more often than not they are omitted from models. In the circumstances it is not possible to say more of foreign usage than that, as far as the few available examples go,[1] save for a tendency to make the ogee rigol rather higher pitched, it seems to have agreed with English practice. Most of the instances are, however, from Spanish ships, in which English fashions were notoriously prominent.

§ 9. CHESSTREES

The chesstree[2] was a timber fitted externally abaft the bow of the ship and pierced with a hole through which the main tack was hauled from within board. Bow being an old word for shoulder, it is logical that the next part of the ship reached when working aft should be the chest, and that a timber placed there should be termed the chest-tree or chesstree.

In early ships presumably the tack came in through a hole close to the gunwale, for so it was in 1600 when ships had grown to two decks of guns. It is interesting to notice that the chesstree

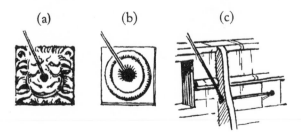

(a)   (b)   (c)

CHESSTREES: ENGLISH

stayed in this place, even when the hull grew higher, so that in three-deckers it remained till the middle of the 18th century on the middle deck, while in two-deckers it was on the upper-deck. In the 17th century the chesstree was commonly no more than a small piece of wood with a hole in it (fig. b), though in important ships it was made bigger and ornamental, the most usual design in which it was carved being a lion's mask with the tack leading in through the mouth (fig. a), though more rarely it was similar in form to a drop hancing piece. In the first half of the 18th century the chesstrees of three-decked ships were mere ornamental holes on the middle deck, but in two-deckers the practice, as in the late 17th century, was to make a hole in the top of the foremost fender, which was sometimes thickened for the purpose (fig. c). After about 1750 this method was followed also in three-deckers, and so continued as long as fenders were fitted.

FOREIGN PRACTICE

When an ornamental chesstree was desired a lion face was usually chosen. This is found in French and in Spanish ships as late as 1760. An example of it is given from the *"Royal Louis"* model at the Louvre, which is the ship of 1758.[3] A mask was sometimes carved on top of a short chock, as in the "Great Dane", said to be of 1600, but probably later,[4] but this form seems to have been confined to early ships. A similar example is found in the chesstree of the *Prins Willem* of 1651, which was fashioned into a goblin

1. Dutch, p. 186, fig. (f); French, p. 187, figs. (f), (g).   2. M.M. IX, 220, 286.   3. P. 197, fig. (o).   4. P. 181, fig. (g).

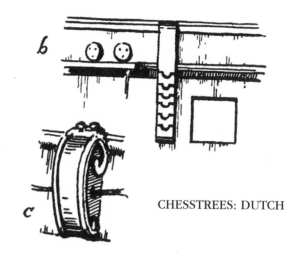

CHESSTREES: DUTCH

(fig. a, above). In Dutch ships of the 18th century, when there was no fender available in which to form a chesstree, a short chock was fitted, usually ornamented with overlapping scales.[1]

An example is given of a Swedish chesstree of Chapman's time, a vertical piece shorter than a fender being used;[2] but in general the practice seems to have been similar to English. The French, however, seem to have taken pains to avoid using the foremost fender as a chesstree. In the *Protecteur* of 1757 a short plain chesstree is worked some

5ft. before the foremost fender; the *Northumberland* of 1780 was similarly fitted;[3] and the Louvre model of a 40-gun frigate of 1785, known as a "vaisseau à rames", has a mere sheave for the tack placed only a foot before a fender.

§ 10. ANCHOR LININGS

This, though a conspicuous, is not an ornamental feature. After the anchor had been hauled up to the cathead, its fluke was raised by the fish to its position

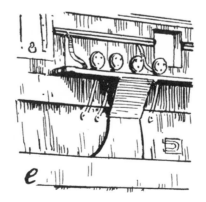

ENGLISH ANCHOR LININGS
(d) The Boyne, 1692.   (e) A frigate of 1741.   (f) A 74-gun ship of *c.* 1780.

1. P. 199, figs. (b), (c); and p. 181 fig. (e).   2. P. 181, fig. (h).   3. *Ibid.* fig. (f).

on the billboard. To prevent the fluke from tearing the side of the ship either in fishing or in cockbilling the anchor (*i.e.*, in getting it to the cathead ready for letting go), a lining was worked to take the chafe; and this naturally took the form of an arc described with the cathead as centre and the length of the anchor as radius. The English fashion always was to place the cathead at the corner of the fore-castle, raking forward very little. The fluke of the anchor therefore came up near the fore end of the fore channel, so that the lining had to be carried up over the chains to the outer edge of the channel. That part of the lining which was on the hull was formed by filling up the space between the wales flush to form an even surface. There were slightly varying forms, those shown representing (d) Restoration usage, (e) normal 18th century practice, and (f) a modification of about 1780.[1]

In Dutch ships the cathead was both lower and further forward than in English ships, with the result that the anchor, and consequently its lining, came up entirely before the channel.[2] Save for this difference it was fitted as in English ships. French ships did not have the lining fitted in a narrow arc as in English ships, but had the spaces between the wales filled in from the stem aft to the fore channel, so that the ship was smooth sided as far aft as the fluke of the anchor would reach. The *Royal Louis* model of 1758[3] also shows a narrow lining carried up over the fore chains, just as in an English ship; but, as few either of the models or draughts available illustrate this feature, it is perhaps risky to say that this was the general French practice in the eighteenth century.

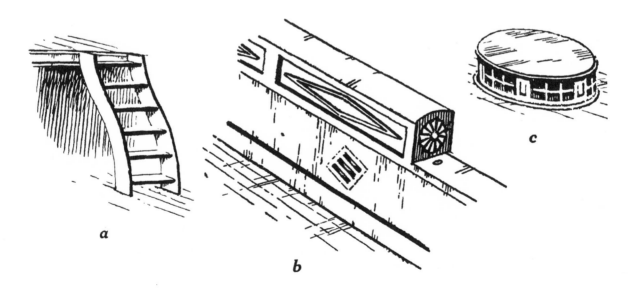

DETAILS FROM MODELS IN THE RIJKS MUSEUM
(a) and (c) Poop-ladder and skylight from line-of-battle ship, late 18th century.
(b) Inboard decoration of rail of the *Prins Frederick der Nederlanden*, *c.* 1830.

1. P. 199.   2. Plates 15 and 36.   3. P. 42, fig. (A).

CHAPTER IX

INBOARD WORKS

There is no intention of attempting to give here any connected account of the ornamentation of the cabins on board ship. From occasional mentions it is known that, especially in important ships, the decoration was lavish; but little written detail and practically no pictorial evidence has survived. We know that even by 1400 there was more ornament than mere hangings, for the *Trinity* then had two large eagles painted in the cabin on a diapered ground, and the barge *Nicholas* had there two large escutcheons of the royal arms and the arms of St. George, together with an image of St. Christopher.[1] This last, however, is probably hardly to be accounted as mere ornament.

Evidence for the 15th and 16th centuries is almost entirely lacking, but we know in general terms what was the state of affairs in the seventeenth. It is on record that in the *Prince Royal* the prince's lodging cabin and the state cabin were "very curiously wrought and gilded with divers histories," and that the room abaft the state-room was "wrought overhead and on each side with sundry figures in oil colours"; but we learn nothing either of the histories or of the figures. It is believed that the same lavish system was followed, no doubt with a steadily decreasing expenditure on fine gold, in other admiral ships from the time of the *Sovereign of the Seas* to the end of William III's reign; and enough details remain to show that such of the Restoration yachts as were intended for royal use were elaborately carved and gilded in their

cabins, and furnished with hangings of embossed and gilded leather. Such decorations were not well suited to the sea, and especially not to fighting ships, wherein "on any prospect of action they were torn to pieces by the sailors"; and it is not remarkable that the order of 1700, which restricted the use of all kinds of ornament in all classes of ships, should have abolished them entirely except for yachts.

It is true that, without calling upon the carvers, a good deal of beautification could be compassed by the joiners; and it is unnecessary to believe that in the long peace which followed Queen Anne's war the regulations were very strictly observed. The probability is that, until the long series of wars began in 1739, the cabins of admirals, and of many captains, were tolerably rich in pilaster work, cornices, panelling and so forth; and that plain slit deals painted in one sad colour were left for such as had no pull in the dockyards.

This is not the place for a description of the internal accommodation of a man-of-war, but as nothing on the subject is generally available save for the cabin establishments of 1673[2] and of 1757,[3] it may be worth while to call attention to two specifications, of 1655[4] and 1702,[5] which give valuable evidence as to the arrangement of the living spaces in those years. As the establishment of 1757 lasted, with minor alterations, till after Trafalgar, it may be said that from these sources alone a tolerably complete history of the subject can be constructed covering a period of a century and a half.

---

1. Nicolas, Hist. of R.N.; II, 445-6.   2. N.R.S.; Cat. of Pepysian MSS., I, 189.   3. M.M. X, 193.   4. Add. MS. 9306. f. 134 b.
5. Admy. Navy Bd. 2507, No. 162.

Carved hancing-piece

Forecastle

Belfry on Forecastle-Bulkhead

Staircase to Forecastle

Upper Deck

THE FORECASTLE-BULKHEAD OF THE "PRINCE", 1670

For the 19th century abundant evidence is available in the Admiralty records.

When the epidemic of ship decoration began at about the end of Elizabeth's reign, the bulkheads which were open to the weather were early chosen for treatment. The *Phœnix* of 1613[1] shows some carved work on the bulkhead of the quarter-deck; the *Sovereign of the Seas*[2] shows much on all her bulkheads. A feature common to these ships, and presumably to others of the same period, is the fashion of building the chief bulkheads in a series of bays or sponsons. There can be no doubt that the purpose of this was defensive. It was designed to give to the small guns mounted in those bulkheads, and also to the small shot men behind them, a wider arc of fire, and to enable them to scour the decks more effectively if an enemy should gain a footing on board. It is difficult, however, to see the need for this complication, for with the forecastle bulkhead loop-holed as well as the several bulkheads aft which faced forward, there cannot have been, even in a ship with flat bulkheads, any spot on deck which was not commanded. Presumably for this reason the sponsoned bulkheads went out of use, and are not found either in Commonwealth or later ships.

Henceforward bulkheads were in theory flat. In practice, as may be seen, they were far from flat, because it was the custom to make the cabins built at the bulkhead project beyond it; and also, in the case of the forecastle bulkhead, because the belfry also projected until late in the Restoration period. When the belfry was got out of the way the galley took its place, and the shape of the bulkhead remained much the same. The quarter-deck and poop bulkheads had

1. Plate 1.　2. Plate 9.

the lateral, or gangway, cabins from soon after 1660, if not earlier; and commonly, though not invariably, in the reign of Charles II there was also a projecting central cabin on the quarter-deck bulkhead. The models of the "*Britannia*, 1700", and the *St. George* of 1701 do not show the central bay, but it frequently occurs again later. When there were three projecting cabins on a bulkhead there was not much flat left, in fact little more than enough to allow a door to be placed on each side.

I have not plotted enough examples to be able to say with certainty when these bulkheads were first covered in by the increasing projection of the deck, but think that the dates were roughly 1715, or a little earlier, for the after bulkheads, and some ten years later for that of the forecastle. The first change made was by carrying the deck square across at the fore part of the cabins, so that the doors between the cabins were under an overhang; but though the decks were progressively lengthened, the cabin bulkheads remained in their old position, so that there came to be a considerable break of the deck beyond them. This was particularly the case with the poop, the break, or awning, of which served to shelter the wheel.

In the Restoration period these bulkheads were all profusely ornamented, chiefly by vertical brackets, which were often carved as terms or whole figures;[1] and the same method was continued until the order of 1703 put a stop to lavish carvings. But the bulkheads did not therefore become plain. Moulded

pilaster work and arcading were used instead of the carved brackets, and the flat spaces were trophied or otherwise painted, so that the bulkheads continued to be decidedly decorative. They remained so until the growth of the decks covered them in out of sight.

The beakhead-bulkhead passed through the same phases of ornamentation as did those of the quarter-deck and forecastle; but it belongs rightly to the head, with which it has already been considered.[2]

Gangways in themselves were not decorative, but they commonly had handsome railings. Their early history is not clear. In the Restoration period it was not the fashion to fit a ladder leading directly down from the break of a deck, but, at least in large ships, to fit a couple of steps down to a gangway, which ran along the ship's side for some six or eight feet, and then ended in a small winding staircase to the deck below. The height of the gangway had to be such as to allow a gun to be fought under it, but it can rarely have been more than 5ft. from the deck.

As these gangways were eventually extended to reach from the quarter-deck to the forecastle, it is of interest that they were used in their complete form in Dutch ships as early as 1675.[3] In England a "spar-deck", which might be the whole width of the ship, or might be only a central strip, often ran between the quarter-deck and forecastle in the early Stuart period. There are no examples of it for a long time before 1693, when

1. Nance, Plates 56, 59.   2. Pp. 48 *sq*.   3. M.M. V, 25.

it turns up again narrowed to a central gangway. The question then was whether such a gangway should be fitted in the *Newark*, one of the new 80-gun ships, but the decision was not to fit it. It may have existed in other ships of that date.

In Anne's reign, perhaps in the course of carrying out the order of 1703, all the other little gangways were got rid of except the pair which led forward from the quarter-deck. These did not yet reach to the entering places, which were just before the main mast, but did so from about 1714. A central gangway from the quarter-deck to the mainmast is first found in 1701, and shortly became universal in ships of 50 guns and upwards. It was not allowed to smaller ships. By the middle of the century the quarter-deck had reached within a few feet of the mainmast, so the central gangway ceased to exist as such. In large ships a grating was still fitted about the mast and forward to the head of the topsail sheet bitts, but even this was soon pushed out by the further growth of the quarter-deck.

In 1744 side gangways were ordered to be carried the whole length of the waist in two-decked ships. Their width at first was only a foot or so, but was quickly increased. In 1782 the steps down to the gangways from quarter-deck and forecastle were abolished and the gangways laid flush, being then about 5ft. wide in ships of the line. The open well between the gangways seems to have had skid beams laid across it first soon after the Seven Years' War; but in spite of these beams the waist remained open till

well into the next century. It is perhaps a little curious that in English ships no railing was fitted round the open waist: in French ships the practice was to fit a solid balustrade.

When the short gangways from the poop and forecastle were abolished the old winding staircases were at first retained, but before the end of Anne's reign gave place to straight ladders. The same change was not made till later in the case of the quarter-deck, and the abolition of the great winding staircase came last of all, in three-deckers not until 1757. This was fitted on the port side of the quarter-deck leading down to the admiral's steerage on the upper-deck, and was so near to the ship's side that it interfered seriously with the fighting of at least one gun. When it went, a straight ladder amidships was substituted for it. The straight ladders going down onto covered decks were in the early part of the century "bell ladders", which meant that the two or three lowest steps were increased in width.

The knights were carved into human heads as far back as can be traced, and continued to be so until 1703. Until a date which may provisionally be placed about 1670 they stood as separate posts, but after it they were joined by cross pieces and became bitts (fig. a, facing page). The working parts of timberheads and kevels were naturally not carved, but their form varied according to nationality and date. Thus fig. (b) shows an English main-rail head, such as was adopted when it was forbidden to carve it, and fig. (d) the form which, after some overlapping,

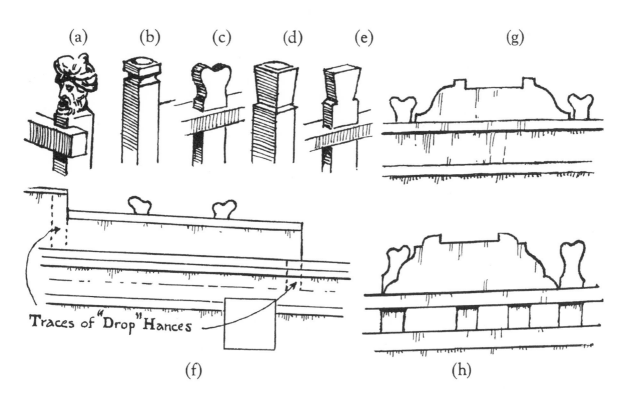

(a) (b) (c) (d) (e) (g)

Traces of "Drop" Hances

(f)

(h)

ENGLISH BITTS, TIMBERHEADS, KEVELS, AND CLEATS

superseded it about 1756. Figs. (c) and (e) are timberheads from the forecastle. The "finger and thumb" pattern (fig. c) was universal in the first half of the 18th century, but about 1756 suddenly gave place to the simpler form. The heads of kevels (fig. f) were fashioned in the same way. Figs. (g) and (h) show another minor inboard feature, the fish-davit cleat. Sometimes a mere block was fitted, but usually there was a slight attempt at decoration. The *Naseby* of 1655 had on the side of her forecastle a pair of brackets carved as terms,[1] seemingly as supports for the fish davit; but this feature has not been found in any other ship.

The belfry is perhaps the most interesting of the inboard features. Henry VII's ships had bells,[2] described as ship bells or watch bells, but there is nothing to show where they were placed. In 1514 the *Gabriel Royal* had "a bell hanging in the deck",[3] by which I understand the summer deck to be implied. This would mean that the bell was under cover, in later phrase "under the half deck". Next, one of Visscher's gallions has a bell at the break of the half deck, in the open, hung on a narrow single arch belfry: this may at least be accepted as good evidence for the position of the belfry about 1600. The *Antelope* of 1619 also shows it aft,[4] but the picture represents the ship as she was in 1648. In 1658 the *Bryer*,[5] a Commonwealth frigate, had her belfry on the quarter-deck; and a Danish church ship attributed to the late 17th century[6] shows it in the same position. Apparently

1. P. 173, fig. (b).   2. M.M. V, 28.   3. S.P. Henry VIII, I, 425.   4. M.M. IX, 59.   5. N.R.S. "First Dutch War", I, 27.   6. Nance, Plate 38.

ENGLISH BELFRIES

(a) ? *St. Andrew,* 1670.   (b) *Mordaunt,* 1682.   (c) *Victory,* 1765.   (d) "*Ruby,* 64, of 1768", really a
70-gun ship of *c.* 1740.   (e) A snow of *c.* 1705.   (f) *Centurion,* 1745.   (g) *Boyne,* 1790.
(h) "*Cleopatra,* 1779."   (i) A 70-gun ship of *c.* 1730-5.
[(c) is from the ship: the rest from models belonging to (a) (e) (i) Mr. R. C. Anderson:
(b) (d) the Mercury Museum: (f) (g) (h) Science Museum S. Kensington.]

its position was the same in other foreign ships, with one notable exception. No one has succeeded in finding a bell in any Dutch ship earlier than the 18th century. Perhaps the Dutch did not use a bell; perhaps, like the English of early Tudor times, they kept it hidden under a deck. As it is, their earliest example of a belfry is from an unnamed 40-gun ship of 1756,[1] which shows a French type of the single arch.

It is not exactly known when the belfry was first moved to the forecastle in English ships, but it must have been very soon after 1660. Its early Restoration position was not on the forecastle, but in a house placed abaft it, the floor of this house being only two or three steps above the upper-deck. Sometimes a few steps were placed for the convenience of the man who struck the bell;[2] and one model shows a bench instead of the steps, so that it is easy to imagine that the warrant officers from the cabins abreast the belfry used it as their smoking room. The belfries of 1670 were big enough to be called little houses, and had for a roof a square dome similar to those used for the turrets on the quarters and ornamented in the same way. The stantions which supported the dome were usually carved as terms, and ran down sometimes the whole height of the forecastle bulkhead.

It may be taken for granted that the turret form of belfry was found only in the largest ships, and that most ships had the single arch type. This was certainly in use soon after 1680, as seen from the *Mordaunt*,[3] in which ship it was

supported by a pair of carved terms, and had two lions lying on the arch or "cap". Probably it had a continuous history from Tudor times. It appears to have been the usual form in William III's time, and until the order of 1703, after which date terms on the stantions and carvings on the cap are no longer to be found. It is easy to over-estimate the change that was made between 1670 and 1700 in the vertical position of the belfry. At the earlier date the lip of the bell seems to have been just below the level of the forecastle; ten years later it was just above it, and therefore in the position in which it remained. The alteration in the form of the belfry is apt to convey the false impression that the bell itself was considerably raised at this time.

The last of the carved belfry caps had solid sides and a single arch of varying pitch. The elaboration of the *Mordaunt*'s belfry carvings was perhaps not surpassed; but, as would be expected, it was equalled, or nearly so, in some of the larger ships of William's reign.

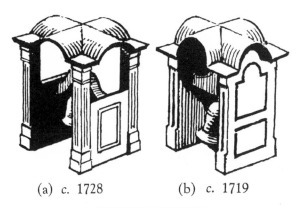

(a) *c.* 1728   (b) *c.* 1719

ENGLISH BELFRIES
(From two models at Greenwich, both called "*Royal William*, 1719".)

1. A model in the Scheepvaart Museum.   2. P. 206, fig. (a).   3. *Ibid.* fig (b).

FRENCH BELFRIES AND TIMBERHEADS

From models of: (A) *Royal Louis*, 1758.   (B) Ship of the line, *c.* 1700, presented by M. Marcotte.
(C) Called the "*Mars*", *c.* 1805.   (D) Called "H.M.S. *Hero*, 1802."   (E) "*Océan*", training model.
(F) Prisoner-of-war three-decker, called "H.M.S. *Caledonia*", *c.* 1805.   (G) *Protecteur*, 64, of 1757.

(a) and (c) *Soleil Royal*, 1690.   (b) The "Pic" model, 1755.   (d) "*Océan*", training model.
[All in the Louvre, except (C), which is in the Mercury Museum, and (D) and (F) in the
Science Museum, S. Kensington.]

The need of finding some decorative substitute for carving and gilding seems to have suggested first the introduction of the crossing arches, which are found, with solid sides, from about 1705. In the earliest form the thwartship arch seems to have been of much wider span than that which went fore and aft, but shortly the arches became equal or nearly so, and the cap approached to square form. Like the contemporary single arches it was somewhat high pitched. The older form had solid sides, but from about 1725 the sides began to be made either open or half open.

There are many seeming contradictions about the form of the belfries used in the 18th century. Forms which are believed to be early occur late, and *vice versa*. In these conditions it does not seem safe to say more than that –

(1) Whether with single or crossing arches, the high pitched form is the earlier, and the arches become flatter as time goes on. Thus it will be seen that the arches of the *Victory*'s cap in 1761[1] are much lower pitched than those of 1719-28;[2] while those of the *Boyne* of 1790[3] are again much flatter than those of the *Victory*.

(2) Later belfries have their sides more open than earlier, the solid side giving way to the half solid, and the half solid in turn to the open four-poster.[4]

But there are contradictions or partial contradictions, due apparently to the fact that there was considerable overlapping of types.[5] Thus the high pitched single arch shown in figs. (e), (h) and (i) may be said to be normal in 1705 and 1730, but much out of date in 1779. There are, in fact, a great many variants of the 18th century belfry, and it would be necessary to spend much time in collecting and plotting examples in order to decide the precise relationship of forms. It has always to be taken into account that such variants as solid sides (fig. h) or perforated sides (fig. f); as straight side bars (fig. c) or curved bars (fig. d) may

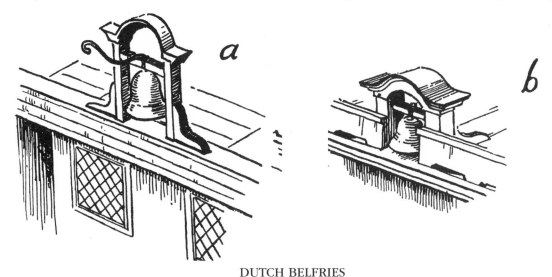

DUTCH BELFRIES

1. P. 206, fig. (c).   2. P. 207, figs. (a), (b).   3. P. 206, fig. (g).   4. *Ibid*. figs. (c), (d), (g).
5. The references which follow in this paragraph are to p. 206.

represent the practice of different yards rather than of different periods. It seems, however, fairly safe to add that the sides of the "four-poster" belfry, after being entirely open for some 30 or 40 years, began to be found partly built up again in some cases towards the end of the century (fig. g).

It will be seen[1] that in the 18th century the French used only the single arch for their belfries, and that, as in England, a high pitch implies an early date, and a lower pitch a later date. There is marked Chinese influence in figs. (D) and (F), belonging to about 1800-05. The drawings also show the breast rails of the forecastle, figs. (A) and (B), with the typical ornament of their respective dates. The pyramidal belfry, not altogether unlike a lych-gate, has not been found except in French models; but more than one instance occurs in models of about 1805.

As has been noticed, belfries are not found in Dutch ships till the second half of the 18th century. When they do occur they are of the single arch type and similar to French forms, not necessarily of the same date. Thus (a)[2], from a line-of-battle ship model in the Rijks Museum, may be compared with the *Protecteur*'s belfry,[3] of only slightly earlier date; but (b),[2] from the model of the *Washington*, 74, in the Mercury Museum, is very like that of the *Royal Louis*[4] of forty years earlier.

On p. 208 figs. (a) and (c) show respectively the fore-bitts and a timber head from the *Soleil Royal*; fig. (b) shows what was French standard pattern in the eighteenth century, and fig. (d) a form which does not seem to have been used till after 1800.

The Dutch timber heads illustrated below are from a line-of-battle ship of the latter part of the eighteenth century. The main-rail head (fig. a) is not unlike English practice, and of the timberheads (d) is like, but shorter than, the English form which went out in 1756; but (b) octagonal, and (c) round seem to be peculiar to the Dutch.

DUTCH TIMBER HEADS

1. The references which follow in this paragraph are to p. 208.   2. P. 209.   3. P. 208, fig. (G).   4. *Ibid*. fig. (A).

CHAPTER X

PAINTING AND GILDING

There never was a time, since ships were ships, when men did not paint them. Mr. Cecil Torr, in his valuable book on "Ancient Ships", has collected and set forth the evidence, from which it appears that the earliest ships, for the sake of staunchness and the preservation of the wood, were pitched (like the Ark) within and without. The earliest form of relief from this sombre scheme seems to have consisted in painting a patch of colour upon either bow, sometimes red, sometimes purple or blue, as found in the Homeric poems. After this came the application of colour to the whole side of the ship, and then, with the use of encaustic wax paint, the painting of elaborate pictures on the sterns, and to a smaller extent on the bows of ships, while occasionally a frieze was painted all along the side. While, however, it is likely that these ornaments were most commonly painted, there is evidence that in some cases they were carved in relief.

Mr. Torr quotes from Pliny the statement that in his time purple, violet, blue, white, green and yellow were used in ship painting. The invisible sea-blue colour which pirates, and others who did not court discovery, applied to hull, sails and gear, is of a later age, the authority for it being Vegetius, a writer of the 4th century, A.D. It is permissible to conjecture that a good deal of disappointment attended its use.

In the later period of the Roman Republic and under the Empire the more important merchantmen measured some 200 tons, which was the usual tonnage of the ocean-going merchant-man down to the 19th century. Roman ships of this size employed in the more important trades, in that with Spain for instance, or in bringing corn from Egypt, were no doubt as much the aristocracy of the sea as were the Indiamen of from sixteen to eighteen hundred years later. They had attained to a three-masted rig with a main top-sail; they had figure-heads, ornamented sterns, frieze work, a half deck aft, and in some cases a gallery abaft and something in the nature of a beakhead. Between such ships and those of the 16th century there is remarkably little difference, and it is a subject for regret that, owing to the scantiness of the records which survive, no more than a superficial comparison of Roman with Tudor ships is possible.

That some of the Roman developments were lost during the dark period following the fall of Rome is certain; but – as may be seen for instance in Jal's "Archéologie" – it is equally certain that others survived. As a matter of conjecture it is conceivable that the painted representations of saints, which still survive on some Sicilian fishing boats, may be in direct descent from the gods and goddesses painted on the sterns of Roman ships; it is conceivable too that, just as the cult of the oculus spread west and north from the Mediterranean, so it may have been with the frieze and the other ornaments of the ship. There was early Scandinavian communication with the Mediterranean, owing chiefly to the demand for the amber of the Baltic, and it seems not impossible that the general

PAINTING AND GILDING   211

idea of ship decoration may thus have been carried north.

We know that in at least one instance a Viking ship of *c.* 800 A.D. was elaborately ornamented with carvings in low relief on the stems and gunwale,[1] but other ships found are not decorated thus. As it is incredible that they were entirely plain, we are at liberty to add conjecture to eke out the few known facts. We know that Viking ships had a figure-head on the fore stem, and sometimes a corresponding decoration on the after stem; and by analogy from the practice of a slightly later date we may decide that they were almost certainly painted in strakes of different colours; and, arguing from still later usage, that probably some at least had the gunwale decorated with a painted frieze where it was not covered with the shields of the crew.

The Bayeux tapestry shows us William's ships painted in strakes of several colours, a method which comes natural in clinker-built vessels. It may even be that the colours there shown are to be accepted literally; but it seems more probable that the Queen and her ladies did not bother about such niceties, and, knowing what was the system in vogue, were content to apply such colours as they had. They used two colours for most of the ships: yellow and green strakes alternately in some; green and red, or red and pale blue in others. In fewer cases they used three colours or more, as for instance: green, yellow, red, yellow, green, red; and green, red, pale blue, yellow, pale blue. No friezing is indicated, and seeing that Duke

William's fleet was distinctly a scratch pack, it is unlikely that it was at all profusely ornamented. For our purpose it would probably be of greater interest to have details of Harold's fleet which disbanded itself, of the ships which Tostig recruited in Flanders, or of those which sailed with Hardrada.

For more than three centuries after the Conquest we have virtually nothing on the subject of ship painting. There is, to be sure, the mention of the "White ship" to show us that at least the ships used as royal yachts were sometimes painted; and a decided difference of fashion is likely to have continued between such ships, which were of the galley type, and the sailing merchantman which formed the bulk of mediæval fleets. But the only attempt at a description of the decoration of a large sailing ship is that of the great Turkish dromon or buss which was destroyed by Richard's fleet in 1191; and even here we are only told that she was painted green and yellow "so elegantly that nothing could exceed her beauty", a description which tantalises rather than satisfies.[2] Fortunately the evidence of seals and coins[3] shows that from about 1340 ships were friezed both on the castles or stages, and under the gunwale, with leopards and fleur-de-lys, quatre foils, and diaper pattern.

The next references are to the ships of Henry IV,[4] and it is again for conjecture whether the painting of the whole side, or of the upper works alone, is intended. One of the King's barges, a long low-oared vessel,[5] was painted red and ornamented, with collars of gold,

---

1. P. 10. 2. Nicolas, Hist. R.N., I, 120. 3. M.M. II, 3, 5, 44; III, 36. 4. M.M. II, 445. 5. M.M. VI, 229.

each with a fleur-de-lys in it; with garters of gold, each with a leopard in it; and with "lyames" (leashes), each with a greyhound in it. This seems to suggest frieze work, especially in a barge which had no height of superstructure on which to dispose much ornament. Red was perhaps one of the hall-marks of a King's ship, for the *Trinity* was also painted red, and the *Goodpace* was red and other colours. Another royal barge, the *Nicholas*, was painted black and powdered with ostrich feathers white, the stems and scrolls being of gold. The mention of scrolls suggests that probably they bore the royal mottoes; and also the manner of the reference implies that such scrolls were not unusual. Undoubtedly the *Nicholas* must have presented a striking appearance. There is also a note of the painting of the *Holigost* in 1415:[1] "Painting the King's great ships with swans, antelopes [*i.e.*, royal badges] and divers arms, also with the royal motto called 'Une sanz pluis' in divers parts of the said ship". The cost was £7 6s. 8d., which at a time when a skilled work-man's wage was 6d. per day, represents a high degree of ornament.

The ships shown in the Rous Roll[2] probably may be accepted as showing what was normal practice late in the 15th century for the best of the ships not belonging to the Crown. Apart from the mediæval custom of beautification by a lavish use of heraldic bearings on flags and pavesses, and in important ships on sails, it seems likely that the side was paid with some bright composition, and only the upper works painted, the colours used being presumably those

of the coat armour of the owner. Thus one of the Warwick ships is shown with her after castle painted checky, presumably in reference to the blue and yellow checks of the second and third quarters of Warwick's arms. We do not know how Henry VII painted his ships, but by analogy from the Rous Roll can probably make a fairly good guess at the method. We have only a list of the colours used,[3] which certainly is full of promise. It includes "vermilion, fine gold, russet, bice, red lead, white lead, brown, Spanish white, verdigris, and aneral [or ashen colour]". The preference for the Tudor colours of white and green does not seem to have been so marked as it became later, though it was already much in evidence in the scheme of decoration by flags.

A statement of the colours used in painting the *Henry Grace à Dieu* in 1514 has also survived,[4] and includes red and white lead, yellow ochre, vermilion, crimson lake, brown, verdigris, and varnish, but not blue. This paper says that the colours were "for peynting of toppys, sails and images in the *Harry Grace à Dieu*"; but another[5] says that they were "for peyntynge of the *Harry Grace Dieu* her toppys and sayles". Thus some doubt remains, as no more infor-mation is available. There seems to have been less profusion towards the end of the reign. From the written records,[6] and from the meagre pictorial records of the Anthony Rolls, it would be impos-sible to discover that the royal ships of about 1540 were not almost entirely destitute of ornament; but fortunately in a MS. of this date[7] we have a number of

1. Nicolas, *Op. cit.* II, 446; M.M. V, 24.   2. Frontispeice.   3. Oppenheim, "Administration of R.N.", 130.   4. Exch. T.R., Misc. Bks. V, f. 231.
5. Exch. accounts, T.R., 61/5. f. 22.   6. Oppenheim, *Op. cit.*, 60.   7. Cott. Aug. 1, ii, 57 b.

well-drawn coloured illustrations of the royal ships.

The colouring is little more than an indication, for the body colour of the hull is not shown; but there are valuable details, which show the use of a partial frieze of simple design along the super-structures, the prevalence of green, and the presence of the royal badges on the stern.[1] The effect is dainty and restrained.

In Elizabeth's reign there was still no approach to uniformity in the painting of the royal ships. The *White Bear* was painted red, the *Lion* was timber colour, the upper works of the *Bonaventure* were black and white, while the *Revenge* and the *Scout* were green and white.[2] It is not to be supposed that these colours were laid on in solid bands, for fortunately we have the extremely hand-some series of coloured illustrations in "Ancient English Shipwrightry" to guide us. Four of the ships from this source are reproduced here,[3] and, though they are neither named nor dated, it is possible to recognise some difference of period from the style of the ornamentation and the manner of building. None of the English ships show the simple herring-bone pattern which seems to have sufficed for frieze work under Henry VIII. What is probably the oldest ship[4] retains the arched ports and windows of former times in her half deck and in her forecastle, and is somewhat half-hearted in her adoption of the geometrical style of ornament. Of the two gallions with half deck, quarter-deck and poop, it will be noticed that one[5] has, in addition to

the decoration of her superstructures, a frieze running right fore and aft down to the upper wale. In her the ornamentation is to an extreme degree geometrical, the only exceptions being the rope mouldings and the "wavy line" *motif* of the little frieze to the poop. In the original drawing this last-named ship is provided with a suit of sails, which is not reproduced here. For the present purpose their only importance is that their dimensions agree with what is known of those of the famous *Ark Royal*, thus making it probable that this is the ship represented. It is very obvious that this drawing differs profoundly from the extremely unsatisfactory traditional portraits of the *Ark*, a fact which seems to speak strongly in its favour.

In 1586, the year before the *Ark* was bought into the Navy, a departure from the conventional style of ornamenta-tion is recorded in the friezing of the *Rainbow* with "planets, rainbows and clouds". For some little time we have no further complete detail of painted works, but it is worth while to notice that the shipbuilding contracts of 1591 contemplated the painting of the ships' sides to two feet below the chain wale, that is to a greater depth than in the ship here called the *Ark Royal*. This carrying of the ornamentation well down the side seems to have had a vogue of some duration in the more important ships, for *mutatis mutandis* the same thing is still found in the *Sovereign of the Seas* of 1637.[6] Also all the records available tend to show that in the end of Elizabeth's reign the geometrical fashion of decoration was giving place

1. P. 108. 2. Oppenheim, *Op. cit.*, 130. 3. Plates 1, 5, 6. 4. Plate 5. 5. Plate 6. 6. Plate 9.

to something more elaborate, in which carvings and gildings, especially of the royal arms and beasts, began to appear. This was certainly so in the *White Bear* and *Elizabeth* when rebuilt in 1598; and Dutch pictures of the opening years of the 17th century point the same way. For these reasons it may be decided that the scheme of painting of our *Ark Royal* belongs to 1587 rather than to 1606; or in other words, that the ship is represented in her original form, and not as she appeared when rebuilt in 1606.

The ascription of the coloured draught titled the *Phœnix* of 1612[1] is again conjectural. The draught itself is preserved in the Admiralty records, and appears to have been made for the guidance of the painters, or for submission as showing the scheme of decoration proposed. The features of the hull are clearly those of a ship of James I and the style of ornament points to her being a King's ship; so that, as no other ship of this size and force was built during the reign, her identification seems inevitable. The development in the style of decoration is as obvious as is the retention of the Tudor green.

In the Vroom picture of 1613 at Haarlem, in which the *Prince Royal* is the central figure, the hulls of the English ships are shown of a greyish tint, which probably represents weathered oak. The *Prince* is green above the waist rail with gold relief and a little white here and there, especially for the large Prince of Wales's feathers on the side of the closed quarter gallery. There is much gold about the head, all

its rails, the cathead, and the serpent for the tacks being gilt, while the lower range of panels shows gold ornamentation on a dark green groundwork. The upper row of panels, or frieze of the head, bears coloured devices. The rails of the waist and quarter-deck are red, as also are the arming cloths. We have the specification[2] of the carvings and gildings of this ship, some of which can be recognised from this picture and from the stern in the portrait of Phineas Pett recently acquired by the National Portrait Gallery.[3] We have also the bill for them, showing that the carving cost £441 0s. 4d., and the painting and gilding, including much profusion within board, £868 6s. 8d. When the *Prince* was rebuilt in 1638-41 the sum allowed for "painting, carving and joining" was £2,000, to which should be added £40 for elm timber supplied for the purpose to the carvers.[4] These estimates were much exceeded, £2,571 being spent on gilding and £756 on carving.[5] Details of this second suit of ornamentation have not been found, but it is clear that the *Prince* in her second state must have been able to hold up her head even in the gorgeous company of the *Sovereign of the Seas*, on whose ornamentation no less than £6,691 was spent.[6] There is the less need to repeat here the well-known description of the *Sovereign's* carvings and gildings as the general scheme, and much of the detail, can be made out from the accompanying illustration.[7]

It so happens that we have at least two representations of the *Prince* as rebuilt in 1641, a draught by Van

1. Plate 1.   2. N.R.S., "Phineas Pett", 207-10.   3. Plate 8.   4. Add. MS., 9294. f. 409.   5. Oppenheim, "Administration of R.N.", 341 n.
6. *Ibid*. 261.   7. Plate 9.

de Velde, and Blankhof's picture at Brussels;[1] and it is not the least remarkable thing that in each case the ship, as compared both with Commonwealth and with Restoration practice, seems distinctly plain. It may be that much of the cost was lavished on inboard works; but again it may be as well to remember that in the early Stuart period the king often paid very heavily for what he did not get. At any rate, to judge by appearances, the second rates *London*[2] and *Henry* of 1655 were more highly ornamented ships, and each of them cost, for painting and gilding, £120; for carving, £150; and for joinery, £150.[3] Two fifth rates at the same time cost £75 each in all, £25 for each item. Obviously the Commonwealth liked value for its money; but it did not like extravagance, for a letter of this same year from the Navy Commissioners to the Admiralty,[4] referring to these same ships, says that half has been abated of what was formerly allowed, and that they now hope there will be another halving, as £80 should serve for painting a second rate ship. To their puritanic and economical minds, elaborate painting was "like feathers in fantastic caps".

The contract with Richard Isaacson for the painting and gilding of the *London* and the *Henry* provided for:

"The figure of their heads to be gilded with the two figures upon the galleries [*i.e.*, quarter pieces], and arms upon the upright of the stern. Their heads, sterns and galleries, rails, brackets and ports, their sides, timber heads and planksheeres all to be primed and blackt as well as ever hath been used in the navy, and painted gold colour proper to the carved work in oil, in

form and manner as the *Resolution*. Their great cabins and state-rooms to be walnut tree colour in oil, grained and revailed, and what is proper to be gilded to be laid gold colour suitable [*i.e.*, similar] to the *Nazeby*. Their round-houses and other cabins to be stone colour and green ... Their half decks, cuddy and forecastle to be of wanescote or other colour according to the direction of the master shipwright. Their bulkhead cabins upon their decks and quarter-decks, bitts, knightheads, brackets and other things usual to be primed and painted as without board."

There is a good deal of interest in this. We see a distinction made apparently between gold leaf and gold paint. If the *Sovereign* and *Prince* (which under the Commonwealth became the *Resolution* and is the ship mentioned in this contract) had all gold leaf, their extravagant cost is in part explained. On the other hand the knowledge that a cheap substitute for gold leaf was in use helps to explain the traditional belief that 17th century ships were habitually gilt on all their carved works from stem to stern. It will be seen too that the use of green paint still survives; but this is the last mention of it for a very long time.

It is admissible to mention "landed work" here, for in it was found a cheap substitute for elaborate ornamentation. Hitherto it has been assumed that the use of "landed work" (that is, clinker-built, lapstrake, or weather-boarding – it has many names, and possibly is what is meant by the 16th century term "cage-work") was entirely confined to Dutch-built ships. It is familiar from many Dutch models, being used in the middle of the 17th century for the topside from the poop down to the quarter

1. M.M. II, 149.   2. M.M. IV, 27.   3. Add. MS. 9306. f. 132 b.   4. Cal. S.P. Dom. 3 Aug. 1655.

gallery, and also for the bulkheads, especially the beakhead-bulkhead. No model shows it in any English ship. Nevertheless it was by no means uncommonly used in English ships from early in the century until after the Restoration. It is found in the *Rainbow*[1] of 1617, and in the *Triumph* of 1623. In the *Triumph*, which cannot have gone through three wars without rebuilding, it survived till 1675, when it was renewed.[2]

Van de Velde's draught of the *Royal Katherine* of 1664[3] shows landed work on the quarters, and explains thereby what the King meant when he said that he would have her and the *Royal Oak* made very plain. Still the carvings of each ship cost £140,[4] which was not quite the royal intention. Perhaps the dockyard officers thought that landed work instead of a carved frieze was concession enough to economy. The stern of the ship seems as highly decorated as any of her contemporaries. The above-mentioned are only some of the English ships in which the use of landed work has been noticed.

The regular practice of the 17th century, certainly under the Commonwealth and Restoration and probably earlier, was to have bright sides from the sheer rail down to the wales. The wales were black, and the ornamentation of the topside was either by the painted or gilded rails and hancing pieces, or else by frieze work on the black background. This frieze work, when it existed, seems normally to have been painted – perhaps with gold paint – and only to have been gilt in yachts intended for the King's own use.[5] There is a further point as to whether the whole of the side was left bright colour. Surgeon Browne, son of Sir Thomas, has left[6] an amateurish but careful drawing of a two-decker of about 1662 showing the side painted black to the sills of the upper-deck ports. This method was not uncommonly used in the 18th century, as it was found effective in disguising the presence of a lower tier of guns, being, in fact, a simple form of camouflage. Again, we have Dryden's comparison of the *London* to a "sea-wasp", which may have been inspired by the normal scheme of painting, black above and below with the yellow of the bright side between; but it also suggests the possibility that the upper wales may have been blacked in some ships, as indeed they are in a few models. On such a point, however, models are very doubtful evidence.

Mr. Oppenheim has formed a very unfavourable opinion[7] of the appearance of these decorated ships: "Probably a 16th or 17th century ship was not a particularly picturesque object …. As for the gilt and painting, a week of rough weather would have converted the original tawdry splendour into a forlorn slatternliness." And yet it was from these tawdry objects that the greatest of marine painters and draughtsmen drew their inspiration. Probably the ornamentation lasted well enough for the usual summer's campaign, but it seems likely enough that ships kept out for the winter guard looked sluttish enough by the time they came in hand for their spring refit. The reign of William III was the

1. S.P. Dom. Car. I, vol. 50, No. 22.   2. Admy. Navy Bd. Misc. 3118. f. 62.   3. Plate 11.   4. Cal. S.P. Dom. 23 Apr. 1664.
5. *Ibid*. 8 Oct. 1663; and 23 June 1664.   6. Sloane MS. 1831A. f. 44.   7. "Administration of R.N.", 263.

high-water of ship ornamentation, and even then it was not thought necessary that a ship should be painted more than once a year.[1]

The contract for building the *Newark* of 80 guns in 1693[2] refers thus to the paint work: "To gild the lion of the head and the King's arms in the stern. To trible paint the ship within and without board with good oil colour, and in like manner all the joiners' work, rails, plancksheers and ladders, gangways and bulkheads and carved works within board: to paint the great cabin and round house with walnut or stone colour, or such manner as is usually done to his Majesty's other ships."

This differs little from the contract of 1655, save that it makes it clear that the carved work was now painted in oil colour, yellow probably being used for the outboard work. It may perhaps be taken for granted that at this date the cost of painting was not less than it was in George I's reign. By 1715 the cost of carving a first rate had been reduced from £896 before 1700 to £323; but the cost of painting her was still over £270. Within four years this figure had been reduced by a third to £180, which sounds ample; but there was the difficulty that painting, being an expensive process, was not allowed very often. Artists who wish to represent the ships of George I at the end of a commission would do well to consider the effect of the following order,[3] issued to all the yards on the 18th July, 1715: –

"You are to use good husbandry in painters' works and not to refresh oftener to the weather than once in a year or two, and the inboard works that are from the weather only upon rebuilding and great repairs, or after a return from a long foreign voyage when the ship hath not been refreshed abroad, and that the outsides of the ships be painted of the usual colour yellow, and the ground black, and that both inside and out be of a plain colour only ... except such part of the head, stern and galleries as are usually friezed ... and that both ship and boats be painted only as the painter's contract directs and not otherwise, though even at a private charge."

It is a somewhat curious point that models usually, and paintings sometimes, show the upper works of the ships of this period painted blue as a ground for the frieze work. The official Navy Board paintings of a little later date quite often show red instead of blue; and yet we know with certainty that there was strict regulation that the colour should be black. And if the order just cited were not enough, we have other references spread over a considerable period: such for instance as is found in the contracts of 1692, already quoted, where the sheer rail is referred to as being placed "to part off the black work". The appearance of the ships moreover can hardly have been improved by a fraud which seems to have had a good innings before it was discovered in 1729.[4] It was then found that the contractors had been using size instead of linseed oil, and Spanish whiting or chalk instead of white lead. If any question arose the painters said the whiting was there to make putty; but the Navy Board told the yard officers that "we cannot think your pretended

1. Admy. Navy Bd. 2507, No. 122.   2. Admy. Library, MS. No. 44.   3. Admy. Navy Bd. 2507, No. 198.   4. Admy. Navy Bd. 2507, No. 281.

inability to discover such frauds any excuse, but that rather your want of knowledge therein should have put you the more upon your guard". From which it would almost seem that the Navy Board may have suspected that fraudulent dealing was not confined to the painters.

The colour plate[1] of a "Fourth-rate of George I", a 50-gun ship, from a model in the Science Museum at South Kensington, shows that the scheme of external decoration, evolved by long usage, was more than merely adequate: it was indeed so handsome, that it would be difficult to suggest how it might be improved. The inboard colour, except in the cabins, was red; but of this little can be seen save at the ports, and where it has, so to speak, been allowed to overflow on the quarters. It will be noticed that the frieze is divided into two strips by the carrying of the waist rail fore and aft, an arrangement which was common, though not universal. When there were two strips the narrower was painted with some variant of the ubiquitous "wavy line"; the wider frequently had trophies, as here, but sometimes a design of seahorses, mermaids, fishes and the like was preferred. The model of the *Coronation* of 1686 has Garter stars on her frieze. The second counter, which came immediately under the lower tier of stern windows, was also treated ornamentally, but its design was usually different from that of the side frieze, and was sometimes, as in the Portsmouth model of Nelson's *Victory*, very handsomely painted in several colours. The

term "pendulum frieze" occurs early in the 18th century for the upper part of the frieze; but why that name should have been given to it is unexplained. Sometimes the space under the windows of the quarter galleries was friezed instead of being balustraded.[2]

There is little, if any, perceptible difference between this fashion of decoration and that of the 17th century. Surviving models afford the chief evidence on this point, but there is reason to believe that in one respect they are to some extent misleading. They invariably, till quite late in the century, show the side bright between the black work and the wales; but there is clear evidence that for a considerable period the regulation was that it should be painted yellow, instead of being paid with "stuff", which may be interpreted as varnish. Thus on 12 July, 1715, the Admiralty ordered[3] "that the outsides of the ships be painted of the usual colour yellow, and the ground black".

It is also known that the order was obeyed; for nearly thirty years later, on 26th March, 1743, Boscawen wrote thus to the Admiralty: "The making H.M. ships-of-war when cruising look small and not like ships of force being the only thing that will make the enemy, when they have the weather gage, bear down to you, I have proposed to the Navy Board the painting the ships under my command black, as I know at any distance it will make the ship look not to be a third of her force; but am told it can't be done without an order from the Lords of the Admiralty, though cheaper

1. Plate 4.   2. Plate 48.   3. Admy. Navy Bd. 2507, No. 198.

than the common way of painting yellow and black: therefore desire their Lordships would please to order it to be done." I have not seen the answer to this request; but after this date there are occasional mentions of ships painted black, and in May, 1780, the Navy Board circularised the yards that ships might be painted yellow or black as their captains should desire.[1] The gallant conduct of the *Monmouth*, of 64 guns, in the battle off Grenada on 6 July, 1779, had perhaps tended to bring black into fashion. It is related that on the evening of the action she was toasted by the officers of d'Estaing's fleet as "the little black ship."

From these references it would appear that there is a continuous history of painted sides from before 1715 until after 1780; but there are difficulties in the way of accepting this as a complete statement of the case. In 1777 there was an order explaining how ships were to pay their sides; and in May, 1780, there was another[2] that when ships' sides were painted, the materials usually allowed for paying them should not be issued. Then we have an unofficial statement[3] that the *Guadeloupe* frigate, when commanded by Cornwallis (which was from 1768 to 1773), was the first ship in the Navy to have a painted side and the figure-head in various colours.

It is possible to reconcile these statements by deciding that some time, perhaps shortly, after 1743 there was a reversion to the older practice of paying the side instead of painting it; that consequently our ships had "bright sides"

in the Seven Years' War; and that from about 1770 till 1780 or later the two methods went on side by side. It is even possible that a reason can be assigned for the order of 1780. In that year the "Armed Neutrality" of the Northern Powers was formed against Great Britain, whereby the immediate interruption of our Baltic trade was threatened. The chief ingredients in the "stuff" used in paying ships were turpentine and rosin, both Baltic products; and there was likely to be a scarcity of these in the near future. Even in a small matter like this it is impossible to get away from the important factors of maritime history.

Harking back to the order of 1715, it is somewhat surprising to see that it mentions only the friezing of the head and stern. Therefore at that time the frieze of the side, if it existed, was irregular; which should mean that it could only be applied by special order. The models of this date bear out this supposition, for some of them show a frieze while others do not,[4] those that show it being the first rates which regularly served as flagships, while the smaller ships, for the most part, are not friezed. The inference seems to be that even from the date of the order, exceptions were made in favour of flagships.

The usage of the Seven Years' War remains somewhat obscure. On the evidence of models and pictures we are accustomed to think of the ships of Hawke and his contemporaries as having bright sides with blue upper works painted with friezes.[5] The bright,

1. M.M. X, 205.   2. Admy. Navy Bd. 2508, No. 706.   3. M.M. X, 89.   4. Plate 4: Nance, Plates 71, 72, 76.   5. Plate 7, fig (b).

or, as they were often called, "turpentine sides", are beyond doubt; but the matter of the friezes is by no means so certain. We know that before this period friezes were exceptional; and, as will be seen presently, in the next war their use was confined to flagships. It is therefore a matter for further discovery whether round about 1760 all ships, or only flagships, were friezed; and, if so, as to how commonly the design was applied on a blue ground instead of upon the regulation black. It is rather disconcerting, when face to face with a difficulty of this kind, to discover that even the Navy Board models cannot be trusted implicitly. There is, for instance, one at Greenwich with the name *Barfleur* painted across her stern in the manner of 1772, and claiming to be the *Barfleur* which was laid down in 1762 and launched in 1768; yet it is certain that she is not that ship, but one of considerably earlier date. If the name of one ship is not contemporary with the model, why should not the frieze or the chequered side of another be equally untrustworthy? For instance, the frieze of the frigate in the Science Museum, South Kensington, which is known as the *Cleopatra*. The *Cleopatra* was launched in 1779, in which year Admiral George Darby, Commander-in-Chief of the Channel fleet, applied to have the *Britannia* "ornamented with paint on the outside, as is customary in flagships". So too the Commander-in-Chief on the North America station, James Gambier, on 1 February, 1778, asked for an order that the *Ardent* might "be friezed and trophied as usual in flagships". The inference is that in the American War

only flagships were friezed, and that the *Cleopatra*, and probably several other models, are seriously deceptive in this particular.

It seems that the reversion to painted sides in 1780 or thereabouts was soon followed by novel developments. Hitherto, with a bright side, the only variation in painting lay in the height to which the black of the wales was carried up, but in the American War, if not earlier, unofficial variants began to come in. There were some captains who liked neither the orthodox "single side", that is a broad band of yellow edged by the black of the topsides and of the bends, nor yet an all black side diversified only by painting the rails yellow. There was a third colour ready to hand, red, which from at least the 17th century had been the invariable colour of inboard works; and the practice began of painting the sides with a red instead of a yellow band. Cornwallis did so in the *Canada*, 74, in 1781; the *Prompte* frigate was so painted in 1798;[1] at the Nile the *Zealous* had "broad red sides with small yellow stripes" and the *Minotaur* double sides red; and, from a seaman's journal in private hands, it appears that in 1797 the *Thalia*, frigate, was painted "red with white borders", giving her the appearance that is shown in fig. E.[2] These instances are from documentary evidence; others occur in pictures. A picture by Elliot, formerly at Kensington Palace, of ships fitting out at Chatham for the Spanish armament of 1790, showed two three-deckers with red strakes;[3] and coloured engravings of the prizes of the 1st of June, by

1. Richardson, "A Mariner of England", 146.   2. Plate 7.   3. Information from Mr. Edward Fraser.

Wells after Livesay,[1] show two French ships, the *Northumberland* and the *Sanspareil*, with "double sides" red. It is also mentioned[2] that the officers of the *Impétueux*, when prisoners of war, claimed that they saw an English ship painted red and black sink in the same battle. As to the sinking they were mistaken; but it is less likely that they were wrong as to the colour. There are a few other instances, but apparently red sides were always exceptional both in English and in French ships, though common in Spanish.

In addition to the use of red, other unofficial fashions were making their way. During the American War some French ships seem already to have had "double sides", *i.e.*, to have broken the broad strake of yellow by painting a black band along the middle of it. On 25 October, 1778, Howe, on his return from North America, reported to the Admiralty that he had sighted two French ships of the line in the Chops of the Channel: "The ship of the commanding officer had the channel wale [*i.e.*, between the lower and upper-deck guns] black, but the rest of her side above and below the channel wale to the main wale was bright and apparently painted. Her quarters were open to the stern aloft [probably it was this that gave her away] and she appeared to have a lion head, which with the rails, her stern and quarters were yellow, with white window bars, to resemble a British ship. The head and stern of the other ship, not having the same opportunity to view them with exactness, were supposed to be painted yellow also; but her sides

were of duller appearance, like a bright-sided ship discoloured by use, without any distinction of the channel wale. Her quarters were closed; the latter had much more the resemblance of a British ship than the other." This is valuable evidence, perhaps more for English than for French usage; but it seems to suggest that the idea of the "double side" did not originate in England.

Several pictures of the battles of the war of the French Revolution show that between 1794 and 1801 English ships often had one or two narrow bands of black between the tiers of guns. Fig. C[3] is from coloured engravings of the 1st of June, 1794, after Livesay, and, besides the black strakes between the tiers, shows the lower deck guns in the black: these same black strakes appear also in Livesay's record of Cornwallis's Retreat; in Pocock's of Copenhagen, 1801; and especially in Col. Fawkes's notes on the battle of the Nile, contributed to the "Mariners' Mirror"[4] by Mr. Louis Paul, from which Fig. D is taken.[3]

There was in fact considerable diversity of practice in these years. Some ships had the old single sides, yellow and black. Some few had red for yellow. Several put one or two narrow bands of black between the ports. A few had a narrow edging of white to their coloured strakes, as seen in Fig. G[3], which, however, is from a picture of later date, representing an English ship in San Sebastian in or about 1813. In a few cases a further "captain's fancy" was to paint the hammock cloths to represent an additional deck of guns, as was done in

1. In the Macpherson collection.   2. Barrow, "Life of Howe", 290.   3. Plate 7.   4. M.M. IV, 266.

the *Theseus* at the Nile,[1] perhaps in the *Victory* when commissioned in 1803, and certainly in the *Cambridge* in 1824.[2]

These fashions approached very nearly to the true "Nelson fashion"[3] which made its début at Trafalgar – so nearly indeed that it is necessary to look somewhat closely in order to see in what the difference consisted. One difference seems to have been that hitherto the divisions of colour followed the line of the wales, that is the sheer of the ship, and this presumably only permitted a fairly narrow black strake to be drawn between the ports. "Nelson fashion" followed the line of the decks, not of the wales, and consequently the black strakes could be, and were, made wider.[4] The fashion was not quite standardised, for apparently in some cases the ports were entirely in the yellow strake, while in others the black was carried a foot or so down the upper-deck ports, *i.e.*, to where the sheer rail, its former boundary, used to be.

Another point of difference was that hitherto, it is believed, the port lids had been of the same colour as the strake: in the "Nelson fashion" they were made black, thus producing a chequer side. The glory of Trafalgar so far hallowed this fashion that, though not adopted officially, it was taken up by the Service at large and became very nearly universal for ships in commission during the rest of the war. The colour of the yellow, both in 1805 and before it, varied considerably, some ships mixing the yellow ochre with a high proportion of white, others using it unmixed. The precise date when yellow gave way to

white has not been discovered, but is believed to have been very shortly after the peace of 1815. From this date till the advent of armoured ships, men-of-war were painted with chequer sides white and black; and indeed the fashion went on through the last of the frigates to the sailing brigs, which survived into the 20th century. The same fashion from a very early date was imitated by the better class of merchant ships, and survived as "frigate painting" long after the ships had ceased to carry guns. Nothing, in fact, but the extinction of sail has killed it. Fig. H and I[5] represent the *Cornwallis* of 1817 and the *Queen* of 1839; and from them it is seen that during this period very little difference was made in the external painting of the ship. From C to I the figures show the bottoms coppered, presenting a marked difference from the white graved bottoms of A and B. It is not necessary to say more of this than that coppering, after being introduced experimentally in 1761, was generally adopted in the American War, and was almost universal by 1780. It is less well known that it was proposed as early as 1707 but set aside, presumably as being too costly.

English ships had not their names painted on their sterns, or elsewhere, till 1771, when by an order of 28 June they were directed to be painted on the second counter in 12 in. letters in a compartment. A year later, on 9 September, 1772, it was ordered that, instead of the above method, they should be painted "as large as the second counter will admit, without any compartment round them". The idea

1. M.M. IV, 272.   2. *Ibid*. IX, 308.   3. See "The Navy", XXIX, 10.   4. Plate 7, fig. (F).   5. These references are to Plate 7.

that this painting of the names was abandoned in 1778 at Keppel's request is mistaken; for though the names were "rubbed out" of the sterns of the ships under Keppel's command in that year, they were left in all other ships, both then and afterwards. The large lettering was the Trafalgar fashion, but how long it survived after that date has not been determined. Some models, *e.g.*, the *Nelson* of 1814 at Greenwich, show the name small in a compartment, and apparently soon after the peace the painting of the names was dropped.

It is a somewhat interesting question, which does not yet admit of a satisfactory answer, whether the green paint, which survived into this century as the mark of an admiral's barge, can justifiably be regarded as being in direct descent from the Tudor green. It was noticed that Tudor green survived under the early Stuarts, and was found even under the Commonwealth on the inboard works; but from 1655 to about 1800 there is no direct mention of green paint. In 1803, however, as judged by the *Victory*, it was in use for some if not all of the boats of a flagship; and all flagships' barges were fitted with green awnings. As in the middle of the 18th century flagships' boats were allowed to be painted when all other boats were bright, it seems possible that even then green may have been the colour of the paint used; but the only 18th century mention of green is in 1709, when it is stated that the *Britannia* had her awning (whether for the ship or for her barge is not stated) lined with green.[1] Many years ago I came across a casual

reference to a flagship which had her stern painted green, with a mention that this was usual in flagships. I did not make a note of it, and have not since been able to find it again; but to the best of my recollection it referred to the *Victory* when she went out to the Mediterranean in 1803. Whether the ship was or was not the *Victory*, I am certain that I found such a mention, and that it referred to a flagship of about 1800. I did not understand it to mean that the whole of the stern was green, but only the window bars, and perhaps the balustrades. Livesay's water colour drawings[2] of some of the Trafalgar ships are of historical and sentimental value, as showing the damage suffered in the battle, especially by the *Téméraire* in her quarter galleries, and by the *Tonnant* from raking fire. They indicate clearly the proportions of the black and yellow strakes; but the treatment is so very light as to suggest rather than to record the colour scheme of individual ships.

Red, as has been mentioned, was from very early the regulation colour for inboard works, but during the French Revolutionary war it began to give way to yellow; and indeed other colours seem to have been used occasionally, for in the *Thalia* frigate in 1797 they painted the quarter-deck and forecastle blue. It appears that in 1801, red being still the regulation colour both for the sides inboard and for gun-carriages, the crews of ships were in the habit of repainting the gun-carriages yellow when they received them from the officers of the Ordnance;[3] and this implies that the inboard works were also yellow, of which

1. Admy. Libry., T. Corbett's Collections, VIII, 20.   2. Plates 32 and 54.   3. Admy. Sec. 4015. 3 Jan., 1801.

there is other evidence.[1] In August, 1807, the Navy Board instructed the dockyard officers to paint the decks (by which is meant the sides and the deck fittings, not the flat of the decks) yellow when requested to do so by the captains. Light yellow was usually chosen. It is likely that both at the Nile and at Trafalgar most ships were yellow inboard, though probably a steadily decreasing number still kept to the old red.

The next colour to be introduced was green, a dark soft green, which is generally believed to have come in for the open decks[2] about 1815, and to have had a vogue of 10 years or more. There is, however, an interesting model at South Kensington, the *Ajax*, which is said to have been made and completed by Sir Joseph Yorke between 1797 and 1808. This shows the lower deck red, the upper-deck pale yellow, and the quarter-deck and forecastle green. The date seems early for green, even if we assign the paint work to 1808; and a further curious point about the model is that the side outboard is painted with a single broad strake of white, an arrangement for which there is not much evidence. It seems worth while to mention that Sir Joseph Yorke did not serve in the *Ajax*, which was burnt in 1807, at any time during the great French wars. There is, however, confirmatory evidence in a contemporary account[3] of the *Neptune* in 1809. She is stated to have had single sides of white, broken only by "three lines of black and red spots, the ports and the guns"; and to have had "the inner side of the bulwarks marked by a fine green colour". She was in the

West Indies at the time, as flagship of Sir Alexander Cochrane; and it may be that the white single side had some vogue as a tropical style of painting.

Whitewashing, instead of painting, the lower deck was introduced experimentally in 1778[4] and quickly became common, and on 14 December, 1815, was made the regular practice.

Apparently about 1830 green in its turn gave way to white for inboard works; but it must be understood that, in default of a definite order, there was always a good deal of latitude about these changes, and a transitional period during which two styles are found. Thus it is quite possible that instances of the use of white may be found as early as 1820, and certainly there were cases when the white was picked out with green.

FOREIGN PRACTICE

With minor differences, the old Tudor method of painting ships may serve as an indication of the early practice of other nations. National differences seem to have been noticeable in the nature of the ornaments used rather than in the general scheme. Thus from the paintings of Vroom and other artists of his period we see all ships with timber-coloured sides, presumably dressed with rosin or Stockholm tar thinned with tallow, as was still the practice in the eighteenth century, with the lower wales commonly blacked, and the topsides and galleries painted in narrow bands in some

1. M.M. VII, 29; *cp*. Plate 7, figs. (F), (G).   2. Plate 7, fig. (H).   3. M.M. VIII, 154.   4. M.M. X, 207.

ornamental scheme which varied from ship to ship. One Dutch ship shown by Vroom has a narrow frieze of herring-bone or chevron pattern in black and white under the poop rail; below that a strake of red; below that again, and down to the waist rail, a timber-coloured strake bearing silver panels with black and gold centres. The galleries of the stern and quarters have red rails with silver panels. Another ship, by Van Antum, has a frieze consisting of a blue and red strake, with a row of white cabossed heads or skulls along the line of junction of the colours, and smaller badges above and below.

These may be taken as typical of early 17th century practice, but from an early date, apart from the frieze, the favourite Dutch colour for the upper works was an olive green, which was applied also to the landed work forming the roof of the quarter gallery. Dark green, varied by dark blue, and relieved by red and gold, also occurs. The green continued in use in Dutch ships apparently in the early part of the 18th century; and was commonly used in yachts both in the middle and end of that century. Yellow ornamentation for the topsides of yachts was not introduced until about the end of the 17th century. A picture of a Dutch yacht of *circa* 1690, by Rietschof,[1] illustrates the transition, showing yellow on the topsides, with the stern painted in the old fashion of colours. This old fashion of painting the principal carved works in proper colours was universal in Dutch ships till about 1670, and is illustrated here from the stern of the *Prins Willem* of 1651.[2]

French ships in the Louis XIV era seem to have used gold or yellow for the carvings, as in England, and often to have friezed the topsides with blue powdered with fleur-de-lys. The beakhead-bulk-head, and the bulwark of the poop, both then and till about the middle of the 18th century, were sometimes, perhaps usually, painted red. It has been noticed that in an admiral galley the whole side down to the water-line might be painted like the frieze of a ship, that is blue, covered with fleur-de-lys.[3]

A model in the Musée de l'Armée at Brussels, known as a "Caravelle de Guerre", and believed to represent an Ostend East Indiaman of the early part of the 18th century, has her upper works aft painted in dark green and light olive, with red inside the bulwarks. This, like most of her fashions, is clearly a reflection of Dutch practice of slightly earlier date. An English model of about 1720, at the Rijks Museum, brought to Holland for technical purposes, has a blue frieze, such as is believed to have been sometimes used in English ships at that date, but instead of trophies has on it a heavy decoration of leaves in gold, which probably may be accepted as a Dutch modification.

In the first half of the 18th century French ships often show trophies instead of the lilies on the frieze,[4] but otherwise do not vary much from the practice of the late 17th century. In the latter part of the century the ships of all nations appear to have approached each other very closely in colour, having bright or yellow sides, black wales and

1. Scheepvaart Museum, Cat. No. 2033.   2. Plate 3.   3. Plate 51.   4. P. 197, fig. (n).

upper works, and frequently, at least in Dutch ships, yellow rails, while the use of red, the traditional colour for inboard works, continued. The side was usually "single", that is paid or painted in a uniform colour which normally ran from the lower wales to the sheer rail, but might be restricted by the carrying of the black either upwards or downwards in order to mask the presence of one tier of ports.

In the War of American Independence we begin to meet with notices of a black strake, or sometimes of two narrow strakes, painted black between the tiers of ports. This occurs both in French, and perhaps more rarely in Dutch ships. Apparently these strakes followed the line of the upper wale, and when they were double were so painted because till shortly before this date the upper wales had still been double in French ships.

The diversities of the end of the century, as described for English ships, seem to have been reflected in those of other nations. In general the tendency during the French Revolutionary War was for the single side to give way to strakes of yellow, now commonly painted instead of paid, but as yet seemingly without black lids to the ports. Also both in France, and more especially in Spain, red was often used for the strakes instead of yellow. I have no notes of red having been used thus either in Dutch or other northern ships, which seem to have been very similar to English in appearance.[1]

The earliest notice of the use of red on the sides of a French ship which I have found dates from 1760, and refers to Thurot's ship the *Maréchal de Belleisle*, which differed from his other frigates by having a red instead of a yellow strake, and also in having a black lion for a figure-head. To mention other and later examples, both the *Northumberland* and the *Sans Pareil*, prizes of 1794, were painted with double red sides. The most conspicuous example, however, of a red-sided ship was the *Santissima Trinidad* at Trafalgar. Many noticed her, and several accounts of the manner of her painting have survived, but unfortunately no two of them agree. The most probable interpretation of the conflicting accounts is that she had four strakes of red, edged with white, and black strakes between; but the mass of red seems to have had such an effect on the beholders that some forget to mention the black, though several notice that there were narrow ribbands of white or yellow. One account even said that she was painted to represent a brick wall.

There is in the Museum of the Royal United Service Institution an interesting sectional model of a Russian ship which was brought from Sevastopol in 1855. She is painted outside in black and light yellow strakes, and inboard in dark green on all decks. It is said that these were her original colours, but, as the model is like a middle 18th century English ship, it is probable that this is not the case. The question concerning her seems to be whether she was repainted at Sevastopol early in the 19th century, in which case we have a valuable record that the

1. See M.M. IV, 218, for Danish practice in 1768.

Russians followed the English fashion of 1815 and thereabouts; or whether she was repainted, in a purposely old-fashioned manner, but not old-fashioned enough, after she was brought to England. In either case she may be accepted as evidence that in the early 19th century some ships, whether English or foreign, were painted green internally on all decks.

It appears to be the case that after Trafalgar yellow strakes, and after about 1815 white strakes, became the ordinary practice everywhere. Perhaps also other nations began to give up the use of red for inboard works about the same time as we did. There is one Dutch model of 1803 which shows the upper-deck painted red inboard, but yellow above it, as might have been found at that date in an English ship.

Secundum Johannem Rous circa MCDLXXX.   Cecilius King inv. et d.ʳ MCMXXIV

(Original) FRONTISPIECE

THE EARL OF WARWICK AT SEA
Water-colour by Cecil King, R.I., after drawings by John Rous,
circa 1480, now preserved in the department of Manuscripts,
British Museum (Cott, MS. Julius E.)

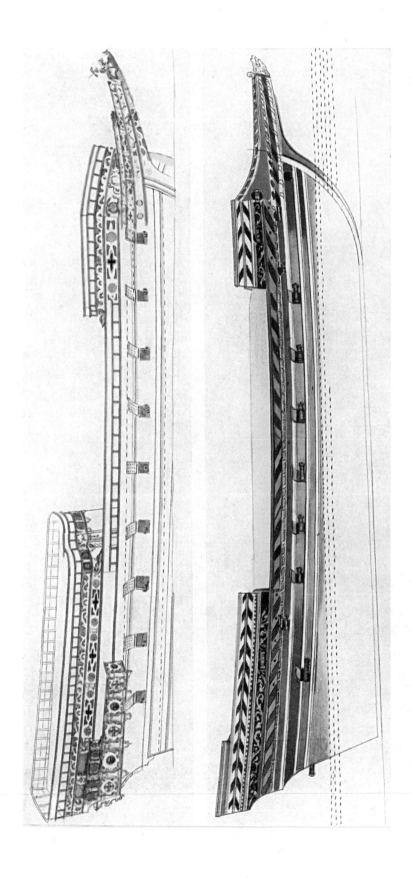

THE "PHŒNIX" OF 1612
(Admiralty Draught of 1613)
A SHIP OF QUEEN ELIZABETH
(From "Ancient English Shipwrightry",
Pepysian MS. at Magd. Coll., Cambridge)

PLATE 1

PLATE 2

FIGURE-HEADS OF THE "PRINCE ROYAL" OF 1610;
OF A TYPICAL DUTCH MAN-OF-WAR, MID-17TH CENTURY;
AND OF H.M.S. "CENTURION", 1745

PLATE 3

STERN OF THE "PRINS WILLEM" OF 1651
(From the model in the Scheepvaart Museum)

PLATE 4

A FOURTH-RATE OF GEORGE I
(After the model in the Science Museum, S. Kensington)

ELIZABETHAN GALLIONS
(From "Ancient English Shipwrightry",
Pepysian MS. at Magd. Coll., Cambridge)

PLATE 5

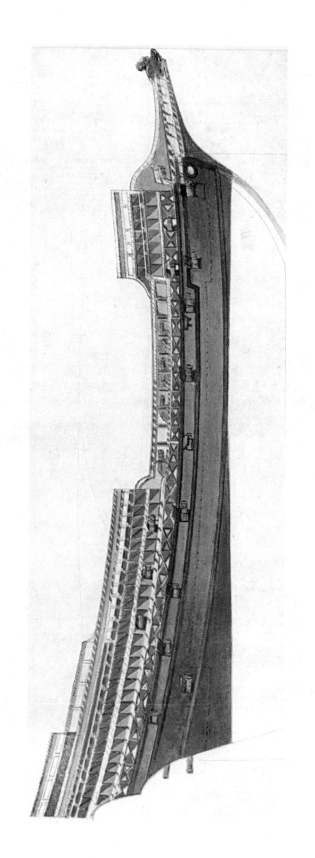

AN ELIZABETHAN GALLION: PROBABLY THE "ARK ROYAL", 1587
(From "Ancient English Shipwrightry",
Pepysian MS. at Magd. Coll., Cambridge)

PLATE 6

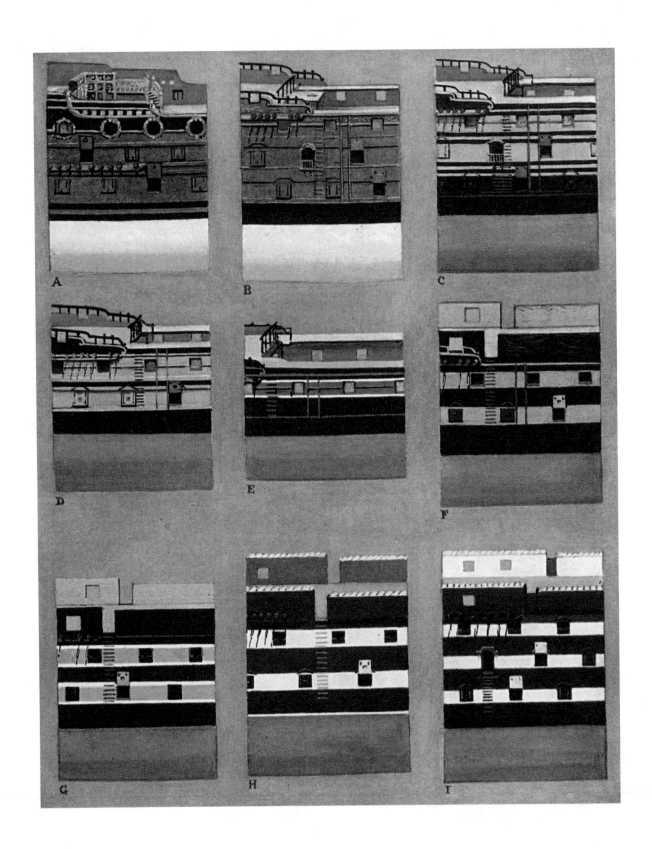

PLATE 7

DIAGRAM SHOWING STYLES OF PAINTING SHIP FROM THE
MID-17TH TO THE MID-19TH CENTURY

THE "PRINCE ROYAL" OF 1610
(From the portrait of Phineas Pett in the
National Portrait Gallery, London)

PLATE 8

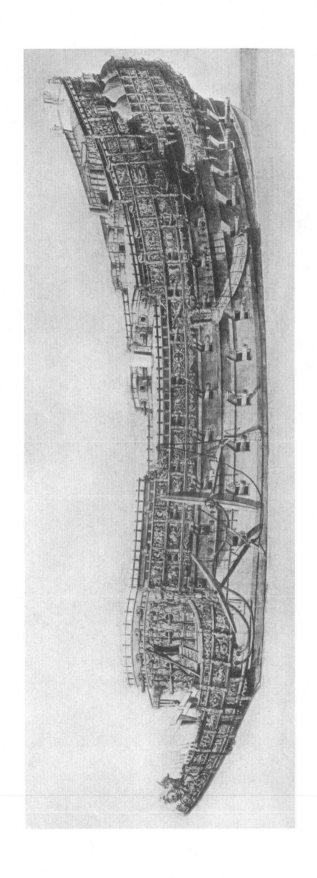

THE "SOVEREIGN OF THE SEAS", 1637
(From a draught by Van de Velde, the elder,
in the collection of Junius S. Morgan, Jr., Esq.)

PLATE 9

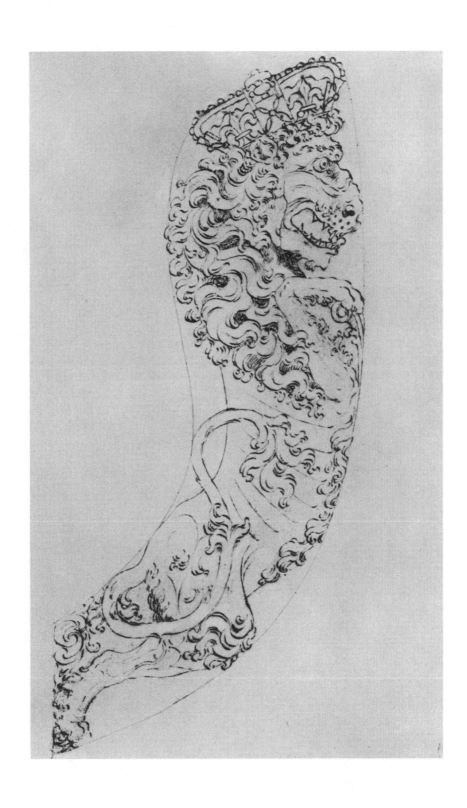

PLATE 10

"LIONS AS THEY ARE IN 1720"
(A contemporary carver's draught, lent by Lt.-Col. Harold Wyllie)

THE "ROYAL KATHERINE" OF 1664
(From a Van de Velde drawing in the Boyman's Museum, Rotterdam)

PLATE 11

THE "OLD JAMES" IN HER RESTORATION FORM

PLATE 12

A SLOOP OF GEORGE I
(From the model in the collection of Col. Rogers)

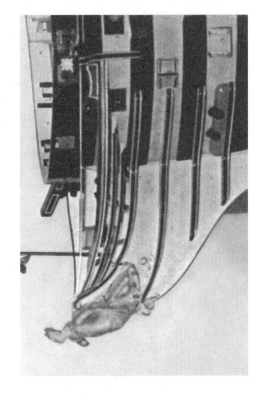

THE "PRINCESS ROYAL" OF 1773
(From the model in the collection of Col. Rogers)

A 74-GUN SHIP OF *circa* 1765
(From the model in the Science Museum, S. Kensington)

THE "ROYAL ADELAIDE" OF 1828
(From the model in the collection of Col. Rogers)

PLATE 13

THE "TERRIBLE" OF 1692
(Hydrographic Library, French Admiralty)

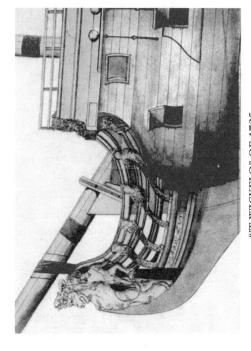

"T WICKELO" OF 1725
(From a draught in the Prins Hendrick's Museum, Rotterdam)

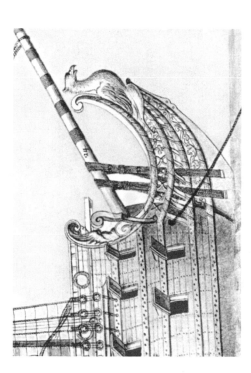

FROM THE COLBERT BOOK, *circa* 1665
(Hydrographic Library, French Admiralty)

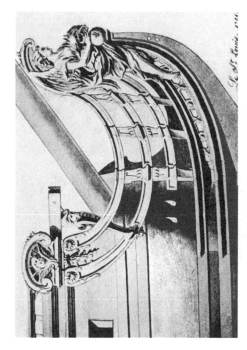

THE "ST. LOUIS" OF 1721
(Hydrographic Library, French Admiralty)

PLATE 14

THE "AMARANTHE" OF 1654
(From the model in the Maritime Museum at Gothenburg)

THE "ARY", DUTCH E. INDIAMAN OF 1725
(From the model in the Scheepvaart Museum, Amsterdam)

PLATE 15

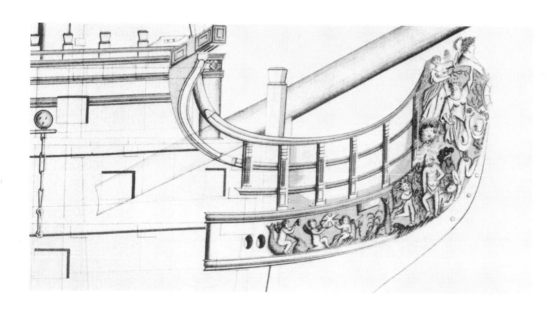

PLATE 16

STERN, QUARTER AND HEAD OF H.M.S. "VICTORY" OF 1765
(From a draught lent by the Director of Naval Construction, Admiralty)

FIGURE-HEAD OF H.M.S. "VICTORY" IN 1815
(Photo, Cribb, Portsmouth, 1925 from the ship in dock)

FIGURE-HEAD OF H.M.S. "VICTORY" OF 1765
(Photo, Cribb, Portsmouth, from the model presented to the
Dockyard Museum by H.M. the King)

PLATE 17

PLATE **18**

H.M. KING EDWARD VII WITH CARVED WORKS FROM
H.M.Y. "ROYAL GEORGE" OF 1817
(Photo, Cribb, Portsmouth)

FIGURE-HEADS OF –
H.M.S. "QUEEN CHARLOTTE" OF 1810
H.M.S. "THE DUKE OF WELLINGTON" OF 1852
H.M.Y. "VICTORIA AND ALBERT" OF 1855
H.M.S. "ROYAL ALBERT" OF 1854
(Photographs, Cribb, Portsmouth)

PLATE 19

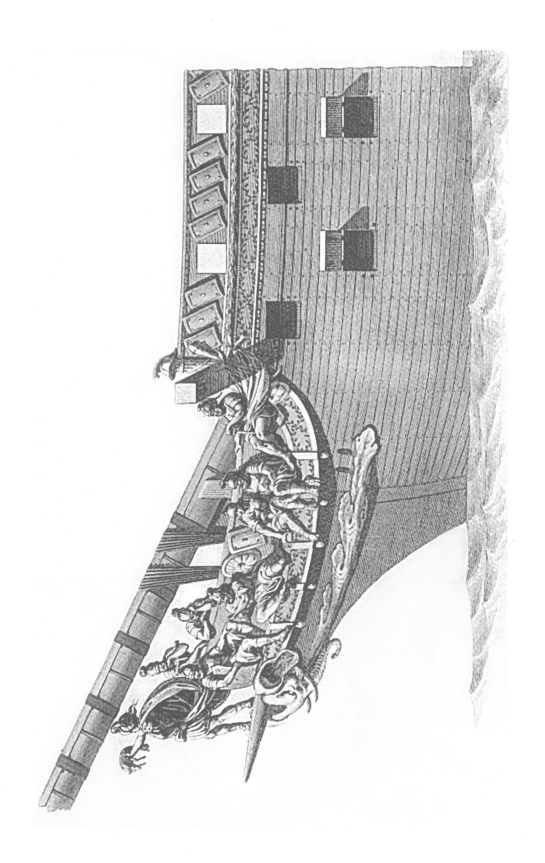

DESIGN BY P. OZANNE FOR THE FIGURE-HEAD OF A SHIP OF
THE LINE, *circa* 1800

(From the collection of R. C. Anderson, Esq.)

PLATE 20

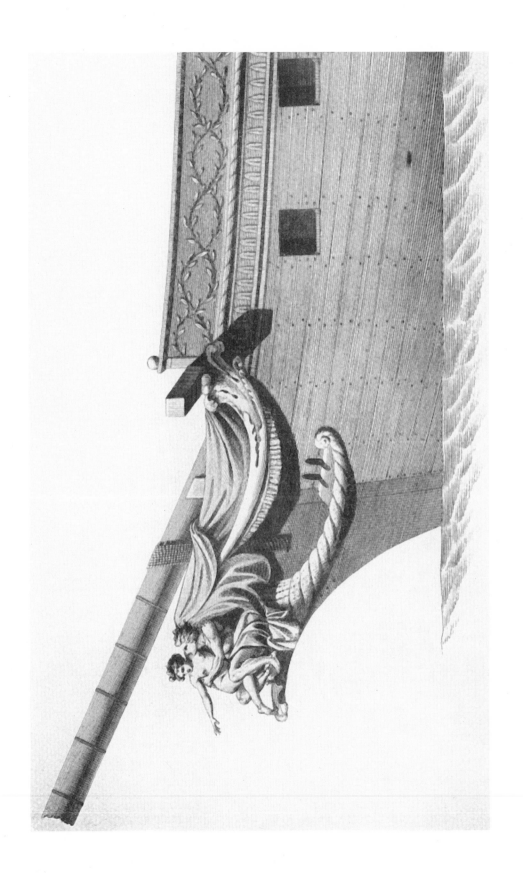

DESIGN BY P. OZANNE FOR A FRIGATE'S FIGURE-HEAD, *circa* 1800
(From the collection of R. C. Anderson, Esq.)

PLATE 21

H.M.S. "WARRIOR", 1860
(From a contemporary photograph lent by Edward Fraser, Esq.)

H.M.S. "TRINCOMALEE", 1817, NOW THE TRAINING-SHIP
"FOUDROYANT" AT FALMOUTH
(Photograph, Opie)

PLATE 22

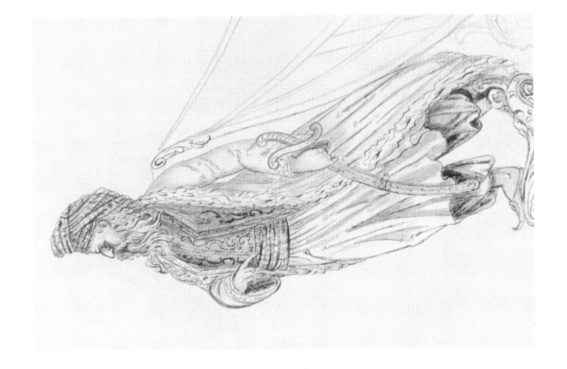

DESIGNS FOR CLIPPER SHIP FIGURE-HEADS, *circa* 1860,
BY THE LATE A. P. ELDER
(From the Macpherson Collection)

PLATE 23

FIGURE-HEADS AND SHIP CARVINGS AT TRESCO, SCILLY ISLES
FIGURE-HEADS OF THE "BENCOOLEN" IN BUDE CHURCHYARD
TOMBSTONE FIGURE-HEAD FROM MORWENSTOW CHURCHYARD
(Photos, Gibson and Sons, Penzance)

PLATE 24

FIGURE-HEAD OF H.M.S.
"AUGUSTA", 1736
(Admiralty draught)

HEAD OF THE "MONARQUE", 1747
STERN OF THE FRENCH FRIGATE "DANAE", 1780
(Admiralty draughts)

FRENCH FRIGATE "OISEAU", *circa* 1770
(Admiralty draught)

PLATE 25

STERN OF THE "SOVEREIGN OF THE SEAS", 1637
(From the portrait of Peter Pett in the possession
of the Earl of Yarborough)

PLATE 26

THE "ST. MICHAEL" OF 1669
(From a drawing by Van de Velde in the collection of
C. G. 'tHooft, Esq., Amsterdam)

PLATE 27

PLATE 28

STERN OF THE "ROYAL WILLIAM" OF 1719
(From a model in the collection of Col. Rogers)

STERN OF THE "VICTORY" OF 1765
(From the model presented to Portsmouth Dockyard by H.M. the King)

PLATE 29

PLATE 30

STERN OF THE "PRINCESS ROYAL" OF 1773
(From the model in the collection of Col. Rogers)

THE SPANISH 80-GUN SHIP "FENIX" LAUNCHED 1749
(Admiralty draught)

H.M.S. "ATLAS", OF 98 GUNS, LAUNCHED 1782
(Admiralty draught)

PLATE 31

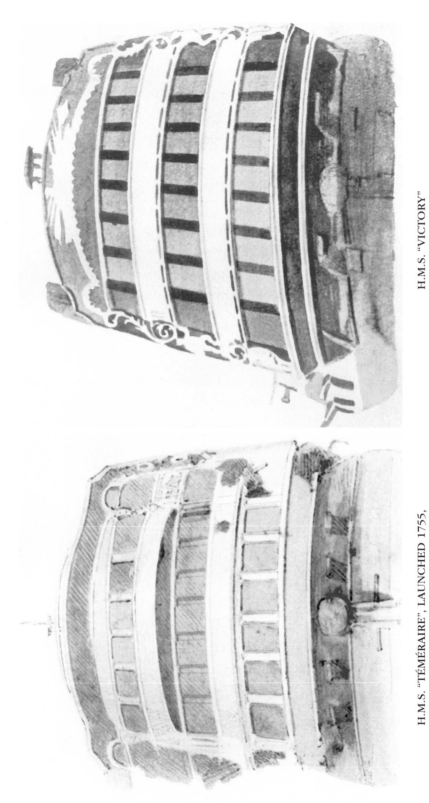

H.M.S. "TÉMÉRAIRE", LAUNCHED 1755,
INTO ROYAL NAVY 1759

H.M.S. "VICTORY"

(From 1805 water col. drawings by R. Livesay, lent by R. Lionel Foster, Esq.)

PLATE 32

PLATE 33

THE "PARIS" OF 1670
(From a 1668 design drawing, attributed to Puget,
in the Scheepvaart Museum, Amsterdam)

THE "GOUDA" OF *circa* 1670

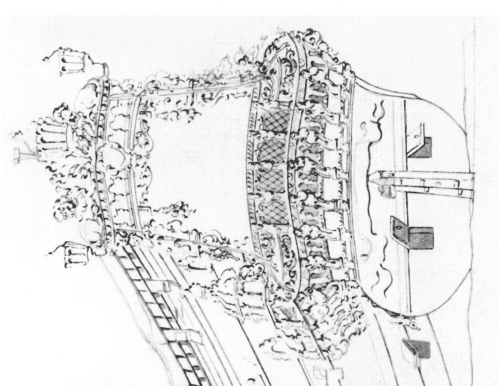

THE "EENDRACHT" OF 1664

(From drawings by Van de Velde in the Boyman's Museum, Rotterdam)

PLATE 34

PLATE 35

THE "HOLLANDIA" OF 1664
(From the model in the Scheepvaart Museum, Amsterdam)

A DUTCH TWO-DECKER, *circa* 1670
A SMALL DANISH TWO-DECKER OF *circa* 1680
(From drawings be Van de Velde in the Boyman's Museum, Rotterdam)

PLATE 36

THE "NEPTUNUS" OF 1803
(From the model in the Prins Hendrik Museum, Rotterdam)
MODEL OF A BRITISH INDIAN-BUILT FRIGATE, *circa* 1809
(Photo lent by Augustus Walker, Esq.)

AN IMPERIAL MAN-OF-WAR OF *circa* 1670
(From the model in the Musée d'Archéologie at Ghent)

PLATE 37

PLATE 38

STERN OF THE "PADMOS", EAST INDIAMAN, OF 1723
(From the model in the Prins Hendrik Museum, Rotterdam)

STERN AND QUARTER OF THE "SOLEIL ROYAL" OF 1690
(From the model in the Louvre)

PLATE 39

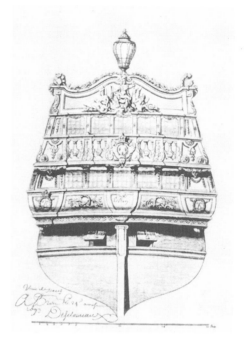

FROM THE COLBERT BOOK, *circa* 1665

"LE BON", 1693

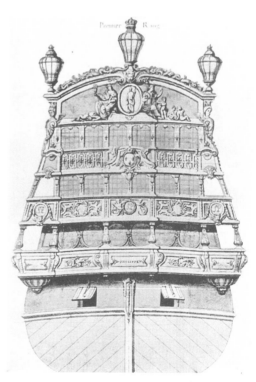

THE "VÉNUS", EARLY 18TH CENTURY

THE "ST. PHILIPPE" OF *circa* 1690

(Hydrographic Library, French Admiralty)

PLATE 40

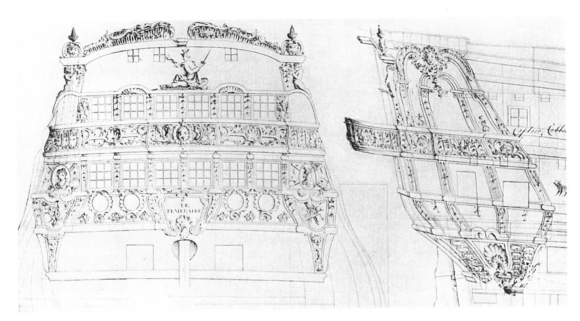

THE FRENCH "TÉMÉRAIRE", 1755
(Admiralty draught of 1759)

A "'S LANDS SCHIP", 1767
(From a draught in the Scheepvaart Museum, Amsterdam)

PLATE 41

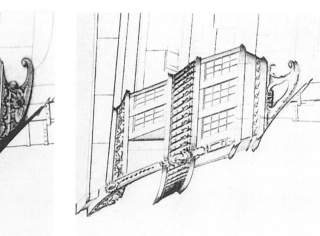

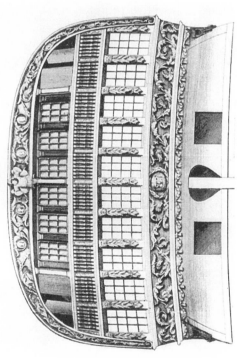

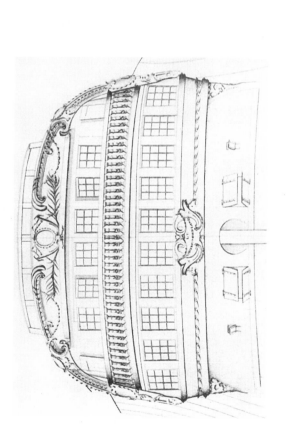

THE FRENCH "SPARTIATE" OF 1796
THE FRENCH "NORTHUMBERLAND" OF 1780
(Admiralty draughts)

PLATE 42

THE "REAL CARLOS" OF 112 GUNS, 1787

SPANISH TWO-DECKER, EARLY 18TH CENTURY

(From the models in the Naval Museum at Madrid)

PLATE 43

DUTCH YACHT, *circa* 1680

DUTCH ADMIRALTY YACHT, *circa* 1750
(From the models in the Scheepvaart Museum, Amsterdam)

PLATE 44

PLATE 45

STERN OF A GALLEY: PERIOD LOUIS XIV
(From a MS. in the Hydrographic Library, French Admiralty)

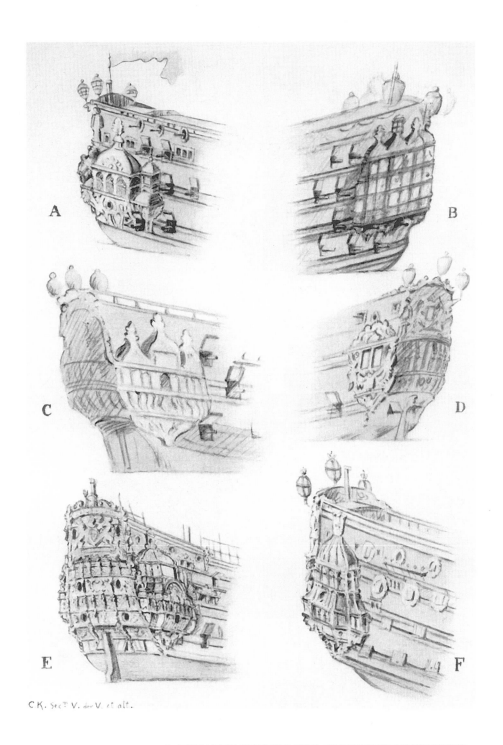

C K. Sec^r V. der V. et alt.

A. UNNAMED ENGLISH SHIP, COMMONWEALTH PERIOD.
B. UNNAMED ENGLISH SHIP, BELIEVED TO BE THE "SOVEREIGN" IN HER
COMMONWEALTH FORM.
C. THE "BRISTOL" OF 1653.   D. THE "OLD TIGER" OF 1647.
(All after drawings by Van de Velde, the Elder, in the Boyman's Museum, Rotterdam)

E. THE "ROYAL CHARLES", EX "NASEBY"
(After a drawing by Van de Velde in the Rijiks Museum, Amsterdam)

F. THE "PRINCE" OF 1670.
(From the model in the Science Museum, S. Kensington)

PLATE 46

AN ENGLISH 80-GUN SHIP OF THE 1690 ACT   AN ENGLISH 70-GUN SHIP *circa* 1716
(From the models in the collection of Col. Rogers)

AN ENGLISH 70-GUN SHIP OF *circa* 1720
(From the model in the collection of Mr. J. A. Howell;
photograph lent by Mr. H. B. Culver)

FRENCH LINE-OF-BATTLE SHIP "TRIOMPHANT"
OF 1809
(From the model in the Louvre)

PLATE 47

"BRITANNIA, 1700"
(From the model in the collection of Col. Rogers)

THE SPANISH "FENIX" OF 1749
(Admiralty draught)

H.M.S. "AUGUSTA" OF 1736
(Admiralty draught)

H.M.S. "ROYAL ADELAIDE" OF 1828
(From the model in the collection of Col. Rogers)

PLATE 48

THE "BRIEL", 1695
"'T WICKELO", 1725
(From draughts in the Prins Hendrik's Museum, Rotterdam)

PLATE 49

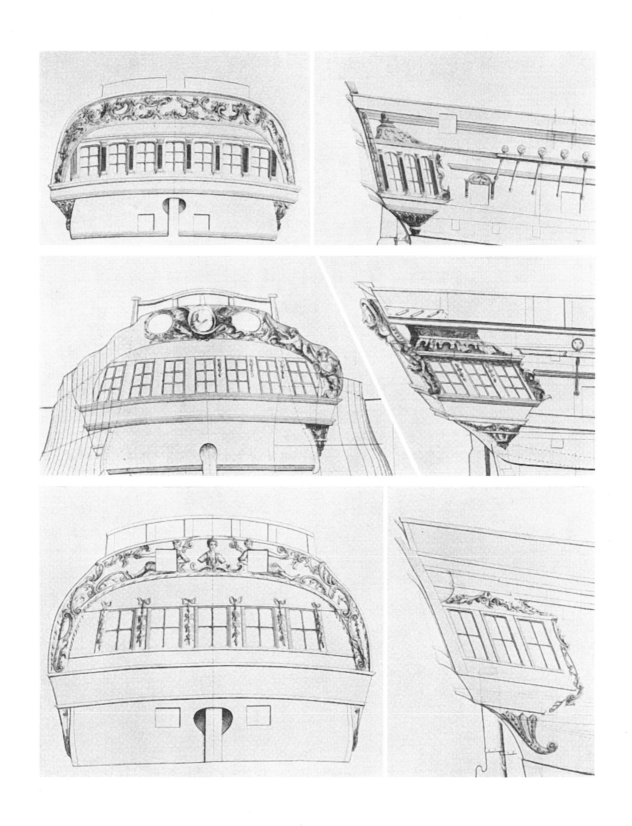

PLATE 50

THE "GRANA", SPANISH FRIGATE, 1780
H.M.S. "TERMAGANT", 1780
THE AMERICAN FRIGATE "RALEIGH", 1775
(Admiralty draught)

QUARTER OF A GALLEY OF LOUIS XIV
(From a MS. book on the Construction of Galleys in the Hydrographic Library, French Admiralty)

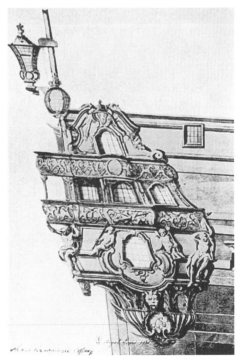

"LA VÉNUS", EARLY 18TH CENTURY   THE "ROYAL LOUIS", 1758
(From drawings in the Hydrographic Library, French Admiralty)

PLATE 51

FIGURE-HEAD OF A "PRISONER-OF-WAR
MODEL", *circa* 1805
(From a model belonging to
C. R. Bosanquet, Esq.)

QUARTER OF THE "PROTECTEUR", 1757
(From the model in the Louvre)

BRITISH STERN GALLERY BRACKET, *circa* 1790,
IN PORTSMOUTH DOCKYARD MUSEUM
(Photo, Cribb)

PLATE 52

H.M.S. "VICTORY" OF 1765

(From the model presented to Portsmouth Dockyard Museum
by H.M. the King)

PLATE 53

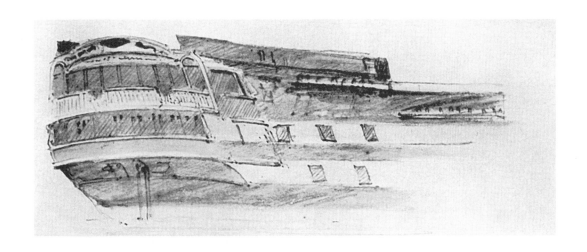

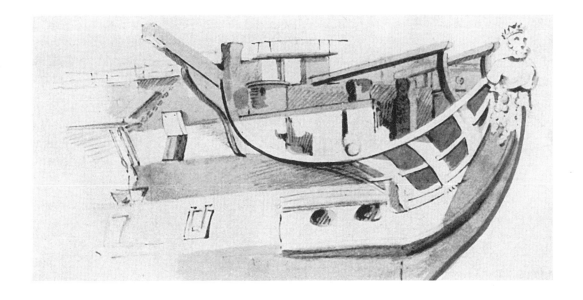

STERN AND HEAD OF H.M.S. "TONNANT", 1805
(From water colour drawings by R. Livesay
in the collection of R. Lionel Foster, Esq.)

PLATE 54

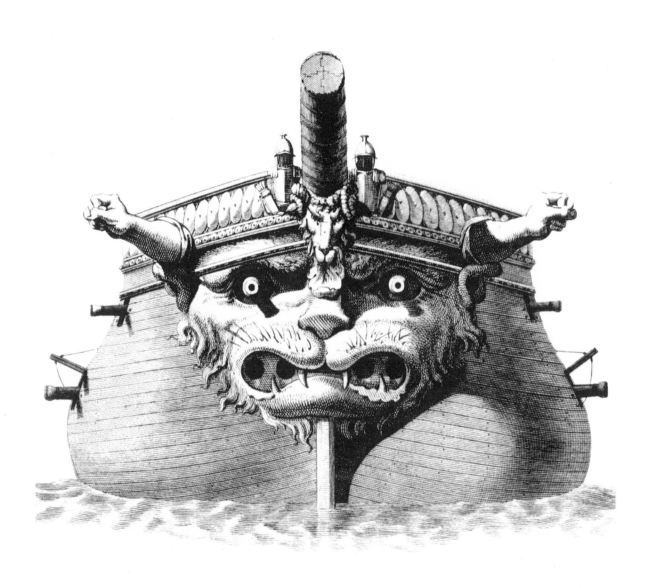

DESIGN BY OZANNE FOR THE HEAD OF A
LINE-OF-BATTLE SHIP, *circa* 1800
(From the collection of R. C. Anderson, Esq.)

PLATE 55

INDEX OF SUBJECTS

INDEX OF SHIPS
(An asterisk means that the identification is conjectural.)